Calming the Family Storm

Calming
the Family
STORM

Anger Management for
Moms, Dads, and All the Kids

Gary D. McKay, Ph.D.
Steven A. Maybell, Ph.D.

Impact Publishers®
ATASCADERO, CALIFORNIA

ATTENTION ORGANIZATIONS AND CORPORATIONS:
This book is available at quantity discounts on bulk purchases for educational,
business, or sales promotional use. For further information, please contact
Impact Publishers, P.O. Box 6016, Atascadero, California 93423-6016.
Phone 805-466-5917, e-mail: info@impactpublishers.com

Library of Congress Cataloging-in-Publication Data

McKay, Gary D.
    Calming the family storm : anger management for moms, dads, and
all the kids / Gary D. McKay and Steven A. Maybell.-- 1st ed.
        p. cm.
    Includes bibliographical references and index.
    ISBN 1-886230-56-0 (alk. paper)
    1. Conflict management. 2. Anger. 3. Family mediation. 4.
Interpersonal communication. I. Maybell, Steven A. II. Title.

HM1126.M43 2004
646.7'8--dc22   2004015128

Impact Publishers and colophon are registered trademarks of Impact Publishers, Inc.

Cover by K.A. White Design, San Luis Obispo, California
Printed in the United States of America on acid-free paper.

Published by **Impact 🕮 Publishers®**
POST OFFICE BOX 6016
ATASCADERO, CALIFORNIA 93423-6016
www.impactpublishers.com

To my family, Dr. Joyce L. McKay, stepson Robert, and nieces Kristin and Jennifer, for the lessons they have taught me about relationships. To the late Dr. Don Dinkmeyer, Sr. who helped me get started as an author. I will be forever thankful for his contribution to my writing career.

— *Gary D. McKay*

To my family, to my amazing wife and life partner Debbie Gregson, to my fine sons Sean and Jason Maybell, and to my inspiring daughter-in-law, Molly Maybell. To Dr. Gary McKay who has contributed such a gift — his belief that I have something valuable to say and the opportunity to say it in writing.

— *Steven A. Maybell*

A special dedication to Mattie J.T. Stepanek (1990–2004), International Ambassador for the Muscular Dystrophy Association. Mattie was a peacemaker and poet who wrote the Heartsongs *series.*

Contents

Acknowledgements

Many have contributed in different and unique ways to the development and publication of this book. We wish to acknowledge with appreciation:

Our wives and partners in life, Dr. Joyce L. McKay and Debbie Gregson for their love, encouragement, support and patience throughout this project, especially during "crunch" time — final deadlines — which required us to spend many extra hours involved in finalizing the book with our editor. Our children, stepson Rob and nieces Kristin and Jennifer (Gary), and, Sean and Jason (Steve) for what they taught us about parenting.

Our lives have also been touched personally and professionally by the following people who, without their contributions, we would not have written this book: James Bitter, Oscar Christensen, Rudolf Dreikurs, Don Dinkmeyer, Sr., Albert Ellis, Bill Hillman, Jane Griffith, Richard Royal Kopp, Harold Mosak, Robert L. Powers, and Frank Walton.

Gary thanks his colleagues in the Adlerian society of Arizona and the North American Society of Adlerian Psychology. Steve shares his appreciation and acknowledgement to those colleagues of his who contributed directly to this book as expert references, Heidi Arizala, Dale Babcock, Joni Ballinger, Lynne Haudenschield, Belinda Lafferty, Peter Kaperick, David Weed, and Ken Wong. He would also like to thank all of his Youth Eastside Services colleagues as well as the Puget Sound Adlerian Society and Idaho Society of Individual Psychology for their ongoing support of his work.

We'd also like to thank all the couples and families we've worked with who have contributed to our knowledge and experience in calming the family storm. Finally, thanks to the staff at Impact Publishers, especially Robert Alberti, our editor, whose contributions to this book have helped make it a solid presentation of our ideas about anger in the family.

— Gary D. McKay

— Steven A. Maybell

1

One Big Happy Family . . . or Is It?

You've been on hold for a half hour, waiting to check on a delivery that was supposed to arrive two days ago. Your spouse promised to be home an hour ago. Janie is screaming, complaining that Johnny took her favorite coloring book. The door bell's ringing; you put your own phone on hold, rush to the door and find someone passing out leaflets for a tree-trimming service. You slam the door, yell at the kids, curse your spouse for being late, run back to the phone . . . and hear a dial tone.

Mary's son Tom — age ten — was a picky eater. He would whine at the dinner table, complaining about what was being served. Mary got angry and threatened to send him to bed without supper if he didn't stop whining and eat his dinner.

Henry and Sandra are the parents of two young children and have been married for seven years. Henry was raised in a "traditional" family: his father made the "important" decisions and his mother focused most of her energies on her husband and the kids. Henry was consequently "threatened" by Sandra's interests outside of the home. Whenever she wanted to socialize with friends or take a class, Henry

lectured her about the importance of caring for the children and would not cooperate by providing childcare or access to the family automobile. Sandra was obviously resentful of this controlling behavior and found herself seething with anger much of the time.

Carl had to win. He looked for opportunities to engage in arguments. His thirteen-year-old daughter Tammy was a good match for him: "Like father, like daughter." One evening dad and Tammy were in a good one — Tammy wanted to skip the two-week summer camp this year; she claimed it was for babies. Carl said that she needed the experience and logically began to present his reasons. Tammy retorted with logic of her own. The discussion became heated with dad finally saying he didn't care what Tammy thought, she was going to camp and that was it! Tammy stomped off to her bedroom.

Ben and Valerie were parents of a blended family, each with two children from previous marriages. Both parents cared deeply about their "own" children and felt bad about how their children had suffered as a result of the divorce. They both were competitive individuals. Their desire to win played out in many family scenarios. An issue of great intensity had recently developed in their new family. Ben's son and Val's daughter quarreled and fought frequently, each blaming the other for starting the conflict. Both Ben and Val would take their own child's side and argue bitterly with the other parent and child over who was to blame. This issue was contaminating the couple's entire relationship and poisoning the family atmosphere.

Sean was an active young teen who enjoyed sports and activities at church. Since his mom worked swing shifts, Dad

usually provided taxi service. Dad was glad that Sean was involved, but the constant running was taking its toll, so he told Sean that he needed his help around the house. Sean agreed to do the dishes after dinner on the days Dad took him to an activity.

The first time went well. Dad put Sean's baby sister Kara in the car seat and took Sean to soccer practice, and Sean cleaned up the dishes after dinner. The next time, however, Sean forgot. When Dad reminded him, Sean complained that he was tired. "You're tired!" Dad said, "What about me? I have to work all day, run you back and forth, fix dinner, and take care of Kara! Now you get in there and clean up those dishes right now!" Sean grumbled and did a sloppy job of doing the dishes. The evening ended with hurt feelings on both sides.

Nicole, a single parent of ten-year-old Corey, has become resentful over how irresponsible her ex-husband has been lately with respect to their visitation arrangement. Frank has been bringing Corey back from "his weekends" late and without making sure Corey had time to complete his homework and prepare for his upcoming week at school. Nicole was angry and resentful toward Frank, and she would "let him have it" whenever he returned late with Corey. This resulted in Frank also feeling mistreated and angry along with a determination to not make things easier for Nicole.

Of course, none of these situations would occur in your family, right? Right?

Well, we're all only human. The fact is, anger and confrontation are a part of our lives, like it or not. The key factor in happy families is how they *handle* anger. And that's what this book is all about. In the pages to come, we're going to get better acquainted with the angry folks you've just read about. And we're going to learn a lot about how to deal effectively with anger in families.

The methods for dealing with family anger that you will find in this book are based on principles of equality and mutual respect — respect for yourself, for your spouse, partner or ex-spouse, and for your children.

In chapter 2, "The Anatomy of Anger," we'll take a look at how anger develops, why we get angry, and the many purposes anger serves in our lives. Chapter 3, "Anger Management Strategies I — First Steps," begins our study of how to handle anger effectively, examining strategies to get anger under control quickly. Chapter 4, "Anger Management Strategies II — For the Long Term," offers you suggestions for longer-term changes, ways to change the "automatic" anger response, and how to change your life so you don't get angry so much. Chapter 5 is brief, bringing you "Five Steps to Less Anger in Your Life." Chapter 6 introduces a very special way to prevent and/or overcome problem anger: "Encouraging Relationships."

Anger can be appropriate at times, and in chapter 7 we'll show you how to communicate in more constructive ways, whether you're angry or not. Similarly, chapter 8, "Problem Solving & Conflict Resolution," and chapter 9, "Family and Couple Meetings," offer techniques that will improve your family relationships and help you to get along better even when you're angry.

Most parents were couples first, of course. Chapter 10, "All's Fair in Love . . ." offers couples a proven approach to dealing with their own intimate communication, including anger.

All parents find child behavior issues to be challenging at times, and chapter 11 will give you a tool kit for "Discipline Without Anger."

The following three chapters — 12, 13, and 14 — continue to explore the problems of parenting and teaching children how to handle their anger with each other, and with adults. Special family circumstances — divorces, single parents, and stepfamilies — are the topic of chapter 15.

Finally, no book on anger in families can avoid the uncomfortable but all-too-common problems of domestic violence and child abuse. It's important to acknowledge that anger can lead to psychological and/or physical abuse, and chapter 16, "When Anger Turns to Violence," presents some helpful thoughts on that very difficult personal and societal issue.

Before we go on to all the important material in the chapters to come, however, let's consider the question of why this book is needed.

WHY IS THERE SO MUCH ANGER IN OUR FAMILIES?

Anger is a universal human emotion that impacts our lives in many ways. But shouldn't the family be a place of comfort, of calm — a place where we can escape the stresses and strains that lead us to angry feelings in the "outside world"? Why do we get so angry with those to whom we're closest?

There may have been a time in history when real families behaved like those on TV sitcoms of the 1950s; times when nobody got angry with anybody else in the family; times when the family was that all-nurturing place that got you ready for dealing with people at school, or the job, or in the neighborhood, or on the highway . . . And indeed, families still are our major sources of **nurturing and preparation.** But if those "TV show" times ever existed, they're not easily found today. Families have changed as the environment around them has changed. The stresses of that world outside the door have leaked into the family room at home.

And those stresses are one of the major contributors to anger in our families.

Dramatic changes in the environment in which we all live are partly responsible for the rise of anger in our families. Among the significant social and economic developments that have increased the stress in families are:

◆ families relocating in search of better jobs or housing, which reduces extended-family suppor and resources;

◆ increase in single-parent households and families where both parents work outside the home;

◆ increase in families living in urban and suburban communities versus rural communities;

◆ limitations on freedom in family and community activities because of fears for personal safety, in light of such high-profile violent incidents as the Columbine and September 11th tragedies (as well as local kidnappings and assaults);

◆ rapid changes in technology, pressuring workers (i.e., parents) to continually upgrade skills or face extinction;

◆ "downsizing" and "outsourcing," where parents are losing jobs due to companies cutting staff and/or moving manufacturing, service, and technology offshore;

◆ kids' schedules filling up with extracurricular activities, leaving little time for family and relaxation.

All of these stressors — and many others — add to the intensity of family life and also to intense emotions, including anger.

Another major impact on families comes from the new technologies — cable and satellite television, high-speed personal computers, MP3 players, digital cameras, instant messaging, video games, picture phones, internet connection to the world — that condition us to expect *immediate* results. We naturally extend this expectation to our social relationships. We expect others to be just as accommodating, just as immediate. When our relationships fall short of these expectations, we may feel angry — and use that anger as an energizing force to get life to meet our expectations.

Reliance on technology in day-to-day activities reduces our direct contact with others, decreases a sense of belonging, and reduces opportunities to learn social skills. E-mail, for example, has largely replaced visiting — or even calling — extended family and friends for many busy people.

The rise of anger in our lives and families is also impacted by a social trend most of us are not fully aware of: the "democratic revolution." We will discuss the democratic revolution and its effects in detail in chapter 6. For now, it's important to realize that society is moving — as it should — from autocratic to democratic models in all aspects of life, including the family, male-female relationships, and the workplace. We are in the midst of the adjustment period and have not quite developed a new tradition of getting along as social equals. There is competition between old traditions and new traditions. During this time of transition, people in the traditional dominant position in relationships (men, parents, whites, management) often attempt to hold onto their status, while those in the traditional subordinate position in relationships (women, kids, people of color, labor) work to rise above that position. The outcome is often anger on both sides.

THE EFFECTS OF ANGER IN RELATIONSHIPS

Anger frequently results in power struggles between people. Your anger, which is intended to achieve a change in the other person's behavior, often results in the exact opposite. The other person is likely to resist and rebel against your anger. Children are especially discouraged when parents are frequently angry with each other or with them. Anger can frighten children, increase rebellion and revenge, and teach them cooperation is not required unless someone is angry with them — if they decide to cooperate at all.[40] Is this the kind of relationship you want with your children? Do you want them to grow up and continue angry relationships in their own adult relationships?

We can't promise this book will bring you relief from anger. It is, after all, a universal human emotion. And indeed, many of the roots of your anger — such as the environmental factors we discussed above — may well be beyond your control. Yet, while you may not have the power to change these factors, you do have the power to decide how you will respond to them. We are confident that you'll find this book to be a practical manual of helpful aids to calming the storms of anger that every family experiences.

We wish you and your family well as you go to work on the changes that will result in less anger in your life, more effective expression of the anger you do experience, and a happier — and less stormy — family environment.

ALERT:

If you or your children are victims of abuse, this book alone is not sufficient. Professional help is needed. If you are dealing with an immediate life threatening domestic or child abuse situation call 911.

GETTING HELP FOR DOMESTIC VIOLENCE AND CHILD ABUSE

Whenever issues of abuse occur within families, it's time to obtain the help of professionals and professional agencies. Domestic violence (abuse between adults age eighteen and above), child abuse (an adult committing emotional, physical or sexual abuse against a child under the age of eighteen), and teen dating violence (abuse between teenagers involved in dating relationships) are nearly always repetitive in nature. There is often a characteristic pattern, involving abusive behavior, periods of relative calm, and periods of remorse with promises that the abuse will cease. The abuse, however, nearly always returns.

Addressing and confronting this complicated, humiliating and overwhelming problem is a major undertaking. It is something not to handle alone. Professional resources are available in nearly every community.

This topic is discussed in greater detail in chapter 16, and you'll also find more child abuse and domestic violence information and resources in Appendix B.

MAJOR POINTS

- Anger is a normal emotion that we all experience. We can calm the family storm by learning to manage anger well.

- Effective anger management in the family requires equality and mutual respect.

- The stress of life today contributes to anger in our families.

- Technology has taught us to expect immediate results. Anger often follows unfulfilled expectations.

- The impact of the democratic revolution accounts for much of the anger and conflict in today's families. It is a major reason that family relationships must be founded on mutual respect to succeed.

- Angry parents can frighten children, increase rebellion and revenge and teach them that cooperation is only required when someone is angry with them (if they decide to cooperate at all!).

- Anger can result in domestic violence and child abuse. If you or your children are victims of abuse, this book alone is not sufficient. *Get professional help.*

2

The Anatomy of Anger

You've been on hold for half an hour, waiting to check on a delivery that was supposed to arrive yesterday. Your spouse promised to be home by an hour ago. Janie is screaming, complaining Johnny took her favorite coloring book. The door bell's ringing, you put your own phone on hold, rush to the door and find someone passing out leaflets on a tree trimming service. You slam the door, yell at the kids, curse your spouse for being late, run back to the phone to find a dial tone . . .

❖ ❖ ❖

Most of us have stressful days like this — one thing after another, enough to tempt us to move to the most remote uninhabited island we can find! Anger is a typical response to the stress we experience in this fast-paced, rapidly changing, highly competitive society. With more stress than ever before, many people feel inadequate, threatened and powerless. Our anger is a statement of protest against our circumstances and a way to feel temporarily powerful.

Anger is a "fight or flight" reaction to situations where we fear our survival is threatened. The loss of survival we fear can be physical or emotional. In addition to the daily aggravations of work and family, we now must face a world that is more physically threatening — violent crime, school shootings, terrorist attacks. All these conditions not only contribute to our stress, they increase our tendency to be angry.

But is anger our best response? Does the anger help us improve our most precious relationships — our families? In most cases the answer is no. It's one thing to be angry at the people and situations that create the violence and rudeness in our world; it's another to have angry relationships in our families. Anger drives people farther apart in a time when feeling close and safe is so important.

This book will help you understand that anger has many dimensions. Among the factors that shape our anger are the changes and developments in the world around us, the kinds of relationships we form with one another, and our creative internal processes of thinking and goal setting. *Understanding anger* is an essential step in becoming more effective in managing and reducing its negative effects upon our lives and the family relationships we care about.

UNDERSTANDING ANGER

Since anger is an emotion, we'll begin our study of anger by looking at emotions. Many people think they are not responsible for their emotions — they just happen. You hear this idea in their language: "It *makes* me so mad!" If this is true, then how can people who experience the same event feel different about it? Emotions don't just happen and nobody *makes* you feel anything. Your feelings are not caused by external events, but are created by your *perceptions of events*. In other words, your emotions are created as a consequence of your beliefs. For example, if you believe the world is a dangerous place, you'll most likely create a lot of fear for yourself. On the other hand, if you believe that the world has its dangers but most people are good, you'll create mostly warm and confident feelings.[21] Thus, the process of emotions proceeds like this:

belief → emotion → action

We aren't aware that we create our emotions; they seem "automatic." Yet we are not on "autopilot" when we create our emotions. It's just that we've held onto our beliefs and practiced them for years.[38] We developed our view of the world and our place in it in early childhood. Further, the brain functions that lead from beliefs to emotions happen so fast that we are not consciously aware of them. When we begin to become aware of our beliefs and learn to slow the process down, we are in a position to manage anger or any other emotion. You will learn how to do this as you continue to read this book.

ANGER: FACTS AND FICTIONS[39]

Since humanity has been engaged in wars throughout history, some believe we humans are naturally aggressive. Yet, throughout the ages humans have also been involved in cooperation. So, are we naturally aggressive or naturally cooperative? The fact is, we have the capacity for both.

Let's put to rest another widespread myth about anger. War is not caused by anger. War is the result of economic, political, territorial, or religious issues where people are unwilling or unable to reach peaceful solutions. Anger is the *fuel* for the actions of war.

Some believe if they internalize their anger they will damage their health, so it's better to express the anger. This is also fiction. Research shows that chronic anger — whether held in or expressed — is dangerous to your health: increased blood pressure, strain on the heart and upset stomachs, to mention a few.[60] Occasional anger, on the other hand, can be healthy if it's not violent and "clears the air" — furthering understanding and cooperation. The success of expressing your anger depends on *how* you express it.

There are those who believe expressing one's anger is *cathartic* — a healthy release of emotional energy. But not everyone finds expressing their anger to be a positive experience. Some people feel guilt and shame when they express their anger. In addition, the person on the receiving end of a "cathartic" expression of anger is the victim, and is unlikely to appreciate the benefits in the same way as does the "expresser."

Finally, some people — including some therapists — believe the way to eliminate your anger is to act it out. While this may relieve one's anger for the moment, such behavior has long-term consequences — most of them negative. Research shows that acting out anger, such as hitting inflatable punching clowns or pillows or screaming, actually helps a person practice being angry. And the more we practice, the better we get — at being angry!

Is Anger a Bad Emotion?

There's no such thing as a good or bad emotion.[42] Obviously some emotions are pleasant and some unpleasant, but that doesn't make the unpleasant ones bad. Instead of thinking of emotions as good or bad, it's more accurate to think of them in terms of whether they are productive and useful (responding to the needs of the situation for all concerned), or non-productive and useless (expressed primarily to elevate our own position or meet our own agenda).

Feeling angry is a natural human experience and has one sure benefit: anger acts as a "warning device." It tells you that something is wrong, that something needs to be addressed, either internally or in your relationships with others. We hope that you'll grow to respect your anger as a "warning device" and that you'll find help from the many ideas in this book for productively addressing your anger and the anger in your family.

Anger "ventilated" upon others is almost always non-productive, as is anger created for the purpose of controlling, winning, or revenge. On the other hand, expressing your anger in respectful ways to address a problem, or to protect yourself and your loved ones, can be productive and useful. The primary purpose of this book is to help you to reduce or eliminate unproductive anger, for your own sake and for the sake of your loved ones.

ANGER, RAGE, AGGRESSION, AND RESENTMENT

To fully understand anger it is important to understand several related issues and terms. *Anger* is a feeling natural to the human condition, it is a feeling every human being experiences especially when we are being challenged, threatened, or hurt. There are obviously degrees of anger, and *rage* is anger at the highest level of intensity. *Aggression* occurs when anger turns from a feeling into a hurtful or harmful action or behavior. When anger turns into rage or aggression, the risk of violence is the greatest. *Resentment* is holding onto and carrying anger as a permanent possession, being weighted down with anger. It usually occurs when you have not fully addressed or resolved being hurt by someone who currently matters, or at one time mattered, in your life.

There are many ideas and choices available to you and your family for dealing with the issue of anger. The concepts and skills you'll be learning in this book are designed to help you to understand, reduce, and manage anger more effectively. Rage, aggression, and resentment are nearly always harmful to you and your family. Our mission in writing this is to help you and your family manage anger so effectively that it never turns into rage, aggression, or resentment.

HOW WE CREATE OUR ANGER

Anger, like other emotions, is created by your beliefs and what you tell yourself about what you experience. You can't always choose what happens to you, but you do have choices about how you *view* what happens. One of the most miraculous human gifts we are endowed with is the ability to choose our attitude toward every situation that we face. Most people are unaware of this gift and don't take the time, effort and practice to develop it. The rewards of being able to *choose* your thoughts and beliefs, however, can transform the most difficult challenge and improve the most challenging relationship. To choose your thoughts and beliefs, you first must become more aware of them. This will take effort, as our thinking tends to occur without our full awareness.

Like anything else you will get better with practice. The following model will help.

You make yourself angry by engaging in "angry thinking." We call angry thinking "hot thoughts" — hostile thoughts make you *hot*.[38, 39, 24] Here are some of the hot thoughts that lead to anger:

Judging an event as unfair or hurtful. Suppose your spouse, partner or child interrupts you when you're involved in a project. You may think it's unfair of them to be so inconsiderate. If you judge an event as unfair or hurtful, you then proceed to the next levels of angry thinking.

Catastrophizing. You believe it's awful or horrible that your spouse or child did such a thing.

"Can't-standing." You tell yourself that you *just can't stand* this awful thing that's happening.

Demanding. You make demands on the other person. "He should (or should not). She must (or must not)." Or you tell yourself, "This should never (or always) happen." In other words, you engage in *absolute thinking*. You think you're Frank Sinatra and believe it should be "my way!"

Blaming. You cast blame on the person (or event) that you judge as unfair or hurtful: "She's a bitch (he's a bastard)"; "He (she) is a bratty (stupid, rotten, worthless) kid."

Another way to analyze angry thinking is to use the acronym MADS. When someone is angry, we can say he or she's got the "mads."[40] MADS is a handy way to label these anger-creating thoughts:

M — *Minimizing* your personal power. This involves "can't-standing": "I can't stand it" or "I can't take this."

A — *"Awfulizing"* or catastrophizing. "It's terrible, horrible" etc.

D — *Demanding.* "He/she should or must (or should not)" etc.

S — *Shaming and blaming.* "She/he is worthless" etc.

We suggest you jot down the four words for "MADS" in your journal. We'll be referring back to this idea from time to time, and it will help you to remember the four key terms.

THE PURPOSES OF ANGER

Because your anger is based on your beliefs, it is also purposeful — designed to get you what you want in life and to help you overcome challenges and difficulties. Like our beliefs, our purposes operate outside full conscious awareness. You'll have to work to be aware of them. This awareness is vital to making better choices and in more effectively managing your emotions and your anger.

Anger grows out of the *expectations* you hold for yourself and others, as well as *interpretations* — what you tell yourself about the events that happen in your life (or don't happen but you think *should* happen.) In short, if things don't go your way, you're likely to get angry. When you do get angry, your anger provides "fuel" for your actions or behavior. As with the fuel in your automobile, emotions provide energy to keep you moving.[21] We all create anger to fuel ourselves to achieve our purposes: to gain (or regain) power; to win; to control; even to exact revenge when we feel hurt and want to get even.

Power moves can involve gaining control, winning or protecting your rights or the rights and safety of others.[39] The person who wants to *control* may believe he or she must be in control in order to be significant. Controllers can seek power in a variety of ways, such as using logic, intimidation, or anger. They believe, "I must be in control." They can also strive to keep distance from others for fear of being controlled by them. They may believe: "Never get close to anyone or they will be your master." Distance-seekers control by being cold or by generating anger.

A person who believes she or he has to be in control can use that purpose in a more positive way. Positive uses of control involve controlling your anger and possibly controlling the situation — setting limits — rather than trying to make the other person behave the way you demand.

The person who *has to win* is highly competitive. These folks can be quite argumentative for the sake of the argument. They say, "I listen to all sides of the argument, mine and the wrong ones!"[36] If you're not in a relationship with this type of person, or don't have a child or other relative like this, you've probably met this person at a party. The evening's going well and you give an opinion on something. Right away, the person takes the opposite point of view and you find yourself in an argument to the point of frustration.

When those who have to win feel they might be losing and logic is not prevailing, anger is a tool they can use to try to get you to agree with them or to back off. Anger gives them a two-to-one advantage: "There are your ideas versus my ideas *plus my anger. I win!*" They essentially believe, "I must win or I'm worthless." These people are especially difficult to deal with when conflict arises. Suppose you're in a discussion with your spouse over an issue you disagree about. If you have to win, you're not interested in compromise, you're interested in getting your way. Are you likely to "win" in the long run?

But having to win isn't all bad. If you believe you have to win, you can redirect your purpose from defeating your opponent to winning cooperation. In other words, you can seek a win-win agreement.

Protecting your rights or someone else's rights or safety — such as your children's — can be positive or negative. If you think someone is denying you your rights, you can choose to be angry to try to reestablish them. You may believe, "You are violating my rights. I won't let you do that. I'll stand up for my rights." While anger is one approach, and may do the job, it also may create bad feelings and lead to future conflict or revenge. There is another way. You can stay calm and firmly state your limits — what you're willing to do and what you're not willing to do.

Protecting others usually applies to your children. If you think your child is being abused, you'll want to step in. Anger can be used to get the person to stop — if you think it will work. It can also lead to conflict and make things worse for the child. Firmly stating what behavior you'll tolerate and what you won't may be more effective. In some cases you may need to seek professional help.[40]

Getting even is never positive. Revenge leads to revenge. The Irish have a saying: "If you want to get revenge, dig two graves — one for your enemy and one for yourself." When you feel hurt as well as angry, revenge is very tempting. You may believe: "How dare you do that to me? I'll get you for that!"

The best way to avoid revenge is to realize that your spouse or child must also be hurting, or he or she would not be behaving this way. When you see it from the other person's point of view — hard as it is — your desire for revenge can turn into compassion and wanting to improve the relationship.

So, we add a new element in our *beliefs-emotions-action* equation — *purpose*. Our emotions are created as a consequence of our beliefs and in service to our goals. Belief leads to purpose which leads to emotions to carry out the action or behavior.

Belief → Purpose → Emotion → Action.

THE LINK BETWEEN ANGER AND OTHER EMOTIONS

We think of anger as a "solution-based emotion," one that advances your purposes, goals, or solutions to life's difficulties. Anger helps you meet the goals of power, revenge, control, victory (winning), as well as protecting your rights and the rights of others. Anger can provide the emotional energy you need to confront and respond to the problems and obstacles you encounter from other people and life situations.

Anger is not the only thing that happens inside you when you're facing a challenging situation, of course. Before the anger, there are often unrecognized "challenge-based emotions" —

feelings that are directly connected to the issues and problems you're confronting. For example, suppose you discover your child is doing something dangerous. You may respond with anger in an attempt to control — trying to make sure the child never does that again, or to punish or protect the child. But, if you think about it, your anger was preceded in this case by anxiety and fear for your child's safety.

The difficulty is that anger tends to overshadow the challenge-based feelings, so that you can easily be unaware of them. It's worth the effort to recognize those feelings, so you can understand where your anger may be coming from, reassess it, and express it more effectively in relationships with your family and other important people in your lives.

Learning to become more aware of the first feelings that may be tied to your anger, and expressing those feelings directly to the person(s) involved — "I feel frightened about your safety when you come home late" — can go a long way to reduce anger and the conflicts that arise from anger. (We'll have more to say in chapter 7 about expressing challenge-based feelings associated with anger.)

The "challenge-based" emotions that often occur before anger may give you a sense of being under attack, weakened, or even powerless, defeated by life's difficulties. Since these "first-response" feelings don't offer you much help in confronting your problems, you may bring your anger "to the rescue," calling upon its empowering energy to overcome or conquer the problem. Thus, although the challenge-based emotions don't cause your anger, they are, in many circumstances, a step in the emotional process that results in anger.

CHALLENGE-BASED FEELINGS ASSOCIATED WITH ANGER

The chart titled "Feelings That Often Go With Anger" on page 25 describes a number of common emotions that are that are challenge-based and often precede anger: *fear, guilt, hurt, impatience, stress,* and others. They represent the ways we emotionally experience a problem, threat, or disadvantage. Anger often becomes an effort — frequently a mistaken one — to rise above these feelings and regain strength, control, or power, or succeed in hurting or getting even.

Here are a few examples of how unrecognized challenge-based emotions can link to anger:

Joshua did something wrong at work and feels ashamed, inadequate and guilty. At home, he "storms" at his wife for the smallest of mistakes — he temporarily feels superior by making her feel inadequate. Nothing like sharing feelings!

Maddie had big expectations for how the day of shopping would go with her kids. She imagined everyone getting along and each child being overjoyed with something special she would buy each one. When instead the children fought with each other and complained about the time it took for a brother or sister to pick out a gift, she felt frustrated and disappointed. To her surprise, Maddie got angry and started yelling and screaming at the kids — punishing them for shattering her expectations.

Gretchen at first felt worried when her fifteen-year-old Kirsty didn't come home at the agreed upon time one Friday night. Gretchen's worry turned to anxiety and then to fear two hours later when her daughter had still not returned home. At 2 a.m. when Kirsty finally arrived home, mom was furious. She aggressively scolded Kirsty and threatened her with severe restrictions if this ever happened again — a misguided effort to reduce the risk by attempting to control and punish her daughter.

It's important to understand that this process of compensating for or covering up a challenge-based feeling like fear, guilt, stress, frustration, or inadequacy by getting angry, then expressing the anger in a harmful or hurtful way, is not a solution at all. It actually creates another problem in your relationship, and often makes the problem you started with worse — much worse!

Let's take a closer look at the feelings of guilt and stress and how they relate to anger.

Guilt and Anger. Guilt usually accompanies anger when one thinks she or he should not have been angry. The person thinks he or she has "sinned" and must pay the price with guilt. The problem is that guilt seldom changes anything. One feels guilty, then feels better and in effect is "free to sin again." Dr. Rudolf Dreikurs, student of Alfred Adler and a major proponent of Adlerian Psychology, stated, "Guilt expresses good intentions we really don't have." He went on to say, "Either do wrong or feel guilty, but don't do both; it's too much work!"

Guilt feelings often have a deceptive quality about them and can actually increase versus decrease harmful behavior toward others. When we have hurt someone by treating them disrespectfully or "loosing our temper" for example, the guilt feelings we generate are often an effort to prove to ourselves and to the person that we hurt that we are really a good person and have good intentions. Dr. Dreikurs still had other things to say about guilt feelings which relates to ones self-deception: "When someone complains about their guilt feelings, watch out for the mischief they are about to do." He went on to say, "Guilt feelings are a preoccupation with what one has done as opposed to what one should do." All of Dreikurs' statements show the fallacy of feeling guilty.

Another Adlerian therapist, teacher and writer, Dr. Harold Mosak, identifies the purposes of guilt feelings. For example, we can use guilt feelings to punish ourselves, to feel superior to those who "sin" but don't have the decency to feel bad as we do, to excuse our bad behavior and to avoid changing. We may also use guilt to protect ourselves from strong angry feelings. In other words, you may think it's safer to feel guilty about your behavior than to let the person know how angry you actually are.[41]

Guilt feelings are most common for people who believe they have to be good or perfect, and can therefore so easily feel "bad" or inadequate when they do something harmful. Their guilt feelings aren't about making amends but are focused on making themselves feel better, by proving they are good. After all, only good people feel guilty, right?

If you feel bad enough to really want to rid yourself of guilt feelings, you need to make a commitment and plan to change your *thinking* as well as your *behavior*. People who feel guilty often believe they must be perfect, or please others, or be right, or be in control. In the name of guilt, some may engage in self-sacrifice: over-commitment to helping others (thereby neglecting themselves); over-concern with success; feelings of inferiority; or extreme discomfort when others are angry with them.

To stop the "guilts" then, you must avoid telling yourself "I did this and it's horrible, I'm a bad person." Don't equate your *behavior* with your *personhood*. Criticize your behavior, but accept yourself as a fallible, yet valuable, human being. Tell yourself, "I behaved badly, but I'm still okay as a person; it's this behavior that's the problem. I will change my behavior."[39]

Stress and Anger. Because stress is so common in our modern and fast paced world and can affect everything about ourselves: our health, our energy level, our relationships, and yes all of our emotions, we want to address it early in this book. Stress is a primary feeling and too much stress makes us vulnerable to all of the other primary feelings and therefore to harmful anger.

Stress often arises from feeling pressured. You tell yourself, "Something awful is happening (or about to happen.) Or "This is too much, I can't stand it." To manage stress, one must first realize that life is full of situations that invite stress. As we said above, while we can't always control what's happening around us, we can control how we respond.

Relaxation and positive self-talk can reduce your stress — just as it can reduce your anger. First, become aware of the anger associated with your fears. Instead of telling yourself it's terrible, I can't stand it, etc., tell yourself positive messages instead, "I can handle it. It's unpleasant but not awful."

In order to get yourself in a state where you can manage these feelings, you may have to use special relaxation techniques, such as deep breathing and muscle relaxation. There are many ways you can learn to relax. (We'll discuss relaxation and self-talk in chapter 4.)

You can also reduce the activities in your life that invite anxiety and stress. You've probably heard the phrase "simplify your life." If you make a list of all the stressful influences in your life, for example, you'll probably find some you can eliminate. One of the stressors on families today is too many activities — especially for the kids! Children are often over-involved with sports, clubs, church activities, etc. This not only contributes to the kids' stress but to yours as well. At the very least, you're probably involved as a chauffeur for many of these activities. Help your kids prioritize their activities. Which ones can be dropped?

If some of the material in this chapter seems a bit theoretical, stay tuned. As you begin to learn strategies for calming anger — the focus of the next two chapters — you'll understand better the importance of these ideas. For now, the most important thing to remember is that you create your own anger, and you can do something about it!

FEELINGS THAT OFTEN GO WITH ANGER

ANGER

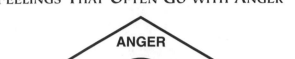

Weak...Tired...Sad...Inadequate...Guilty   Disappointed...Frustrated...Impatient

Stress...Pressure...Overwhelmed   Fear...Anxiety...Worry...Threatened

Hurt...Embarrassed...Betrayed...Cheated   Powerless...Defeated...Devalued...Rejected

Major Points

- For people who feel inadequate, threatened and powerless, anger can be a form of protest, a way to feel temporarily powerful.

- Anger is a "fight or flight" reaction to situations where we fear our survival is threatened.

- Emotions do not "just happen." You create most of your anger by your beliefs and interpretation of events.

- Among the many myths about anger: humans are naturally aggressive; holding anger is dangerous to your health; expressing anger is cathartic; acting out anger gets rid of it.

- Anger — like all emotions — is neither "good" nor "bad; it depends on how the emotion is used.

- Anger can act as a "warning device," telling you that something is wrong — in yourself or in your relationship — and needs to be addressed.

- You can't always choose what happens to you but you do have choices about how you interpret what happens.

- You make yourself angry by "angry thinking" or "hot thoughts" — judging; catastrophizing; "can't-standing"; demanding; blaming.

- Anger often comes from the "MADS": Minimizing your personal power; Awfulizing or catastrophizing; Demanding; Shaming and blaming.

- Anger expression may be a "power move," to gain control, win, get even, or protect rights.

- Anger is often related to fear, anxiety, stress, guilt, depression, annoyance, hurt, frustration, disappointment, or other emotions. Look carefully for the source of your anger.

3

Anger Management Strategies
I

— First Steps —

In chapter 2 you learned how your anger is created by your beliefs and purposes. In this chapter, we'll discuss specific strategies you can use to manage your anger.

"Wait a minute! I thought this book was going to help me with the anger in my family! How come all of a sudden the spotlight is on me?"

Good question. The answer lies in the idea that your family is a *system,* and what affects one of you affects all of you. By starting with yourself, you're in the best position to understand what's happening with the other members of your family as well. (Trust us on this.)

As you've read the first couple of chapters, it's likely that you've discovered some of the factors that may lead to anger in your own life, and in the lives of those you love. To get started on the process of *calming* that anger, we suggest you begin an *anger journal.* You can use the journal to keep track of anger-related events in your life: things like "triggers" (what sets off your anger?) and your body language (do you get frequent headaches, upset digestion?). It's an action step you can take right now to help you focus attention on the messages your body is sending you about your anger. As you proceed through the book, we'll ask you to record other items in your journal. Any kind of notebook will do, although you may find that an 8½ by 11 three-ring binder will work best for your journal.

WHAT ARE YOUR ANGER TRIGGERS?

To begin to deal effectively with anger, you have to learn what it takes to "push your anger buttons." We all have triggers — "hot spots" — situations or behavior of others, or ourselves, that invite or stimulate anger.[40] Some common triggers are: feeling stressed, frightened, anxious, guilty, unjustly accused, pushed, hurried, betrayed, or tired; being interrupted; having your wants denied. Sometimes a spouse, partner, ex or child can act in a way that sets you off: whining, yelling, an insensitive word, certain facial expressions or gestures. The person may behave in a way that reminds you of someone in the past, violates your values, or reminds you of past issues.

Think about your triggers. Do any of the ones we've mentioned ring a bell? Do you have other triggers?

TUNE INTO YOUR BODY

Another way to get in touch with your anger is to learn to recognize when your body's telling you that you're "heating up." Do you experience tenseness, sweating, feel hot or cold, twitch, breathe rapidly, get an upset stomach, clench your fists or grit your teeth, narrow or widen your eyes, raise your voice, speak rapidly, or stiffen up? All these can be signs that you're angry. Consider how you use your body language to communicate your anger to others. Pay attention to your body; it will give you important clues.[39]

Triggers and body language are "storm warnings" — a kind of "internal weather forecast" that let you know the family storm is about to erupt. Once you are aware of your triggers and your body language, you're in a position to begin serious work on managing your anger. Being aware puts you in an active — rather than reactive — position: you are in charge of yourself and your feelings.

The "Storm Warnings: Anger Triggers/Body Language" chart on pages 30–31 will help you identify your triggers and body language. You may want to photocopy the chart and put it in your journal.

You Can Decide to Take Charge of Your Anger

To paraphrase Shakespeare: "To be (angry) or not to be (angry); that is the question." When you catch yourself feeling angry, realize that you have three choices: suppress it, express it or reassess it.

Taking charge of your anger doesn't mean suppressing it. Suppressing anger seldom gets rid of it. You'll find yourself ruminating later — going over and over the situation. When you do this, you usually end up feeling more angry than you were in the first place.

Reacting with anger — expressing it — during a confrontation often produces more confrontation. So that's not the way to go, either. What to do?

There are some immediate steps that can help you take charge of your anger in the moment of confrontation. By taking charge of your anger you are making a decision to reassess it — and to change your thinking, behavior and emotion.

Techniques to Interrupt Your Anger on the Spot

Reacting instantly with anger is where we often get ourselves in trouble. Recognize that you can *be* angry, but you don't have to *act* angry. So when you find yourself becoming angry with another family member while in his or her presence, it's important that you take some time out to give yourself a chance to cool off and *think before you act*. During your time-out, don't berate yourself for feeling angry — this won't help, you'll just feel worse. You need to concentrate on *feeling better* in order to get over your anger so you can address the problem in a positive way. Think about

STORM WARNINGS: ANGER TRIGGERS/BODY LANGUAGE

Anger Triggers

Rate each of the following feelings and conditions as well as others' behavior on a scale of 1–10 for the level of provocation each situation has for you. 1 is the lowest level of provocation and 10 the highest.

Feelings and Conditions	Others' Behavior
____ Being tired	____ Certain look: _____
____ Busy	_____
____ Hurried	_____
____ Pressured	____ Certain gesture: _____
____ Cornered	_____
____ Getting interrupted	_____
____ Making mistakes	____ Tone of voice: _____
____ Seeing things as unfair	_____
____ Frightened	_____
____ Anxious	____ Certain phrase: _____
____ Impatience	_____
____ Non-compliance with my wishes	_____
	____ Certain characteristic:
____ My failure to live up to my own expectations	_____
	_____
____ Frustration	_____
____ Under stress	____ Mannerisms of a past antagonist: _____
____ Think I've been betrayed	_____
____ Feeling guilty	_____
____ Unjustly accused	_____
____ Pushed	____ Other: _____
____ Other: _____	_____
_____	_____

Body Language

Check (✓) each situation below that applies. How is your body signaling you that you are getting angry? What is your body telling others about your feelings? What body language communicates that you are angry?

Body Signals that Tell You You're Getting Angry	Body Language that Communicates to Others You're Angry
___ Stomach upset	___ Clenched fists
___ Increased heart rate	___ Pointing finger
___ Rapid breathing	___ Crossing arms on your chest
___ Tight muscles	___ Hands on hips
___ Grinding or clenching teeth	___ Rigid stance
___ Sweating	___ Moving toward person in threatening manner
___ Feeling hot or cold	
___ Dry mouth	___ Turning away
___ Twitching	___ Raised voice
___ Stiffening up	___ Harsh voice
___ Goose bumps	___ Rapid speech
___ Clenched fists	___ Slowed speech
___ Numbness	___ Mumbling
___ Clammy hands	___ Glaring
___ Raised voice	___ Tightened facial muscles
___ Pacing	___ Raised eyebrows
___ Tenseness	___ Squinting eyes
___ Other _____	___ Widening eyes
_____	___ Other: _____
_____	_____
	_____

what's going on for you and what you can do that may make things better.

You may have a way for immediate management of your anger that has worked for you in the past. If so, use it. If you're having trouble interrupting your anger, you may find one of the following techniques helpful.[38, 39, 40] It's important to have a plan so you don't get caught off guard.

Avoid Your First Impulse. In many cases you will feel like lashing out. Don't. Avoid doing what the other person expects you to do; this will just reinforce the person's behavior that you find disturbing. Do the opposite of what you feel like doing (or do nothing at all).[19]

Walk Away Whenever Possible. Don't walk away in a huff, just remove yourself from the situation. You could say, "I don't think this is the best time to talk about this so I'm going to take some time out. Maybe we can talk about it later when we both feel better." If such incidents keep happening with the same person, the next time you could just say, "I'm going to take some time out" — the rest of your message is obvious.

Tell Yourself Calming Phrases. Create and memorize calming phrases such as "calm down," "take it easy," "keep your cool," "chill out," "cool off." Develop some of your own calming phrases.

Count to Ten. This old technique can be very helpful. By concentrating on the counting, you can calm yourself down, become aware of your body language and think of an appropriate response.

Visualize. Create some peaceful scenes in your mind, such as a lake, the oceanside, or whatever you find calming. Keep these visualizations handy to manage your angry feelings.

Tell Yourself to Stop. You may have to call a halt to your anger before you can use the other techniques we mentioned above. Silently (in your head) shout "stop" when you notice yourself becoming angry. Then tell yourself calming phrases, count to ten, or use your peaceful visualization. You can also take a deep breath to help calm yourself down. Be careful, though; you don't want your deep breath to be interpreted as a sigh as this will just fuel the fire.

Telling yourself to stop is not suppressing your anger. When you tell yourself to stop, you're taking charge — you're making a decision not to allow your anger to escalate and do harm. You also provide yourself an opportunity to handle the situation and your anger in another way. When you suppress your anger, you're telling yourself you *shouldn't* be angry. When you engage in "shoulding," you're actually in a battle with yourself — a battle "you" usually lose.

Everyone gets angry at times and has a right to feel anger. You're not a bad person for feeling angry. Consider what course of action would best address the situation. What can you choose to do or not do, to help solve the problem or improve the situation or relationship?

Stop, Think and Act. Using the above suggestions, you can apply a formula for on-the-spot anger management called *Stop, Think and Act*.[7, 30] In this approach, you first *Stop* — preventing the escalation of angry feelings by avoiding your first impulse, telling yourself to stop, inserting calm phrases or visualizations, counting to ten, taking a time-out — whatever it takes to calm yourself. Then you *Think* about what is going on for you and what an appropriate action might be. Finally, *Act* on that thought — replace reaction with action. Instead of allowing your emotions to control you, take charge of your emotions for your own benefit and the benefit of the other person. In other words, replace going on "autopilot" with making a choice.

DECIDING WHETHER OR NOT TO EXPRESS YOUR ANGER

Sometimes respectfully expressing your anger can clear the air and make things better. At other times the expression may make things worse. So how do you decide? In chapter 7, we'll detail the conditions for appropriate anger expression. For now, it's important for you to simply assess how you think the other person will accept your anger. By and large, how the other person will most likely respond is your key to deciding if expression is your best choice.

Rating Your Anger

Relationships can be filled with irritating situations. Think of something you're angry about and ask yourself whether it's really worth it to be angry. Rate it on a "worth-it scale" from 1–10. If you score the situation at six or below, it's probably not worth it.

You can also make a two-column list in your notebook: Column 1: "Things worth being angry about"; Column 2: "Things not worth being angry about." Study your lists. Can you move some of the "worth-its" to the "not worth it" column?[39] If you find being angry and expressing it won't help the situation, then you may decide it's not worth it to be angry.

You could begin to consider your anger like an exceptional meal or fine wine: to be served only on special occasions!

We've begun our exploration of anger management by emphasizing brief, short-term steps you can take to defuse your anger at the point of an angry episode. Chapter 4 offers aids to help you deal with the anger in your life over the long term.

Major Points

- Anger management begins by recognizing your "storm warnings" — triggers and body language.

- Triggers — "hot spots" — are situations or behavior of others that invite or stimulate your anger.

- Body language can tell you that you're "heating up," and can communicate your anger to others. Pay attention to it.

- When you're feeling angry, you have three choices: suppress it (don't: you'll go over and over it later), express it (be careful: you may produce an unwanted confrontation), or reassess it (good choice: change your thinking and behavior about the situation).

- Interrupt your anger on the spot: avoid your first impulse; walk away; tell yourself calming phrases; count to ten; visualize; tell yourself to "Stop, Think and Act."

- Consciously decide whether or not to express your anger. Will it clear the air or make things worse? Consider how the other person will feel and react.

- Rate your anger. Is it worth it — on a scale of 1–10 — to express your anger in this situation?

4

Anger Management Strategies II

— For the Long Term —

While immediate techniques are important — they help you get control of your anger for the moment — if you are to reduce your angry actions and reactions, then you also need strategies for the long term. Long-term anger management involves taking time to work on your beliefs and purposes.

DISPUTE YOUR IRRATIONAL "HOT" THOUGHTS AND PURPOSES
In chapter 2 you learned that we make ourselves angry by engaging in hostile or "hot" thoughts. Such thoughts are, as psychologist and author Dr. Albert Ellis says, *irrational* because they won't stand the test of reality. Dr. Ellis suggests we dispute our thoughts to see how irrational they are.[23]

Begin by writing down your hot thoughts about a particular anger-provoking situation. Then examine your belief — consider your "MADS" — those beliefs you hold which most commonly create anger.[40]

M — Minimizing. How are you *minimizing* your personal power? What are you telling yourself about the situation — your "can't-standing" statements — that indicates you believe you are incapable of handling this event?

What evidence exists that you just "can't stand" what happened? You've stood many things in your life; what makes this one different?

A further note about minimizing your personal power. People tell themselves other types of passive language besides "I can't stand . . ." Some tell themselves, "It makes me so mad!" No one *makes* you mad but you. When you think someone makes you mad, you're giving your power away. Others say, "I can't help it." This is a very weak belief and disrespectful of yourself. If you really believe you can't help it, you should stop reading this book now! Some say, "I lost my temper." Your temper is not something you carry around that can be "lost." As Dr. Dreikurs said, "We don't lose our tempers, we throw them away." Others say, "Something came over me." It's as if there's an alien spacecraft directing your behavior! Some say, "I'm not myself today." We are always ourselves — with all our faults and good points — we don't temporarily become someone else. We may not be our best selves today, but we are ourselves.[39] All these things we tell ourselves to excuse our anger are BS — Bad Self-analysis!

A — Awfulizing. Examine your *"awfulizing"* statements. What evidence exists that this situation is awful, terrible or catastrophic? Catastrophes involve things like people dying in terrorist attacks, terminal illnesses and the death of a child. It is logical that one would judge these events as awful.

In your journal, make a list of things in your life you would find catastrophic and those you would find frustrating, disappointing, annoying, but not awful. Examine your list. Which of the things you think are "awful" could actually be moved to the "frustrating" column? How does your present situation rank — is it really catastrophic or just really frustrating, disappointing or annoying?

D — Demanding. Search for your *demanding* statements — your should, must, always, or never statements — the narrow expectations you place on others or life. Why do you think that just because you really want or wish this disturbing situation to be different, that it *actually* should or must be different? Why must your spouse, partner, ex or child always do what you want or never displease you? Your demands are really your wishes, not the other way around.

S — Shaming and Blaming. Look at your judgments about the other person's character — your *shaming and blaming* statements. How does not following your wishes make this person bad, rotten, or worthless? Make another list with two columns — what you see as the person's good points and what you see as the bad points. Realize that you're actually judging the person's *behavior* as bad in this situation, not the total *person*. Don't equate the deed with the doer!

Finally, examine the purpose of your anger in this situation — are you trying to control, win, get even or protect your rights? Sometimes you can have more than one purpose. For example, you want to control the person's behavior or, failing that, you want to seek revenge. Your purpose is often revealed in your self-talk. For example, if you believe, "He must do what I say," you're probably seeking control.

Let's look at an example of using the above disputing techniques.

> *Suppose you think your seven-year-old watches too much TV. You tell her this and attempt to limit her TV time. She throws a temper tantrum the next time you tell her it's time to do something else. You get angry, turn off the TV and order her to her room. You end up swatting her on the bottom and dragging her, screaming, to her room — threatening to suspend her TV watching privileges forever. While she's screaming in her room, you're smoldering in the living room.*

Let's examine and dispute your "hot" thoughts. You could be telling yourself something such as, "I can't stand this! She should do what I tell her to do — I'm the parent! This is terrible. Who does she think she is, saying no to me and throwing a fit? Such a little brat. I'll fix her!"

Why do you think you *can't stand* this? It's certainly not pleasant when a child defies you, but what makes it *intolerable*? While you really want her to do what you wish, what makes you think she *should* do it — just because you're the parent? This is a tough one, because most parents think they are the boss. But kids don't really see their parents as the boss anymore. That doesn't mean parents aren't responsible for setting guidelines and limits, but the kids will test them, and anger doesn't really solve the problem (more on this in chapter 12).

Does this situation really qualify as a catastrophe? Did someone become seriously ill or die? Also, is this kid *always* a brat, or just behaving bratty in this situation?

What's your purpose here? By telling yourself, "She should do what I tell her to do . . ." you're probably trying to control or win the argument. By hitting her and threatening to suspend her TV privileges and telling yourself, "I'll fix her," you probably also want to get even. Maybe it's time to stop for a moment and ask yourself, "Who's the adult here?"

CREATE "COOL" THOUGHTS AND POSITIVE PURPOSES

Once you've disputed your "hot" thoughts and hopefully concluded they are indeed irrational and not really based on reality, then it's time to create "cool" thoughts and revise your purpose or purposes.

In the situation involving your daughter and the TV, you can tell yourself something like, "I don't like this, but I can stand it. It's certainly frustrating, but it hardly qualifies as awful. I really wish she would abide by my instructions, but there's really no logical reason why she should, from her point of view. While I find her behavior very frustrating, she's not a total brat; she's a good kid most of the time." Notice that you are focusing on your ability to handle unpleasant situations, re-evaluating the importance of the situation (it isn't a catastrophe), realizing that you can't effectively *demand* that she obey and, finally, refraining from judging her total personality based on this incident.

Now, reassess your purpose. How can you change from trying to control your daughter to controlling the situation? Perhaps you can give her a choice in a calm voice: "When it's time to turn off the TV, you may do it, or I will do it." In this way, you are sticking to your limits, but you aren't demanding; you are giving her a choice within the limits you set. If she doesn't turn off the TV, then she's made her choice and you turn it off. If she throws a fit, resist the temptation to control her or get even. You could simply walk away. It's hard to have a temper tantrum without an audience. She may increase her tirade to try to get you involved, but if you stick to your resolve, she'll eventually give it up because it isn't working.

If you think she'll do herself or your property harm if you leave her alone in the family room, you could give her another choice: "You may settle down here or have your fit in your room. You decide." If she doesn't settle down, you could say. "Do you want to go to your room on your own, or shall I help you?" If she balks, you simply take her by the hand and usher her to her room saying. "Come on out when you feel better."

If your daughter has frequent temper tantrums, you can set up a positive time-out system. We discuss positive time-out in chapter 12.

If you've taken the time to analyze, dispute, create "cool" thoughts, and change your purpose, you'll be prepared for a reoccurrence of this situation or a similar one. If necessary, use the "techniques to interrupt your anger on the spot" listed in chapter 3 to help you remain calm when the situation occurs.

Be aware that by creating "cool" thoughts we're not just talking about playing word games with yourself. If you are to be effective you must really *believe* your new self-talk.

OTHER TECHNIQUES FOR MANAGING ANGER

The following techniques can help you when you are creating "cool" thoughts.[38, 39, 40]

Reframe the Situation. Reframing involves looking at the situation in a different way. When we encounter a situation, we perceive it in a certain way — "frame" it — according to our beliefs. When you "reframe" a situation, you look at it differently. Reframing involves seeing if the person's behavior could mean something different than you first thought, looking for the positive potential in an otherwise negative situation, seeing if there's an opportunity in the situation, or, if the situation has passed, concentrating on what can be learned.

Looking again at our example of the conflict with your daughter over watching too much TV, ask yourself, "Could this behavior have a different meaning than the way I'm interpreting it?" You could be thinking that she's just being defiant, but you could also choose to think: "She's just testing the limits — something nearly all kids do." "What's the positive potential here?" Although you don't like your child throwing a temper tantrum, at least she's standing up for herself, even if temper tantrums aren't the best way to do that. Ask yourself "What's the opportunity in this situation? Your daughter has an opportunity to learn to accept limits, even if she doesn't like them. You have an opportunity to learn to apply limits and follow through without becoming angry. Then ask yourself, "What did I learn from this experience?" You learned that anger often doesn't work very well; both of you end up feeling worse.

Sometimes reframing involves looking at the positive "flip side" of a particular trait that you see as negative. A person who is stubborn is also determined; the picky person is also discriminating, the argumentative person is also able to see alternatives; the complainer knows what she or he wants. Even one who's lazy has a positive side — he or she is selective!

Take a few minutes to list in your notebook traits your spouse, partner, ex or child has that you consider negative. Search for the flip sides — the positives — and write them down.

Find the Humor. Your sense of humor is one of your best assets. When we are able to see humor in otherwise disturbing situations, we can defuse our anger. By finding the humorous side, you are actually reframing the event. Of course you don't want to use your humor to belittle the person — just attempt to find what's humorous. If your daughter throws a temper tantrum over your TV limits, you might tell yourself (not her), "Boy, she does that well; maybe she should be on TV!"

See if you can find some humor in your own beliefs and behavior. In this situation, you might tell yourself. "My performance wasn't bad either; maybe I could play second to her leading role!"

Think of some behaviors of your family members including yourself. What humor can you find? Write it in your journal.

Don't Revisit Past Hurts and Failures. "She will never change." "You never listen." "He always . . ." These and other negative ways of describing your spouse, partner, child, ex, or yourself only reinforce your angry feelings and prevent progress. Just because someone did something in the past doesn't necessarily mean that person will always behave the same way. Of course, if you're consistently behaving in a certain way in response to that person, you may be establishing a pattern. You can break the pattern: if you change the way you think, feel and behave, the other person may also begin to change.

Do Revisit Past Successes. When you're faced with an anger-provoking situation, think of situations in the past, similar to this one, that you handled successfully. How did you do it? What did you tell yourself to keep you calm? How did you behave? How can you apply your discoveries to your present situation? Again, write this all down in your journal. The past successes you find will help you see that you are capable of handling anger provocations and find solutions.

Think About What the Other Person is Experiencing. When you're angry with someone, you're focusing on your own anger and trying to win, control, get even, or protect your rights. Remember the other person has beliefs and purposes as well. If you shift your focus from yourself to what the other person might be experiencing, you may be able to diffuse the anger and solve the problem.

Your TV-watching daughter may be thinking you're unfair. She's trying to demonstrate her power and perhaps to get even with you for taking from her what she thinks is her right — to watch TV. She's had experience with you so she expects you to get angry and when you do, you fall right into her trap. She may not be able to force you to let her watch more TV (unless you give in, of course), but at least she can get a big adult out of control. Either way she has power and therefore — guess what? — she wins the power contest!

So when faced with an anger-provoking situation, instead of focusing on your anger, ask yourself: "What might she be thinking? What's her purpose?" "Did I do something to bring this on?" "What does she expect me to do?" "If I do what she expects, what will most likely happen?" "Could something else outside our relationship be influencing her anger?" Your answers to these questions will help you decide what to do. Write out your answers in your journal. With practice, you will be able to do this on the spur of the moment as well.

Talk It Over With a Third Party. Sharing your concerns with someone you trust can be helpful. Sometimes a friend will have insights that don't occur to you. Of course, if things aren't getting any better or are threatening, you may need to consult a therapist or other professional.

Seek Spiritual Guidance. If you're a religious or spiritually focused person, you may want to use prayer or meditation to help you find the guidance and strength to handle anger challenges. Your faith and prayers may help you find the courage and inspiration to more peacefully handle these challenges.

Exercise. Physical activity can help you drain the tension you experience when you're angry or under stress. Exercise can help "clear your head." Also, exercise has been proven to brighten our moods by enhancing certain beneficial chemical processes in the body. Often, creative ways of thinking about challenging situations, or creative solutions, to them surface while exercising.

As you're exercising, think about the situation, examining your hot thoughts and considering the cool thoughts you could have. When you get through exercising, write down what you were thinking.

Establishing regular exercise periods not only helps you physically but can help you emotionally as well. It helps in your ability to manage anger and stress. When you feel better physically, you have more energy, and maintaining good relationships requires energy.

Minimize or Eliminate the Use of Alcohol and Other Drugs. Alcohol and other drugs reduce the ability to develop cool thoughts and raise the temperature of hot thoughts. It is common for people to rely upon intoxicating substances to reduce stress and "take the edge off" of emotions that are uncomfortable or painful. The irony is that this "solution" has only very short-term benefits, if any. Drugs and alcohol in the short or long term actually intensify painful emotions and erode the ability to function physically, socially, and economically. If substance use progresses into addiction, the common defenses of denial and delusion result in conflict, alienation, and anger for everyone in the family. If you or a loved one has a drug or alcohol problem, it's important to realize that the affected person has a limited ability to control their emotions. We strongly recommend that you seek out the support of substance abuse treatment agencies or counselors trained in substance abuse treatment in your community.

Create a Things To Do List. Having a plan to meet anger-provoking situations helps you avoid behaviors that may make the situation worse. So be a good boy or girl scout and "be prepared." Write a list of things that you can do when anger triggers arise, and look at it frequently so that you commit it to memory.

Practice Deep Breathing and Relaxation. When you're angry, your breath usually comes in short, shallow bursts. You can slow yourself down by concentrating on taking deep breaths. Deep breathing will help you start to relax.

Get yourself in a relaxed state by doing whatever helps you relax, such as exercise, listening to music, a warm bath, or relaxation exercises. Here's a simple relaxation exercise that many have found helpful:[9]

1. Get comfortable. Lie down or recline in a comfortable chair. If you choose a chair, make sure it has a head support.

2. Get calm by taking several deep breaths.

3. Relax your muscles by tensing them and then releasing the tension. Do this for five seconds for each of your body's muscle groups. When you let go of the tension, say "relax and let go." Start with your forehead — wrinkle it, hold, let go and tell yourself to relax. Proceed to your eyes, squint them tightly. Open your mouth widely. Next, clench your jaw. Push your head back against the support. Touch your chest with your chin. Slowly roll your head to your shoulders: to the right, then to the left. Shrug both shoulders up toward your ears. Then shrug your right shoulder toward your ear, then your left. With each shrug, pretend you're trying to touch your ears. Proceed to your upper and lower arms, tensing and relaxing, then your hands and fingers. Now tense and relax your chest, stomach, upper and lower back. Continue with your buttocks, thighs,

calves, ankles, feet, and toes. (You may begin with your toes and reverse the procedure if that's more comfortable for you.) With each muscle group, make sure you hold the tension for five seconds, release and tell yourself to relax and let go. Feel the tension drain out of your body. Take slow, deep breaths, and exhale slowly. Keep letting go and relaxing the tension more and more, breathing deeply and slowly, for several minutes. Get up slowly after the exercise.

Practice this relaxation exercise twice a day — it only takes a few minutes. You can also use it to get yourself into a relaxed state just before you work on changing your thinking and purposes. After a few weeks of practice with this exercise, you'll find you can become completely relaxed without tensing your muscles first.

Practice Visualization and Positive Self-Talk. In the previous chapter, we suggested you create brief, calming visualizations to help you manage your anger in the heat of the moment. The following visualization exercise will help you develop long-term non-angry responses.

Begin by choosing a mildly anger-provoking scene from your past, or one that occurs frequently. As you gain experience in visualizing, you will be able to handle stronger anger-provoking situations. Close your eyes and take a few deep breaths to help you relax. (You may wish to do the deep breathing and relaxation exercise above as you begin this one.) Then imagine the scene in detail; let yourself see and hear the other person and yourself. As soon as you start feeling angry, insert a calming phrase such as "take it easy," "keep calm," or any self-talk that helps you calm down. If you have trouble interrupting your anger with calming phrases, firmly tell yourself to "stop." You may need to take some deep breaths as you tell yourself to stop. Once you've got control of yourself, insert the calming phrase. Repeat the scene several times, using self-talk to calm yourself down. Work on calming yourself, no matter what the other person is doing in your scene. Keep at it until you feel calm.

As you get more practice with developing "cool" thoughts as opposed to "hot" thoughts, you can insert your cool thoughts after you get yourself calm. "I can stand this, even though I don't like it. It's very disappointing, but not a catastrophe. I really want . . . but there's no reason why Chitra should complete the project just because I wish it. I think she's acting badly here, but she is not a bad person."

Practice visualizing with positive self-talk three times a day for ten minutes each session. As you practice visualizing, you'll notice you can calm yourself down quickly. Visualization can be useful in helping you prepare for future events where you may have a tendency to be angry.

We know that some folks do not easily visualize images. If that's a problem for you, focus on any of your senses that are active when you're angry: sound, touch, smell. You'll find it will help you to get in touch with your anger if you can concentrate on the senses you experience. You can also substitute your other senses for visual images in the visualization exercise above, giving you another way to practice long-term non-angry responses. The sensory information you gain about your body's response to anger can serve as a storm warning, telling you when it's time to call on the anger management skills you're developing as you read this book.

Now that you have learned some immediate and long-term strategies for anger management, we're going to introduce yet another approach — a simple five-step procedure that will pull together all of your new resources for preventing and dealing with storms in your family. Keep reading!

Major Points

- Long-term anger management takes time. Get started by writing down your hot thoughts.

- Examine your "MADS." (Minimizing, Awfulizing, Demanding, Shaming)

- Examine the purpose of your anger in a situation: Control, win, get even, or protect your rights.

- Create "cool" thoughts: You can handle unpleasant situations; this isn't a catastrophe; your wishes are not the other person's command.

- Reassess your purpose: (For example: You can control your anger; you can't control the other person.)

- Reframe the situation: What's another way to look at this?

- Find the humor: There must be something funny in all this.

- Don't revisit past hurts and failures; do revisit past successes.

- Look at it from the other person's view.

- Talk it over with a third party or spiritual guide.

- Exercise away the tension you experience when you're angry or stressed.

- Minimize or eliminate the use of alcohol and other drugs.

- List things to do about your anger.

- Practice deep breathing, relaxation, and visualization.

5

Five Steps to Less Anger in Your Life

We've given you several techniques you can use to manage your anger, including "on-the-spot" methods (such as "Stop, Think and Act") to handle anger when you're caught off guard. Now we'll discuss the five steps of an anger management process you can use to reduce anger in your life. You can use these steps to prepare for anger-provoking events in your relationships. As you learn to handle such events, you'll find yourself better prepared for other anger-provoking situations. In short, the more you work on your anger, the more you'll reduce it in your life.

The essence of this process is to help you become more responsive and less reactive. *Reacting* without pausing or thinking — behaving "automatically" when you're emotionally distressed — is exactly what leads to harmful and hurtful behavior toward the people that you care about. Allow yourself instead to *respond*, to pause and take the few seconds — or few minutes — you need for reflection, assessment, and choice. You'll significantly increase the likelihood of an effective and respectful relationship with your family and other important people in your life.

As you proceed through the five steps in this chapter, use the techniques discussed to help you change your thoughts, purposes, feelings, and actions. Choose the techniques you think will work best for you. Write down your answers to the questions listed in each step in your anger journal. (See the sample format at the end of this chapter.)

STEP 1: EXAMINE THE ANGER-PROVOKING SITUATION
Ask yourself these questions:

1. *"What happened?"* What stressor or situation did you encounter? What did the other person do (or not do)? What specifically triggered your anger?

2. *"How did I respond?"* What did you do? What did your body feel like and tell you?

3. *"What were the consequences of my action?"* What happened as a result of your angry response?

4. *"How angry was I?"* Rate from 1-10.

STEP 2: EXAMINE YOUR INNER PROCESSES
Taking time to think about what is going on for you is a very important step in becoming more effective in managing your anger. First of all, be kind to yourself. Remind yourself that anger is a natural human emotion and that you have value even when you're angry.

Look for your "hot" thoughts, your "MADS." Here are more questions to ask yourself:

1. *"How am I **Minimizing** my personal power?"* Are you saying, "I can't stand it," or "I can't take this"? Do you hear yourself making other passive statements, such as, "He makes me so mad!"?

2. *"How am I Awfulizing?"* Do you tell yourself how awful, terrible, horrible, catastrophic this is?

3. *"How am I Demanding?"* Look for your "shoulds" and "musts," or "always" and "never" statements.

4. *"How am I Shaming and blaming?"* Watch for calling the other person names, such as "worthless," "rotten," "a bad person" or worse.)

Look at your "hot spots," those emotionally painful experiences from the past and/or your most cherished values. Ask yourself, "Have any of my hot spots been activated in this situation, leading to my angry thoughts and strong reaction?"

Next, consider your purpose: *"What was I trying to achieve?"* Decide whether you were trying to control, win, get even, or protect your rights.

Reflect on any other emotions your anger may be covering up, such as anxiety, fear, embarrassment, frustration, threat, hurt, powerlessness, inadequacy. Ask yourself, "What am I feeling besides the anger?"

STEP 3: RETHINK THE SITUATION

Dispute your "hot" thoughts. Ask yourself:

1. *"What evidence exists that I 'can't stand' what happened?"*

2. *"What evidence exists that this situation is 'awful, terrible or catastrophic'?"*

3. *"Just because I really want or wish this disturbing situation to be different, why should or must the situation be different?"* Or, *"Why must it always (or never) be a certain way, even though I really want it to?"*

4. *"How does not following my wishes make this person bad, rotten, or worthless?"*

If the situation activated your hot spots, think about the *connection between the present situation and your past* and how this leads to hot thoughts in the current situation. Admit to yourself that your anger makes sense, given your past life experiences. Remind yourself that the past is the past, that this is a new challenge requiring new resources and solutions, and that as an adult you can find the inner resources you need.

Look at the possible results of your purpose. If you want to *control*, ask yourself: "What will happen if I try to control Amanda?" If your purpose is to *win*, ask yourself: "What will happen if I try to win this argument?" If what you want is to *get even*, ask yourself: "What will happen if I get even?" If your purpose is to *protect your rights* (or someone else's), ask yourself. "Will anger really help me protect my rights (or the rights of others)? At what expense?"

STEP 4: CREATE "COOL THOUGHTS" AND A POSITIVE PURPOSE

To create cool thoughts, you have to change the way you think about the situation and *really believe* your new language.

Realize that, hard as it is, you *can* stand whatever you're faced with. "I don't like it, but I can stand it." Change your demands — your shoulds or musts — to what they really are: strong desires, wants or wishes. Your demands are the root of your irrational hot thoughts. If you did not demand that others be (or not be) a certain way, or demand that things always (or never) occur, you would not awfulize, proclaim you can't stand it, or shame and blame. You can tell yourself something such as: "While I really wish he'd do what I want, there's no reason why he *should*." Or, "While it certainly would be better if it never happened, there's no law that says it must turn out that way."

Realize what you're encountering is unfortunate, frustrating, disappointing, or inconvenient, but it's far from a catastrophe — it's not awful, terrible or horrible. You can tell yourself something such as: "This is frustrating, but it's not awful."

Finally, reject the behavior but not the person. Realize that the person is not a total jerk — even though you think he or she is behaving like one in this instance. "Even though I don't like this behavior, Geoff is okay as a person."

You can also use some of the techniques we've discussed to help you create your cool thoughts: Reframe, find the humor, revisit past successes (don't revisit past hurts and failures), think about what the other person is experiencing, talk it over with a third party, talk to your God or your spiritual resource, exercise, create a things-to-do list, practice deep breathing and relaxation, and use visualization.

By creating these cool thoughts, you may still end up disappointed, annoyed or frustrated, but you won't be angry. As Dr. Ellis says, "These healthy negative feelings (disappointment, etc.) help you live happily and productively without unnecessary frustration and pain. On the other hand, unhealthy negative feelings (such as too much anger) tend to stop you from achieving many of your main goals."[23]

With practice, you can get past the annoyance, disappointment, and frustration and learn to turn your anger into determination. You can add another positive self-statement to your cool thoughts by telling yourself: "I will not continue to be angry. I will work for cooperation instead." This type of thinking will strengthen your determination.

Once you've created your cool thoughts, create a positive purpose. Here are a few questions to ask yourself, depending on your purpose:

Control: "How can I change my focus from controlling others to controlling my own anger and the situation?" Realize that trying to control others often provokes a battle. Although most people don't like to be controlled, there are exceptions. If a person doesn't want to shoulder any responsibility for the outcome of a decision, she or he may let you be in control. Then, if the decision goes wrong, guess who's to blame! When you focus on controlling your anger (reminding yourself that the only person you can control is you), you stand a much better chance of gaining cooperation. Controlling the situation involves setting limits. Limits offer the person a choice within boundaries — much more effective than demanding that the person submit to your will.

Win: "How can I work for the win-win?" Remember that trying to win usually increases the conflict. It often becomes a contest of who's right, which only increases the anger. (Unless, again, the person decides to let you win in order to avoid responsibility.) Working for the win-win helps each "opponent" feel that she or he has a part in the solution.

Get even: "How can I work to make things fair rather than getting even?" Realize that you can never really "get even." Revenge provokes revenge. You may think you got 'em, but when you least expect it, watch out! Working for fairness helps both you and your adversary feel better and committed to the decision.

Protect rights: "What are some other ways to protect my rights besides anger?" Using anger to protect your rights (or someone else's) may work with some people but not with others. Only you know whether using anger stands a chance of being effective with a particular person. Firmly but respectfully stating what you are willing to accept and what you are not willing to accept is often more effective.

STEP 5: CHOOSE NEW BEHAVIOR AND FOLLOW THROUGH

Once you've got yourself calmed down, it's time to decide what you will do. What changes in your behavior are you willing to make to improve the relationship? Do limits need to be defined here? (Chapters 11 and 12 will discuss how to effectively set limits with kids.) Is this a situation that needs to be talked about, or is it best to let it go? If you decide to talk it over, clarify the other emotions that accompany the anger (e.g., fear, embarrassment, frustration, threat, hurt, powerlessness, inadequacy). Validate (accept) those feelings in yourself, and ask yourself if it would be more effective to express *those feelings* to the person, or is it better to communicate your anger directly.

When you've decided what to do, do it; don't just "try" to do it. Trying and doing aren't the same things. "I'll try" usually means you aren't convinced that what you've decided to do will work — trying is a weak commitment. It's like buying insurance for failure. While you don't know if what you've decided to do will improve the situation, you stand a much better chance of being successful if you make a firm commitment: "I will" rather than "I'll try to." You cannot promise an outcome, of course, but you can take positive steps toward it.

For example, if you've decided to ignore your child's whining rather than get angry or giving in — which usually makes it worse — stick to your decision. Don't just "try" to ignore the whining, really ignore it! How? With conviction, you can choose to think about something else — your shopping list, a favorite activity, or your plans for the weekend — while your child is whining. Create determination and make a commitment to do this every time she whines. Experiment with this technique for a week, and see what happens. The whining will probably get worse before it gets better because the child is used to you losing your cool or giving in. If you do either of these things, your child has successfully demonstrated his power. But if you stick to it, the child will most likely give it up because the whining no longer works!

Watch out for the "yes, but" game. You've probably played this game before — most people do. The rules of the game go like this: You read or hear an idea and you think you should do it, but you really don't intend to do it. "Well, I agree with Toni's proposal, but . . ." Then you argue why it won't work. Instead of first agreeing, "yes," and then canceling with "but" (or synonyms), why play this game with yourself or someone else? If you don't want to do it, don't do it. If you "yes, but" it, you're only fooling yourself.[39]

THE FIVE STEPS IN ACTION

Here's an example of how the five steps can help with anger problems:

Jennifer's anger toward Rick — her husband of ten years — has been growing. It erupted recently when Jennifer felt strongly that Rick was being too rough in his discipline of Bethany, their eight-year-old. He sometimes shouts at Bethany and says, in Jennifer's view, harsh and threatening words to her. He has "swatted" her as well for recent misbehavior, including an incident where Bethany refused to do her chores. In this instance, Jennifer reproached Rick in front of Bethany. Rick obviously felt humiliated and undermined by Jennifer, and stormed out of the room in anger. They didn't speak the rest of the day.

While both partners are playing a role in this conflict, we will focus on Jennifer and how she might address the situation, incorporating the anger management strategies we've discussed.

Step 1 — Examine the Anger-provoking Situation: As Jennifer thought about the incident, she recognized that her own anger was intense — a 10. She noted that she stiffened up, pointed her finger at Rick, and yelled at him.

While still believing that Rick's approach to discipline is ineffective and harmful, she realized her own response was also ineffective and harmful. She recognized that correcting Rick's parenting approach in Bethany's presence fueled Rick's anger, provoking him to be even more resistant to considering a more respectful approach. Her response actually increased the likelihood that his behavior would continue and that anger would escalate for them both.

Step 2 — Examine Your Inner Processes: Jennifer was able to remind herself that she is human, her anger is natural, and is a sign of how much she cares for her family. In examining her MADS, Jennifer saw that she was telling herself that she just *couldn't stand* Rick's behavior and that he was the cause of her anger. She was able to recognize that her belief and behavior were in fact awfulizing Rick's behavior, concluding that he will *always* be this way, and as Bethany gets older, things will only get worse. She also realized that she was actually demanding, shaming and blaming — believing that Rick should never behave this way, that he was a *lousy* parent for doing so, and that he'll never learn! She recognized that her purpose was to punish him for harshly punishing their daughter.

Step 3 — Rethink the Situation: Jennifer realized that Rick was, in fact, very capable of learning, and that there was ample evidence of this. She admitted to herself that Rick is doing what he learned to do, as his father was a strict disciplinarian. She also realized that Rick cares deeply about his daughter, and that his discipline of her, though perhaps misguided, was proof of how much he cared for Bethany and her development. In examining her purpose, Jennifer, with a smile, was able to see that her own punishment of Rick was very similar to what she objected to in Rick's discipline of Bethany!

Step 4— Create "Cool Thoughts" and a Positive Purpose: Jennifer converted her hot thoughts and original purpose to cool thoughts and a positive purpose: "Even though I don't like Rick's behavior, it's not awful, just very unfortunate because it's discouraging. Rick cares about Bethany, he's capable of learning, and so am I. I can only control my own approach to parenting and not Rick's. I will respectfully share with Rick my thoughts and feelings about parenting, and model these every day. I will start discussions about parenting only when we are not in the heat of a conflict. If I am feeling angry when observing Rick with Bethany, I will interrupt my anger by walking away. I will be more conscious of pointing out what I appreciate about Rick as a father. We can both benefit from reading more about parenting and attending parenting classes together."

By concentrating on these cool thoughts, Jennifer found that she still felt sad and somewhat frustrated by Rick's behavior, but she no longer felt so angry. She also was determined to do her best to win Rick's cooperation.

Step 5 — Choose New Behavior and Follow Through: Jennifer found that as she followed through with her cool thoughts, positive purpose, and behavior, her relationship with Rick became closer and more positive. Over time they were able to have meaningful discussions about parenting, and after several months passed, Rick was receptive to attending a parenting class together. While their parenting styles remain different, they are overlapping and complementing each other much more than in the past.

Self-Anger

In this chapter, we've discussed anger in terms of how you feel about others' behavior. We've talked about accepting other people while not accepting some of their behaviors that disturb you. What about *your anger at yourself?* You're a person too. You will probably never totally eliminate your anger; you are, like other people, not perfect. Besides, sometimes anger is necessary. But you can greatly decrease your anger if you are willing to accept yourself and others as imperfect beings and realize that making demands on others — or yourself — usually gains you nothing but grief.[39]

When you do feel angry with yourself, use the five-step process to examine that anger.

Anger Journal

You can become more effective in handling your anger toward others or yourself if you take the time to write out your answers and plans to the five steps in your journal/notebook. Journaling will help you study your answers and act on your new thoughts and decisions. You'll find it helpful to create the following chart in "landscape" (horizontal) format so you can see the entire process on one page and have room to write. Or use two pages with columns facing each other. You may want to make a template and photocopy it so you don't have to keep designing a form each time you fill up a page.

In this chapter we've discussed several ways to manage your anger and to become more responsive and less reactive when you are emotionally distressed. The more time, effort and practice you put into your anger work, the better you'll get. You may find it helpful to re-read some of the material we've covered — there is a lot to know about anger!

The remaining chapters in this book will show you how to apply what you've learned to your family relationships — helping you discover how to calm the family storm. For example, chapter 6 talks about encouragement — a basic skill to manage and reduce anger.

My Anger Journal: Five Steps for Managing Anger

STEP 1	STEP 2	STEP 3	STEP 4	STEP 5
Examine the Anger-provoking Situation *(Include any triggers — "hot spots")*	**Examine Your Inner Processes** *("Hot thoughts" — MADS & purpose)*	**Rethink the Situation** *(Dispute your thoughts & purpose)*	**Create "Cool Thoughts" and a Positive Purpose** *(Include any reframes, humor you can see, etc.)*	**Choose New Behavior and Follow Through**

MAJOR POINTS

◆ *Step 1: Examine the anger-provoking situation:* What happened? How did you respond? What were the consequences of your action? How angry were you?

◆ *Step 2: Examine your inner processes — your MADS:* How are you Minimizing personal power? How are you Awfulizing? How are you Demanding? How are you Shaming and blaming?

◆ *Step 3: Rethink the situation.* Is it really true that you can't stand it? That it's a catastrophe? That it must be different? That the other person is bad, rotten, worthless?

◆ *Step 4: Create "cool thoughts" and a positive purpose.* You can stand it. It's frustrating but not awful. Your demands are really wishes. The person is okay, even if the behavior is not. Change your purpose to controlling the situation or yourself, not the other person. Work for the win-win. Make things fair, not even. Protect your rights without anger.

◆ *Step 5: Choose to change your own behavior, and follow through.* What changes will you make to improve the relationship? Act on your decision, don't just "try" to do it.

Use the 5 steps to deal with your self-anger as well as your anger toward others.

6

Encouraging Relationships

T he basic skills of encouragement, communication, and problem solving are the building blocks for all relationships, and provide important resources for preventing, managing, and reducing the intensity of family storms.

This chapter will focus on encouragement — a central feature of healthy relationships. (Effective communication comes up in chapter 7, problem solving in chapter 8.) We'll start by exploring what *encouragement* actually is. You may hear the word frequently, but not have the same understanding of the concept that we'd like you to consider.

WHAT IS ENCOURAGEMENT?

Encouragement is based on *courage* — its root word. When we encourage, we focus on building courage in those we care for, helping them to believe in themselves and their own abilities. That means recognizing what one can do, and being independent enough to do it. Courage requires the determination to contribute your efforts and abilities in spite of obstacles and dangers, all of which builds *resilience*, the internal strength to weather hardship.

A vivid term for what we're referring to here is *"psychological muscle"*.[59] When you consistently encourage the people you care for, you help build their psychological muscle, their inner strength, and their resilience. You're preparing them to weather the many storms that life will bring their way — including those that occur in the family.

Encouragement is also the process of building *self-esteem* in yourself and your family members, and courage is an integral part of self-esteem. To have positive self-esteem is to accept and value yourself and others. We humans are social beings with a strong sense of belonging, and our self-esteem includes a sense of mutual respect, of concern for the self-esteem of others — such as family members — as well as ourselves. In other words, healthy self-esteem includes "people-esteem" or, in the case of families, "family-esteem."

If you attempt to build your self-esteem at the expense of others — building yourself up by putting others down — you actually possess what we call "ego-esteem." Ego-esteem is different from self- or people-esteem; ego-esteem implies that to feel good about yourself you must be better than others.[40]

Anger can discourage self-esteem in others as well as in yourself. If you're frequently angry with family members, you may be engaged in power contests, trying to win, control or get even. Power contests discourage cooperation in families, as each member is more concerned with her or his own desires — building ego-esteem — rather than promoting cooperation or increasing family-esteem.

Even in families where the parents are separated or divorced, sustained anger and disrespect of one's estranged partner affects the kids. Parents may use the kids as ploys in their war with each other. Obviously this discourages kids and impacts their self-esteem. (See chapter 15 for information on reducing anger in divorced relationships.)

Encouragement, on the other hand, conveys the message that "I believe in you, I appreciate you, I recognize your effort, I celebrate your accomplishments, and I'm on your side." While anger exists to one degree or another in every relationship, anger can never flourish; can never become a pattern in any relationship with an encouraging atmosphere. As we have discussed, we don't lose our tempers, we *use* our tempers. Anger is often an emotion that we use in order to be more effective in fighting against and defeating a perceived enemy. When encouragement is consistently applied in a relationship, there can be no perceived enemy and anger has no useful place.

ENCOURAGEMENT AND RELATIONSHIP STYLES

The way adults involved together in the task of parenting behave toward one another has tremendous impact on their kids. These relationships form our children's frame of reference for how to get along with others. Ultimately, the way kids interact with their parents, their siblings, and their peers is largely learned from parents and other adults involved in their care. Children learn much more from observing their parents' behavior and relationships than from any words the parents might use in their effort to correct or influence them. The old adage of "do what I say, not what I do," has been relegated to obsolescence in our democratic world. With today's children picturing themselves as equals to their parents, it's much more likely that they will do what we do and not what we say.

Even in families where there's a degree of equality between parents, the parents may not see the children that way. The kids, in their sense of equality, will often use anger to rebel against the edicts of their parents.

THE DEMOCRATIC REVOLUTION
AND ITS IMPACT ON RELATIONSHIPS

Relationships have never been more complicated. Every relationship has been impacted by the "democratic revolution," which refers to the upheaval in all of our social institutions: government, education, the workplace, race relationships, gender relationships, and families. This upheaval has resulted in the traditional roles of domination/submission, which previously defined all of our social institutions and social relationships, giving way to egalitarian democratic relationships. Whether the president of the country or a common citizen, the boss of a company or the employee, a person of color or a person of fair skin, a woman or a man, a parent or a child — each of us now operates on an "equality identity." The equality identity includes an attitude that says, "regardless of my status in the relationship, I am not inferior, I have equal value, I deserve respect."

In the past, relationships were clear and simple. The old tradition was easy to understand and easy to apply. Whoever was in the dominant position had the right to make the decisions, to control and to punish. Whoever occupied the subordinate position merely had to figure out what was expected and to conform. Clear, simple, easy — but no longer true! Getting along as equals requires a whole new tradition, consisting of a completely new attitude toward one's self and toward others, plus entirely new sets of knowledge and skills.

Being in a democratic, equal relationship — adult to adult or child to adult — does not imply that each person is the same. Sameness is not the definition of equality. No two people, adults or children, are the same — everyone is unique with their own talents and responsibilities. Equality refers to respect and dignity to which every family member is entitled. Furthermore, while each person has rights, no one has the right to do whatever she or he wants. There are rules in families and in society.

Anger is an emotion that has an important role in this time of transition. Those who traditionally occupied the superior position often used anger to maintain their advantaged status, a tool to maintain their power and control. But times are changing. Those who traditionally occupied the inferior position now have significant social support to overthrow their oppression. Anger can energize them to effectively resist and rebel, and at times to get even. This dynamic and the resultant rise in anger often describe today's relationships, including parent-child and couple relationships. Tension, conflict, anger, and even violence often result from the volatility that comes from these changing times, as we move from the old autocratic tradition to a new democratic one.

THE DEMOCRATIC REVOLUTION AND COUPLE RELATIONSHIPS

Given what you are learning about the democratic revolution and its impact on relationships, is it any wonder that our divorce rate continues to hover around the fifty percent mark? The democratic revolution has shown us that equality and mutual respect are the keys to mutually satisfying relationships.

To realize just how quickly times have changed in couple relationships between men and women, we think you'll enjoy an excerpt from a magazine article published in May of 1955 in the *Housekeeping Monthly*. This article is titled "The Good Wife's Guide." The following are four of the thirteen points on how to be a "good wife" stated in the article.

* *Prepare yourself. Take 15 minutes to rest so you'll be refreshed when he arrives. Touch up your makeup, put a ribbon in your hair and be fresh looking. He has just been with a lot of work weary people. Be a little gay and a little more interesting for him. His boring day may need a lift and one of your duties is to provide it.*

* *Listen to him. You may have a dozen important things to tell him, but the moment of his arrival is not the time. Let him talk first — remember, his topics of conversation are more important than yours.*

* *Don't complain if he's late home for dinner or even if he stays out all night. Count this as minor compared to what he might have gone through all day.*

* *Don't ask him questions about his actions or question his judgment or integrity. Remember, he is the master of the house and as such will always exercise his will with fairness and truthfulness. You have no right to question him, a good wife always knows her place.*

Now back to the present reality. Obviously, the only true antidote for destructive anger is a relationship based upon mutual respect. This requires each of us to develop the attitude, knowledge, and skills necessary to work out life's difficulties together, where each person's inherent worth as a human being is taken into account. Alfred Adler — a forward thinker — recognized this principle long ago when he said:

Two people cannot live together fruitfully if one wishes to rule and force and the other to obey. In our present conditions many men and, indeed, many women are convinced that it is the man's part to rule and dictate, to play the leading role, to be the master. This is the reason why we have so many unhappy marriages. Nobody can bear a position of inferiority without anger and disgust. Partners must be equal, and when people are equal, they will always find a way to settle their difficulties.[2]

An important implication of the democratic revolution is the importance of taking responsibility for your behavior. If you are in a couple relationship, you'll recognize this pattern. When you get into a conflict with your partner, you may be concentrating on what you can do *to change him or her.* In our democratic world this strategy always backfires. It leads to resistance, alienation, and rebellion. The democratic alternative is to focus your energy and efforts on the only thing you can change — the choices you make about *your own* behavior. By letting go of changing the other person, by focusing your attention on your role in the relationship and what you can do to contribute to it, a whole new energy is set in motion, and real change in the relationship becomes possible.

A New "Golden Rule" for Couples

One way to understand how the relationship between partners breaks down over time is to reflect upon the early stage of the relationship when the partners are first discovering each other, taking joy in being together, and appreciating all the qualities they recognize in one another. Think back on your own current or former relationship, and how natural it was for you to encourage and appreciate your partner and how good it felt to be encouraged and appreciated in return. Over time, as life's responsibilities, stresses, trials and tribulations increase, as jobs, kids, and financial challenges take the place of the fun and joy of your early relationship, what happens to the encouragement? Too often it's replaced by discouragement, criticism, blame, ridicule, and distance. After a time, couples can become strangers and even enemies. These are the conditions where anger flourishes, and becomes a tool to defeat your perceived enemy and maintain your distance.

So, if you are in a committed relationship, *make your relationship a priority.* As the stress of raising a family increases over time, as the children and work become centers of each partner's life, as the sense of discovery, spark, interest, joy, and appreciation is less present than it was in the beginning, it's vital to keep your partner and her or his welfare as a top priority in your life. The adult partnership is the foundation of every family, and when the adults are at odds with each other, the tension, conflict and alienation profoundly affect the children. Making the relationship a priority requires work and effort, and like everything important in life, the "law of the harvest" applies: *we reap what we sow.* As Lennon and McCartney wrote in one profound passage of a favorite Beatles song, "and in the end . . . the love we take . . . is equal to the love . . . we make."[35]

Being an encouraging partner is more complicated than it may seem at first. Many adults understand that relationships are strengthened when they regard their mate with appreciation and support. It's not uncommon, however, for partners who intend to encourage each other to actually create discomfort and tension instead. When this occurs, it's unintentional and therefore perplexing and alienating. It can result in the partners feeling hesitant and distrustful of each other and reluctant to be deliberately encouraging. In our years of working with couples we have discovered what tends to be behind this. The best way we can describe it is the "fallacy of the golden rule."

When we set out to be encouraging of our partners, most of us make the same mistake; we apply the golden rule . . . to a fault! How is this possible you ask? We all know that the golden rule —

"do unto others as you would have them do unto you" — is a wonderful rule to live by — in general. However, in a specific sense, as applied to couples, it can be disastrous. What is encouraging to one may not at all be encouraging to the other. Consider an example:

> *Peter and Carmen had been married for a little more than a year when they entered marriage counseling. They had barely made it through their first year together, which was marked by strife, confusion, conflict, and now alienation. In spite of what they both describe as a real effort to please the other, each has found that their best intentions have resulted in conflict. They gave as an example their celebration of each of other's birthdays during their first year of marriage. When Carmen's birthday arrived, Peter decided to surprise her by taking her out to dinner and by letting her choose the restaurant. He bought her a birthday card with a loving sentiment. At the end of the evening, Carmen was in tears, and thoroughly disappointed about the birthday Peter had planned, leaving Peter feeling unappreciated for his efforts and bewildered. When Peter's birthday arrived, Carmen threw him a huge surprise party, complete with friends and family, cake and presents galore. Peter seemed embarrassed by the lavish event, and at the end of the evening when everyone had left, shared concern about how they could possibly afford such an expensive party. Now Carmen felt unappreciated.*

When reviewing the issue in counseling with this couple, their childhood backgrounds came to light. Peter was raised as the fourth of seven children in a midwestern farm family. Life consisted of hard work and significant chores for all of the children. Economically, the family struggled to make ends meet. When each child's birthday came along, that child was excused from his or her daily chores and was able to select, within reason, what meal would be served for the birthday. There were no presents.

In striking contrast, Carmen was raised in an upscale suburban area as the younger of two children in an affluent family. Birthdays were treated as holidays. Carmen remembers a carnival-like atmosphere, which included clowns, horseback rides, fireworks, and many presents.

In chapter 5 we discussed "hot spots" — emotionally painful experiences from the past or violations of your values. It's obvious that, for Carmen, a hot spot was activated when her birthday was not celebrated as she was accustomed. For Peter, the over-celebration of his birthday touched a hot spot.

The golden rule for couples needs to be re-written and be phrased as follows, "do unto my partner as my partner *wishes* to have done unto her/him." One qualifier is called for here: "as long as it's mutually respectful." If what is required to encourage any partner is disrespectful to either party, then it will have a discouraging, rather than encouraging, influence in the long run.

Single Parents

If you're a single parent, you may be in a relationship where much of the above couple material will apply. If you're not currently in a relationship, we hope you have — or are building — a support system through extended family, friends or organizations. You already know that parenting is a tough go when you're doing it by yourself or sharing it with an ex-spouse. If you don't have a supportive relationship in your life, spend some time building that support. Getting involved with other adults will help you establish encouraging relationships. You can join clubs and organizations, cultivate former friendships, or join a support group. Get to know other single parents and team up with them to share child care, car pooling, play dates, children's parties, and other activities of mutual interest.

Encouraging and Discouraging Parenting Styles

Even parents who operate on the principle of equality between adults may not interact with the kids in this way. So let's look at parenting styles and how they affect kids.

While no parent has purely one style, there is a tendency for each of us to parent in a preferred style, although the consistency and degree of the style varies from parent to parent. Understanding your style and its effects upon your children can be most beneficial in knowing where you're most vulnerable as a parent and what patterns you can begin to change.[14, 40]

Some styles are discouraging and some are encouraging. We'll begin with a discussion of common, but discouraging parenting styles.

Discouraging Parenting Styles. The *Coercive Parenting Style* is defined by a focus on controlling children "for their own good." Coercive parents play the role of the boss, giving orders, setting all the rules, making demands, rewarding obedient behavior and punishing non-obedient behavior. The model for this style is *limits without freedom.* Parents who tend toward this style have the best of intentions, want to make sure their children have productive lives, avoid the pitfalls of life, and profit from all that the parent has learned along the way. This style was the traditional and accepted style prior to the "democratic revolution." When children accepted a "subordinate" identity in relationship to their parents, this style "worked."

Now that kids operate on an "equality identity" this parenting style results in conflict, power struggles, and anger on both sides — definitely a discouraging atmosphere for any family. Kids become experts on *not doing* what their parents want them to do and on doing exactly what their parents *don't want!* The irony, therefore, for today's parents who employ this style is that in their effort to control their children, they may lose all control.

When parents do succeed in controlling, two results are possible. If kids feel they lose, they may get even. Then a war of revenge ensues. For kids who decide to submit to the coercion, another consequence is possible: They rely on those in power to make all the decisions. When they become preteens and teens, this power shifts to the peer group and negative influences — such as drug use — may prevail.

The *Pampering or Permissive Parenting Style* is defined by a focus on making children comfortable and happy by indulging them (pampering) and/or by letting them do whatever they please (permissiveness). These parents love their children and are very well intentioned in their efforts. The model of this style is *freedom without limits*.

Pampering parents consistently do for their children what their children can do for themselves. In our modern democratic world the impact of the pampering style can be tragic. When today's children, who picture themselves as equals to their parents, are pampered, they quickly move to a "superiority identity," seeing themselves as the family "prince" or "princess," and their parents as "subjects" — their servants. In other words, they develop a strong sense of ego-esteem with little true self- or people-esteem. At the same time, pampered kids don't develop normally. Since their parents are doing so much for them, children who are pampered tend to be under-developed and lack "psychological muscle" and are in actuality dependent upon others for strength.[59] Parents then feel even more justified in doing too much for the child. This pattern often leads to relationship conflict, power struggles, and anger as well as parents who feel exhausted, frightened and under appreciated.

Permissive parents set no limits for their children, who then tend to operate on the notion that they can do anything they want, anytime they want. The children of permissive parents often develop little internal discipline or sense of responsibility to others. When any limits are set, these kids tend to resist and to rebel, with anger as a common reaction. The irony for today's parents who give in and/or serve their kids is that, in their effort to make their children happy, they make their children miserable.

It's not uncommon for parents to vacillate between these styles, compounding one mistake by adding another. This can occur within one parent who goes back and forth between pampering and coercion. Here's a typical example:

> *Jessica, single parent of Caleb, often feels sorry for her seven-year-old, whose father is away often for out-of-town work assignments. Jessica attempts to make up for this loss by pampering Caleb, doing everything she can to make him feel comfortable and happy. Caleb has become increasingly self-centered and demanding. When he doesn't get what he wants, he lashes out at his mom with angry and hurtful words, and actually has hit her on occasion. During these moments Jessica naturally feels hurt and angry and feels justified in using controlling and punitive tactics.*

Pampering or permissive parents like Jessica, who realize after a time that the child has gone way too far in the direction of rude, self-centered, and irresponsible behavior, often decide to "crack down" and become coercive. This is one mistake on top of another.

Another common family dynamic happens when one parent is naturally pampering and the other naturally coercive. When this occurs each parent tends to become even more exaggerated in applying his or her mistaken parenting style. Juan and Maria offer an example:

> *Juan, who tends to be a strict disciplinarian and who resorts frequently to controlling and punitive tactics, is concerned about how lenient and indulging his wife frequently is with their five-year-old son, Tomas. Juan consequently feels as if he needs to be even more firm in his discipline to prevent Tomas from being too timid and too dependent. Maria, in her concern for how punitive Juan is with their son, feels compelled to protect and comfort Tomas from this harsh treatment, and so is even more indulging and protective of their son.*

This common combination exists in many families, in which one parent is basically coercive and the other is basically pampering — as we see in the example of Juan and Maria. When this is the case, the styles tend to become even more exaggerated. The pampering parent is concerned about the coercive parent being too cruel and harming the child, so she or he ramps up the pampering. The coercive parent fears that the pampering parent is way too soft and might weaken the child, so this parent decides to be tough by accelerating the control. The child receives the worst of the two mistaken styles.

An Encouraging Parenting Style. We advocate for neither coercion nor pampering. It's important to avoid the pitfalls of both control and permissiveness. A third option is the style of *Respectful Leadership.* In this style there is both firmness and kindness. The model for this style is *freedom within limits.* This is an encouraging style where parents — as leaders in the family — value the child and value themselves at the same time. Mutual respect is the guiding principle of respectful leadership and is applied to all areas of parent-child interaction. These parents focus on giving choices instead of giving orders or giving in. (See chapter 12.) Simply put: when mutual respect exists, damaging anger does not. Therefore, *Respectful Leadership* is a fundamental principle of this book.

Now that you've seen how your relationships with your spouse/partner/ex and with your kids can benefit from establishing an encouraging atmosphere, we'll concentrate on skills to help you bring this about. In order to be an encouraging partner or parent, certain skills are necessary.

ENCOURAGEMENT SKILLS

An encouraging person is accepting, instills faith and confidence, builds on strengths, accentuates the positive, and promotes responsibility.[40, 14]

Accepting. In chapter 4, we discussed "shaming and blaming" by angry people who don't separate the deed from the doer. Yet separating the deed from the doer is essential in encouraging adults and kids. Regardless of how a loved one behaves, you can learn to reject the behavior without rejecting the person. The message is: "While I don't accept how you're behaving, I still love (and/or respect) you."

So, when you're upset about your child's, partner's or ex's *behavior*, realize that it's just the behavior you're concerned about, not the *total person*. When you find yourself condemning the total person, force yourself to look at the person's good points as well. This will help you realize that your judgment is directed at the person's deeds, not his or her personhood.

Accepting is the cornerstone encouragement skill. If you don't accept people as they are, not just as they could be, the other skills of encouragement will be useless.

Most of us are more prone to make comments when we don't like what someone is doing. We can be more encouraging by making an effort to comment when we enjoy being with the person: "It was really fun being with you today."

Instilling Faith and Confidence. Once you're willing to accept the person as is, despite his or her behavior, you're in a position to have faith and confidence in that person to behave or perform differently. For example, if your child throws a temper tantrum, instead of joining him in the tantrum, you could withdraw and leave the child to himself to get over the tantrum (or you could use a positive time-out, described in chapter 12). In this way, you show the child he can't manipulate you with tantrums, and that you believe he's capable of handling his feelings.

Once the child has calmed down, it may be appropriate to discuss his feelings as well as your own. The skills of reflective listening and I-messages can facilitate a positive discussion (see chapter 7).

Also, look for other ways to show your faith and confidence. For example, when someone is facing a challenging task you could say: "It looks really difficult, but I'm sure you can handle it."

Building on Strengths. All of us have our strengths and weaknesses. We may be more prone to dwell on another family member's weaknesses rather than emphasizing strengths. Most of us are quick to point out mistakes, especially when someone behaves in a way we don't like.

Concentrating on focusing and building on strengths promotes positive relationships. When a family member, child or adult, believes she can contribute and that her contributions are worthwhile and valued, cooperation increases.

Become a talent scout. List the strengths of each of your children, your spouse, or even your ex. How can you help the family member use his or her strengths to assist the family? Write your ideas in your journal.

Some strengths are obvious, others are hidden. Some are hidden simply because you may only see the negative side of a particular characteristic. In chapter 4 we discussed the skill of *reframing*, which often involves seeing the positive potential in the negative. A reframe can involve the "flip side" of a trait you consider negative. If you describe your partner or child's behavior as "stubborn," you can also choose to see the person as "determined" or "persistent." Determined is a more positive way to view the same behavior. Consider how you can help the person use that strength in a positive way.

Comment on the strengths you see: "You're so skilled with computers! Would you show me how to get online?" "You seem to enjoy cooking a lot. Would you like to help fix dinner for the family sometimes?" The more strengths you dwell on, instead of weaknesses, the stronger the person will be.

Accentuating the Positive. The lyrics of an old song go: "You've got to accentuate the positive, eliminate the negative, latch on to the affirmative, and don't mess with Mr. In-between." How true!

The more you emphasize the positive, the more the negative will be de-emphasized. The more people feel valued and appreciated, the more they want to cooperate.

You can accentuate the positive in several ways. First, stop making negative comments to your child or partner. Use the positive methods you're learning in this book to address problems such as examining your angry beliefs and behavior — getting rid of the "MADS" (see pages 37–38). Use positive communication and problem solving skills and discipline your kids respectfully. You'll learn about these skills later in the book.

Next, consider mistakes as simply opportunities to learn. Everybody makes mistakes. There's no reason to dwell on them unless you want to further discourage the person. Focus on effort and improvement. None of us are "finished products," and it's very difficult to improve and develop unless progress is recognized. So, pay attention to your loved-ones' efforts. Point out improvements and the progress you see. "You're really working hard on that." "Look how far you've come." "You're making real progress."

Accepting mistakes — yours and others — reflects what Dr. Rudolf Dreikurs called "the courage to be imperfect." Since we are all imperfect beings, in order to accept ourselves, we must accept our imperfection, and that often takes courage. The more you're accepting of your family members — and yourself — despite mistakes, the more you help in developing courage.

Promoting Responsibility. When family members accept responsibilities they're capable of handling, the family runs more smoothly (not so stormy!) and there's less anger in relationships. Even young children can accept certain responsibilities, such as learning to how to dress themselves, helping set or clear the table, hanging up their clothes on low hooks, choosing between breakfast cereals, and cleaning up spills to the best of their abilities when they have an accident.

As kids grow, they can accept more responsibilities such as learning to use an alarm clock to get themselves up and ready for school, making their own lunches, deciding how to spend their allowances, sharing family chores. (As children grow, "Sharing family chores" should include taking initiative — seeing what needs to be done and doing it without being asked.) Teens can be given a clothing allowance and permitted to purchase their clothes. As they learn to drive, they can help with family errands. And everyone eventually needs to learn to cook!

Married parents can also share responsibilities. Who says women should be the only cooks in the house or men (or children) should always take out the garbage? In these busy times, when both parents work outside the home in many families, it's important that partners share the family responsibilities.

When family members pitch in, they often feel good about being able to contribute. Contribution builds people-esteem and self-esteem and psychological muscle. When your kids or your partner participates, you can encourage them by showing your appreciation: "Thanks for helping out. Things run a lot more smoothly around here when everyone pitches in."

Some think that encouragement is just another word for praise — but there is a vast difference, as you shall see.

THE DIFFERENCE BETWEEN PRAISE AND ENCOURAGEMENT

Encouragement focuses on accepting people as they are and promoting self-esteem and people-esteem by building on the positive. Also, encouragement can be given when a child or adult doesn't succeed. *Praise*, on the other hand, is a type of reward and is based strictly on accomplishment and meeting a standard set by the one handing out the reward. Encouragement is a gift, freely given; praise has to be earned.[14]

Because praise is strictly accomplishment-oriented, it can actually be discouraging. If you make an effort but don't succeed, you didn't just fail — *you are* a failure. Praise equates the deed and the doer — you're only worthwhile when you meet certain standards.

While it's important to acknowledge accomplishment, it's just as important to acknowledge effort and improvement. We don't

Some Words of Encouragement

In the text, we've given some examples of ways to give verbal encouragement. This chart will give you some additional encouraging words.

Accepting

"How do you feel about your effort?"

"I enjoyed going to the movie together."

"I love you." (No conditions attached!)

Instilling Faith and Confidence

"I have faith in you."

"Knowing you, I'm sure you'll be able to do it."

"I trust your judgment."

Accentuating the Positive

"So you made some mistakes, but look how many you got right."

"You're improving. Last report card you had a C;
this time you brought it up to a B!"

"I can see you're unhappy with the results.
What do you think you can do make it more the way you'd like it to be?"

Building on Strengths

"You have a talent for drawing. Would you help Johnny with his project?"

"I'm having trouble moving this table. Would you lend me a hand?"

"Your persistence helped you get the job done."

Promoting Responsibility

"I've got to get cleaned up before our guests arrive.
I could really use your help."

"Thanks for cleaning the windshield.
It really helped us get on the road faster."

"I really appreciate it when you unload the dishwasher
without being asked."

always succeed in our endeavors, but if our efforts are ignored, we may give up.

Instead of praising with words such as "good," "great," "wonderful," "I'm so proud of you," encourage your family members by concentrating on how *they feel* when they accomplish something. You can say something like: "You must really feel good about that" or, "I bet you're proud of that accomplishment." This is much more encouraging — stimulating self-evaluation of one's endeavors rather than imposing external judgments. In addition, it helps family members by providing an internal language for developing their self-esteem. "Goods," "greats," and "wonderfuls" are value-judging words that tend to foster "ego esteem" or a sense of superiority.

Judging people with "goods" can be discouraging. Why? Because what will they think of themselves if they don't measure up? "Does that mean I'm not *good* — and therefore *bad*?"

There are some adults and kids who don't believe they are worthy of praise and may become further discouraged when they occasionally do something that the praising person considers praiseworthy. Since the adult or child doesn't believe he's worthy of praise, he may feel the need to prove his lack of worth. The person may believe that if he doesn't perform according to the praiser's standards that he's an unworthy person. His behavior deteriorates rather than improving after being praised.

Also, be aware that praise, like reward and punishment, is often used in an attempt to establish control. "I am the boss. You'll do what I want you to do and I'll reward you for it — I'll tell you how good you are." And, of course, if the person doesn't do what the boss wants, watch out! Also realize that kids and adults who are in rebellion will often reject the praise, sensing the controlling efforts or their parent or partner. The praise may actually encourage further rebellion.

The chart on page 81 illustrates the difference between praise and encouragement.

Praise				Encouragement			
Message Sent	Example	Message Received	Likely Results	Message Sent	Example	Message Received	Likely Results
"I am the boss."	Now that's the right way to do it.	"I'm okay only when I obey."	Measures worth by conformity, or rebels.	"I trust your ability."	You can do it.	"I am trusted."	Willing to make effort. Gains confidence.
"You must please me."	I'm so proud of you!	"I'm okay only when I please." (Please or perish.)	Measures worth by how well pleases others. Fears disapproval.	"You can please yourself."	I'll bet you're proud of yourself.	"How I feel about myself and my efforts is important."	Evaluates own progress. Makes own decisions.
"You must do things well."	You can do better than that!	"My worth depends on meeting your expectations."	Develops unrealistic expectations, strives for perfection and fears failure.	"Your efforts and improvements are important.	You're trying hard and you're improving.	"My efforts and progress are valued. I don't need to be perfect."	Accepts efforts of self and others. Develops persistence.
"You must be better than others."	You were the best on the team.	"My worth depends on being the best or at least better."	Is overcompetitive and strives to be on top at expense of others.	"Your strengths and contributions ae what matter most."	You helped your team by ___.	"I am valued and appreciated."	Uses strengths to make contributions, rather than just personal gain.

So, what I say and how I say it can be encouraging or discouraging.
True, but encouragement is more than words, it's attitude.

THE ENCOURAGING ATTITUDE

We've discussed encouragement skills and how you can encourage by what you say to your family members. We want to also stress that not all encouragement is verbal. For example, remaining silent when you feel like giving advice or criticizing can be encouraging as well. After all, you do have "the right to remain silent." Catching yourself and exercising this right when you would otherwise criticize is a powerful way to begin to be more encouraging. Allowing adults or children to work through problems they can manage without your interference shows your faith in them. If they ask for help, encourage them to think for themselves or make suggestions, without telling them what to do: "What do you think would happen if you told him how you feel?"

Silent encouragement can also include a hug, kiss, wink or smile. Such actions can be encouraging because they show you love and accept the person.

In short, when you have an encouraging attitude, you believe in and appreciate your family. Encouragement must underlie everything you do with your family members if you're to build positive relationships and foster cooperation.

SELF-ENCOURAGEMENT

So far we've concentrated on how to encourage others. What about you? You can't give away what you don't have, so it's important that you learn to encourage yourself. You build your own self- and people-esteem by first accepting yourself as you are. You realize that you can improve — we all can — but that doesn't negate your worth as a human being.

Concentrate on the positive things you do as a parent and partner (or ex). How can you increase your positiveness? In the areas where you feel you need improvement, map out a plan and include it in your journal.

Give yourself credit for your efforts and improvements. Don't wait until you've reached your goal to recognize your progress.

Use your sense of humor to encourage yourself. As our friend Mac Logan, managing director of a major business in Scotland, tells his people: "Don't take yourself seriously; nobody else does!" The more you can lighten up and laugh at yourself, the more human and less discouraged you'll feel. You'll be a good model for your family members as well.

Believe in yourself and your ability. If you don't believe in yourself, who will? Having faith and confidence in yourself is the only way you'll make changes.

Become involved with others outside your family. If you view your worth simply as a parent or partner, your life will be over-invested in your family and you'll miss opportunities to grow as a person. Spend time with friends, join clubs or volunteer in the community. Take a parenting class to gain even more skills for calming the family storm.

Need even more support or help? If things get too tough, consider family or personal counseling. Incidentally, to seek

---

"MY PERSONAL ENCOURAGER" EXERCISE

The following exercise will help you personalize and apply what you've learned in this chapter to yourself and your family members.[15]

1. Think of a person in your present or past who is (or was) especially encouraging to you.

2. Write down in your journal three to five specific things that person has said or done to help you feel encouraged.

3. How do (or did) you feel being around this person? Write your answers in your journal.

4. Make a list of ways you can use the actions and example of your personal encourager to encourage yourself as a parent and to encourage your family members.

5. Start your own encouraging actions now!

counseling is a sign of strength, not weakness. It means you've recognized your limits and are taking action.

In this chapter we've discussed the skills of encouragement. You've learned how to accept others despite their unacceptable behavior, instill faith and confidence, build on strengths, accentuate the positive, and promote responsibility. We discussed how couples can encourage each other, and how you can encourage your kids and yourself. The more encouraging you are, the less angry you are. You could say that a high-encouragement family is a less stormy family.

Communication gets the blame for lots of problems between people — including a major share of family storms. Who doesn't want to learn how to communicate better with the people most important to us? The next chapter gives you a chance to develop new skills for letting each other know how you feel. You'll learn encouraging ways to communicate anger and other emotions you experience, and how to show understanding of another's feelings.

MAJOR POINTS

◆ Encouragement means building courage and self-esteem in yourself and your family members.

◆ Encouragement says "I believe in you, I appreciate you, I recognize your effort, I celebrate your accomplishments, and I am on your side."

◆ If you're frequently angry with family members, you may be engaged in power contests, trying to win, control or get even.

◆ The democratic revolution has changed relationships and social institutions to an "equality identity," so each person can say, "I am not inferior, I have equal value, I deserve respect."

◆ Real change in a relationship becomes possible when each person lets go of trying to change the other, and focuses attention on her role and what she can contribute.

◆ A new "golden rule" for couples: "Do unto my partner as my partner wishes to have done unto her/him" (as long as it's mutually respectful).

◆ Discouraging parenting style I: The Coercive Parenting Style -- controlling children "for their own good." The model for this style is *limits without freedom.*

◆ Discouraging parenting style II: The Pampering or Permissive Parenting Style — making children comfortable and happy by indulging them (pampering) or letting them do whatever they please (permissiveness). The model for this style is *freedom without limits.*

◆ Encouraging parenting style: Respectful Leadership — exhibits mutual respect, firmness, and kindness. The model for this style is *freedom within limits.*

◆ Encouragement skills include: accepting; instilling faith and confidence; building on strengths; accentuating the positive; and promoting responsibility.

◆ Praise and encouragement are not the same. Praise is a reward based on accomplishment. Encouragement accepts people and promotes self- and people-esteem.

◆ Encouragement must underlie everything you do with your family members if you're to build positive relationships and foster cooperation.

7

Healthy Communication

What the H...'s your problem?!
Can't you see I'm trying to . . . ?
There you go again!
You never listen to me!

Is this communication? Well, of a sort, yes, but does this type of communication help a relationship?

Anger in relationships is often fueled by poor communication. Misunderstanding often invites anger. Inappropriately expressed anger can provoke constant battles and hurt feelings. In this chapter, we'll discuss some ways to improve communication in your family. You'll learn how to really listen to the feelings of others, as well as how to respectfully communicate your own feelings.

We'll begin with listening. When you learn to really listen to another family member's feelings, the person feels understood and will be more willing to listen to how you feel.

LISTENING OR "RECEIVING" SKILLS

Listening involves really hearing how a person feels; by doing your best to understand the emotions behind the words, tone of voice and body language. Setting the stage for listening begins with connecting.[40, 14]

Connecting. Your kids, partner or ex will seldom come to you and say, "I'd like to discuss my feelings." (It would be great if they did! Maybe this will happen eventually as you practice listening skills.) So, how do you make a connection with your loved ones to let them know you care about their feelings and want to listen and help if you can?

Pay Attention. If you're going to listen, make sure you really pay attention. Get rid of distractions — turn off the TV, put down the newspaper, etc. Make eye contact. Touch or hold your loved one if that seems to be what's called for. If you just can't listen at the moment, make an appointment to talk later. "I really want to hear and try to understand what you're feeling. The problem is I have an appointment and I have to get going. Can we talk when I get back?"

Notice Non-Verbal Behavior. You know your family members. What nonverbal actions — body language — tell you they're upset? Maybe it's a frown, a scowl, raising eyes toward the ceiling, or looking down or away. It could be tapping a foot, clenched fists, stiffness, pacing, walking rapidly or slowly, mumbling, raising or lowering the pitch or volume of voice, sighing, making expressive gestures, giving one-word answers, or being too quiet. Or maybe it's one of those behaviors that's hard to miss, such as slamming a door, dropping a book on the table, or throwing things.

So when you see that frown, angry (or sad) look, or angry action, or hear that unpleasant tone, how do you respond? Ignore it in the hope it will go away? Yell, "Don't give me attitude!" or "Keep it down!"? Say, "What's up with you?" Or maybe ask quietly, "Looks (sounds) like you're angry. Do you want to talk about it?"

The latter response is a *connection statement* that may open the flood gates, or be denied: "No, I'm okay." Respect the person's desire to share or not share feelings. If your loved one shares, it's important to show you care and understand. We've listed below several things you can do — keep reading. If the person declines, however, you can keep the door open by saying something like, "If you change your mind, I'll be glad to listen."

Listen for Both Feelings and Content. How do you think she feels? What situation led to this feeling? Ask a question to clarify if you need to. Check out your perceptions by paraphrasing (restating) the person's remarks in your own words. "Let me see if I understand. You said Jimmy promised he'd meet you after class and he never showed up, right? Now you're mad at him because he's done this before and you think he really doesn't care about you any more. Sounds like you're pretty angry with him. Is that what's going on?"

Leave the Analyzing to the Professionals. It's important to listen but don't put your loved one on the couch — don't interpret. When someone's upset and tells you about it, he doesn't want to be analyzed, he wants to be heard. He's usually not looking for advice, either, although he may be interested in talking about solutions. You can certainly help with that (and we'll discuss how to effectively problem solve in chapter 8), but since helping a person solve his problem requires effective listening, let's continue to focus on listening first.

A very useful skill that will help you communicate what you're hearing and help the other person feel understood is *reflective listening*.

Reflective Listening. Reflective listening lets the other person know you understood by "reflecting" what you're seeing and hearing into your own words. It's important not to just echo or parrot the other's feelings. Just repeating their words may give the impression that you really don't understand, you're simply being courteous. Reflective listening concentrates on the *feelings* and the *content* of the person's story, and restates your understanding *in your own words.* That's the only way the other person will really know you got it.

A simple formula can help you get started with reflective listening statements: "You feel (*state the feeling you think the person is experiencing*) because (*state the situation that led to the feeling.*)" "You feel *hurt* because *George called you a name.*" "You feel *angry* because *your boss ignored your suggestions for improving the work conditions."*

The formula can be varied to fit your style of communication. You could say, "Sounds like you feel hurt." "I'm sensing you're feeling sad." "Could it be you're feeling frustrated about this?" The important thing is to communicate your understanding of how the person is feeling.

A word of caution: avoid "I understand how you feel," or "I know just how you feel." The person may think that there's no way you could understand and may feel turned off. It's much better to guess at the feeling from clues you have, such as body language and tone of voice, as well as from the statements the person makes. If you guess incorrectly, the person will sense your attempt to understand and will correct you. Your attempt to grasp the feelings will be encouraging. Be as accurate as you can, given the clues. If you haven't a clue, ask: "I'm not sure I understand; could you tell me a little more about how you feel about it?"

When you're listening to someone who seems angry, you can reflect the anger, the solution-based feeling: "Jacob, it sounds like you're feeling angry about the way Mr. Donovan treated you at school today." If you have a clue that another feeling may be behind the anger, you could also reflect that challenge-based feeling: "Sounds like you felt embarrassed about the way Mr. Donovan treated you in front of your classmates." Both are valid. Both also help you connect, and help Jacob work through whatever is concerning him. It's ideal if you are able to reflect both the anger and the challenge-based feeling connected to it.

Here are some examples of reflective listening statements:

"You're angry because I don't want to go to the ball game tonight."

"You're feeling frustrated because your brother won't help you with your mother."

"I'm sensing you're sad because Marsha doesn't seem to enjoy her visits with you."

"You feel lonely because Billy had to move away."

"Sounds like you're angry because I said you can't go out tonight."

"Maybe you're feeling hurt because it seems to you that I don't trust you?"

Here are some examples for practicing reflective listening. You may want to use your journal to write your responses if you prefer not to write them on the lines provided here.

Incident: Your partner says: "I thought I was going to get a raise, but the company's complaining of lost revenue."
   Your response: _____

Incident: Your partner or ex says: "What! You think I'm a lousy parent because I won't put up with Cheryl lying to me?"
   Your response: _____

Incident: Your fifteen-year-old son says: "Why can't I go to the party? Everyone else is going!" (You don't know the parents and aren't sure the party will be supervised.)
   Your response: _____

Incident: Your eleven-year-old daughter complains: "Mr. Jenkins asked me a question in class and I didn't know the answer! Why did he have to ask me?"
   Your response: _____

Incident: Your three-year-old cries and complains when you put her down for a nap.
   Your response: _____

Once you've successfully identified the feeling and the circumstances associated with it, the person may want to continue to share. Follow along as best you can, reflecting and asking for clarification if you need to. Silence can also be effective, simply listening and nodding to indicate, "I hear you." Don't overdo silence, though; the person may think you don't get it.

Incident: Suppose your partner is quieter than usual. You sense that something is wrong.

You: "You seem upset about something."

Partner: "I am. I'm sick and tired of working so hard and nobody appreciates it!"

You: "Something happen at work?"

Partner: "Yes, we got our evaluations today and Kurtner was really displeased with my work. I was so embarrassed!"

You: "Sounds like that must have been a real blow, after all your hard work."

Partner: "It sure was. He didn't recognize any of the ideas I've had for increasing sales; just complained because the sales are down. Seems like he thinks it's my fault!"

You: "So you're feeling pretty angry because you were ignored and blamed."

Partner: "That's for sure! . . . Thanks for listening, hon'. I'm sure I'll get over it."

Incident: Your ten-year-old daughter comes home from school with her shoulders slumped and a frown on her face. Melinda says: "They chose the girls' softball team today and I didn't make it."

You: "You must be really sad about that."

Melinda: (Tears welling up.) "Yeah, I mean, I really practiced so hard."

You: "Sounds like you're really discouraged too, giving it all that effort."

Melinda: (Crying, sniffing, wiping her eyes and developing a scowl on her face.) "Yeah . . . I mean, I'm as good as Kim, and the coach picked her!"

You: (After being silent for a moment to show acceptance of Melinda's feelings.) "I'm sensing you're also angry at the coach?"

Melinda: "I don't know, maybe . . . I just don't know why she picked Kim instead of me."

You: "It sounds like you're confused about the decision. I can see how you would feel so strongly about this."

Melinda: "Yeah, it really hurts . . . Thanks for listening, Mom; it helps to talk about it."

At this point, you could offer to help Melinda figure out what she might do next to respond to the situation, if she wanted to. In the next chapter we'll discuss problem solving — a more advanced skill. For now, let's continue with reflective listening.

Reflect Pleasant Feelings, Too. So far we've concentrated on reflecting upset feelings. But noticing and commenting on pleasant feelings helps build relationships too, because it shows you're tuned in. People who feel good often want to share it. Here are some examples of reflecting pleasant feelings.

> *"You got a promotion! Wow! You must really feel good about that! Congratulations."*

> *"It seems to me that you're really pleased because Jarel enjoyed going to the game with you."*

> *"You're excited because your teacher liked your report."*

> *"You're feeling really happy (excited, satisfied, etc.) because . . ."*

> *"You're looking very pleased about that."*

> *"That must have been exciting."*

> *"I bet you're proud of yourself for . . ."*

So far our examples have given you some words to "label" emotions. In order to reflect, or "send" feelings effectively it's important to have a number of words for feelings on hand. The chart, "Increasing Your Feeling Vocabulary" lists several feeling words. See how many synonyms you can add for each feeling word.

INCREASE YOUR FEELING VOCABULARY

In order to reflect or "send" feelings, it's important to have a number of feelings words on hand. Here are some basic feeling words. See how many synonyms you can add for each feeling word.

Feeling Word	Synonyms	Feeling Word	Synonyms
Accepted		Guilty	
Accused		Happy	
Afraid		Hopeless	
Angry		Hurt	
Anxious		Inadequate	
Appreciated		Left out	
Bored		Loved	
Capable		Miserable	
Confident		Pleased	
Defeated		Proud	
Discouraged		Rejected	
Disrespected		Respected	
Embarrassed		Sad	
Encouraged		Unhappy	
Excited		Worried	
Glad			

COMMUNICATING YOUR FEELINGS — "SENDING SKILLS"

We've been concentrating on how you can use listening skills to show a loved one you understand how he or she feels. But what about *your* feelings; how can you effectively help someone to listen to you?

We'd like to describe for you two ways people communicate their feelings, one ineffective and one effective.[27] We'll begin with "you-messages" — the ineffective way.

You-messages — How *Not* to Express Your Feelings. A *you-message* is a statement of how you feel which makes the other person responsible for your feelings. It may attack, blame, put down, or even praise the other person. "You make me so mad." "You hurt me." "What's the matter with you!" "You'd better stop that!" "You make me feel really good." Notice that while these messages convey feelings — stated or unstated — the negative statements are discouraging remarks, place the other person in an inferior and defensive position, and can invite a fight or retaliation. Even a positive statement may put the other person on the defensive ("Man, I've got to watch myself. I guess how she feels is up to me!")

Also notice that each message contains the word "you." Whenever you start a message this way, the person is likely to be on the defensive. A much better, and more effective, way to express your feeling is with an "I-message." Let's take a closer look at I-messages, both for expressing unpleasant and — a little later in the chapter — pleasant feelings.

I-messages — How to Express Your Feelings Effectively. You've learned that you alone are responsible for your feelings. You can take responsibility for your feelings by using I-messages to express them. I-messages let you communicate from a position of personal responsibility, conveying that *how you feel is up to you* — not the other person. Such messages are more likely to stimulate cooperation because they are respectful.

An I-message simply states how you feel, without going on the attack or attaching blame or making the other person(s) responsible for how you feel. You can say it like this:

"When _____ (*what triggers your reaction?*)
I feel _____ (*what feeling do you get?*)
because _____ (*what happens to you as a result?*)."

The "When" states the behavior you're concerned with. You then state your feelings with an "I feel" statement. Finally, your "because" tells how the person's behavior is affecting you. It's important to recognize that *your upset is really connected to the way the behavior affects you, not the behavior itself.*

For example, if your children are playing loudly, laughing and carrying on, it may not bother you at all — until the phone rings. Then their behavior interferes with your trying to hear the caller. It's important to let them know *how their behavior is affecting you* or they may think it's their behavior that's the problem, when it's actually the circumstances. If you make it seem that the problem is with their behavior, they're likely to feel blamed. To avoid that, it's important to connect the consequences of the behavior with your feelings. Thus, you could say, "When I'm on the phone and there's so much noise, I feel frustrated because I can't hear what the person is saying." This is a simple statement of facts, not an attack or trying to place blame.

Here are more examples that contrast You-messages and I-messages:

Incident: Your partner promises to stop at the store on the way home from work and forgets.

You-message: "You're so inconsiderate! Now I don't have what I need for supper. You can just make your own ~$#! dinner!"

I-Message: "When you say you'll pick up the groceries and you forget, I feel frustrated. Now one of us will have to go to the store, and dinner will be late. I have lots to do tonight."

Incident: Your partner is yelling angrily at you.

You-message: "Don't you dare yell at me!"

I-Message: "When I'm yelled at, I feel disrespected because it seems you don't care about my feelings."

Incident: Your ex wants to take your child to a movie you think is too violent.

You-message: "You know Tom's not old enough for that kind of film!"

I-Message: "I'm really worried that the film will make the wrong impression on Tom because it's so violent."

Incident: Your child tracks mud into the house.

You-message: "You tracked mud into the house again! How many times have I told you to take off your shoes when it's muddy out? You clean that up right now!"

I-Message: "When mud is tracked into the house, I feel discouraged because I work hard to keep the house clean for all of us."

Incident: Your three-year-old throws food at the table.

You-message: "Stop that! Don't you dare throw food!"

I-Message: "When food is thrown, I get upset because the table gets messy. It's not nice for the other people at the table, and somebody has to clean up the mess."

Notice the difference in the messages in these examples. The you-messages attacked and blamed the adults and children. The I-messages simply stated what happened, how you felt and why you felt that way. In the first message, the word "you" was used. Sometimes the word "you" can't be avoided. It's okay to use the word "you" if it simply describes the situation and your intention and tone are respectful and non-blaming. But, whenever possible, avoid the word "you," and say something like: "When *people drive too fast,* I feel *anxious,* because *it's dangerous.*"

Also, you don't always have to use the formula. You can express your feelings in a way that fits your style, as long as you're clear that you're taking responsibility and not blaming. "I feel sad when you say 'I hate you'."

With some people, a simple respectful statement of your feelings will help you gain consideration. With others, you may have to give them ideas on how to help you out. You can do this by adding an "I'd appreciate"statement, which tells them what you'd like.

"I'd Appreciate" Statements. "When mud is tracked into the house, I feel discouraged because I work hard to keep the house clean for all of us. I'd appreciate it if you would remove your muddy shoes before you come in." Such a statement describes what happened, how you feel about the consequences the behavior has for you, and lets the person know what he or she can do to improve the situation in the future.

Here are some examples from our above discussion of I-messages. Notice the "I'd appreciate" statement in each example.

"When you say you'll pick up the groceries and you forget, I feel frustrated. Now one of us will have to go to the store, and dinner will be late. I have lots to do tonight, and I'd appreciate it if you could help prepare dinner."

"I'm really worried that the film will make the wrong impression on Tom because it's so violent. I'd appreciate a chance for us to talk about some standards for movies he can see."

"When food is thrown, I get upset because the table gets messy. It's not nice for the other people at the table, and somebody has to clean up the mess. I'd like it if we could all agree not to throw food."

Be cautious with adding "I'd appreciate" statements. Use them only when your feeling statements aren't getting through. Otherwise the receiver may think you're trying to give orders.

Now let's look at how I-messages can be used to communicate anger.

Using I-messages to Express Your Anger. I-messages can be useful for communicating a range of feelings, including anger. The decision on whether or not to express your anger depends upon several factors.[39, 53]

Ask yourself, "Will expressing my anger influence *positive* change or make things *worse*?" You've had experience with your partner, ex or child before; decide whether or not expressing your anger has helped in the past. Consider how the person is likely to respond and whether directly communicating your anger will effectively address the issue. Will the person become more cooperative or retaliate? Weigh the consequences of short-term versus long-term cooperation and the nature of the relationship.

If you decide to express your anger, make sure you express it to the person you're angry with. If you're angry at your spouse, don't take it out on the kids or the dog, or vice versa. And, as we said in chapter 2, don't beat pillows or shout in an effort to "get rid of the anger." You'll only end up reinforcing it.

Make sure your expression is directed at establishing justice and fair treatment.

Suppose your twelve-year-old daughter leaves her jacket, backpack, books, and soccer gear all over the family room. You feel unfairly treated because you have to pick them up before you can sit down and read or watch TV. You could say, "When I find your stuff all over the family room, I feel angry because I have to pick everything up before I can sit down."

Perhaps your son comes home late from a party: "I feel angry when you come home late without calling, because I worry that something may have happened to you."

Or suppose your partner or ex blames you when your son breaks a lamp after you denied him permission to go to a concert with an inexperienced driver. You feel blamed for what you considered a good decision. You could respond with, "I feel angry when I'm blamed for Sasha's behavior because I think I made an appropriate decision. Sasha chose to respond the way he did."

Some adults or children will respond positively to a direct expression of anger such as in the above "messy room" example. They may reply with something like, "I'm sorry" and take care of the problem. Others may get defensive. "Well, I was going to pick them up!"

With family members who get defensive, an indirect expression may be more effective. As you've learned, there are many challenge-based feelings associated with anger, including frustration, disappointment, embarrassment, fear, hurt, put down, blame. You could identify this feeling and express it instead of expressing your anger directly. "When I find stuff all over the family room, I feel frustrated because I have to pick everything up before I can sit down." "I feel frightened when you come home late without calling, because I worry that something may have happened to you." "I feel hurt when I'm blamed for Sasha's behavior because I think I made an appropriate decision and Sasha chose to respond the way he did." Many people will respond more positively to the expression of the feelings associated with anger, rather than anger. These feelings tend to be easier to hear. Expressing anger directly may be too frightening or too challenging, making it difficult for the person to listen and to cooperatively respond.

Make sure your expression of anger or an associated feeling is done in a calm, matter-of-fact way. If you express yourself in an angry tone or with angry non-verbal behavior, you're more likely to get a defensive or revengeful response.

Timing of your message is important. Expressing your feelings at the time an anger-provoking incident occurs could lead to a conflict. It's usually best to calm down, and to let the other person calm down, before discussing the incident. If you're having difficulty responding with calmness and respect, just return to the "stop" and "think" and "act" steps described chapter 4. You could say, "I can tell I am still not calm enough to deal with this. I need more time to calm down and think. I'm willing to talk with you about it later."

While it's best to express your feelings at non-conflict times, there will be incidents where it's best to express your feelings on the spot. For example, if your two-year-old runs toward the street, you would grab him and say: "When you run toward the street, I get very scared because a car might come too fast and hit you." You could also tell him how angry you are at him running toward the street but this is more likely to influence him to be afraid of getting run over by you than by a car!

Examples of I-messages. Here are some examples of situations that could invite your anger. Remember that you can express your anger directly, or you could decide to express any challenge-based feelings that may be connected to your anger. Again, your choice of expression depends on how you think the person will respond.

Incident: You're trying to teach the kids about budgeting. You give them an allowance and tell them it's to last the week. Your partner gives in when they ask for more money.

I-Message: "When you give the kids money before allowance day, I really get angry (or frustrated, or worried) because I'm trying to teach them how to budget."

Incident: Your ex brings the kids home late after a visitation.

I-Message: "I feel angry (or disrespected) when the kids are late because I worry, and I don't know when to plan dinner."

Incident: Your partner unloads the dishwasher and puts things in the wrong place. You've had a discussion with your partner about where things go.

I-Message: "When things aren't put in the correct place, I feel angry (or disappointed, or frustrated) because I can't find them when I need them.

Incident: Your teenage son promises to be home at 10:00 and doesn't show up until 11:30.

I-Message: "When you're late, I feel angry (or worried, or scared) because something might have happened to you."

Incident: Your kids are playing, chasing each other through the house.

I-Message: "I feel angry (or scared, or worried) when you guys run through the house because someone might get hurt or something might be broken."

Here are some situations which could provoke your anger. Writing your responses to these situations will help you practice recognizing and expressing your anger or associated feelings.

Practice Situation: Whenever you share your feelings with your partner, instead of listening she or he immediately gives you advice.

How could you respectfully express your anger? _____

_____

Besides anger, what else are you feeling? _____

_____

How could you respectfully express that feeling? _____

_____

Practice Situation: Your ex is supposed to pick up the kids. She or he backs out at the last minute complaining of "too much work to do." You've made a commitment during this visitation time which would be extremely difficult to cancel.

How could you respectfully express your anger? _____

_____

Besides anger, what else are you feeling? _____

_____

How could you respectfully express that feeling? _____

_____

Practice Situation: Your ten-year-old leaves a mess in the kitchen, making it difficult for you to make dinner.

How could you respectfully express your anger? _____

_____

Besides anger, what else are you feeling? _____

_____

How could you respectfully express that feeling? _____

I-messages aren't just for communicating your displeasure at behavior that interferes with you; they are also for sharing your pleasant feelings. The sharing of pleasant feelings helps build a relationship which also makes the sharing of unpleasant feeling more acceptable to the receiver.[14]

Using I-Messages to Express Your Pleasant Feelings. The more pleasant feelings you share, the more encouraging you are and the greater your chances of gaining cooperation with your family and other important people in your life.

Suppose your partner or child compliments you on your choice of clothing for a particular outing. You could say, "Thank you. I'm glad you like it. It really feels good to hear your compliment."

Other examples of using I-messages to communicate pleasant feelings:

"I appreciated your finding time to take Mandy to the dentist. My schedule's been so crazy lately."

"I really enjoyed going to the movie with you. It feels great to spend some time together."

"When you bring Toby home on time, I really appreciate it because he still has homework to do and he'll have time to get it done."

"Thanks for helping me with the dishes. It sure makes cleaning up go faster, and it's fun working together."

"It's nice to see you petting the kitty gently. She really seems to enjoy being with you."

Think of pleasant feelings you have about your family members' behavior. Decide how you will share your feelings. Make notes in your journal.

The skills of reflective listening and I-messages often go together. When you send an I-message about a problem you're having with a family member, you may get one in return. This is the time to use your reflective listening skills.

Using Reflective Listening and I-messages Together. Earlier in the chapter we asked you to write an I-message for this situation: *Whenever you share your feelings with your partner, instead of listening she or he immediately gives you advice.* Suppose you said: "I would really appreciate it if you would listen to how I feel. I find it discouraging to be given advice when I just want to be heard." Suppose the conversation continued this way:

Partner: (Defensive.) "Well, I'm just trying to help!"

You: "Sounds like you're angry because I'm sharing with you how I feel about this."

Partner: "Well, yeah. Why do you tell me things if you don't want my help? I believe in solving problems."

You: "I know you're trying to help, but I'd find it most helpful if I could just share my feelings."

Partner: "You mean you don't want to solve the problem, just ventilate?"

You: "I want to solve the problem, but first it really helps just to know you understand how I feel."

Partner: "Well, okay, but I thought I was doing that."

You: "I love it that you care, but sometimes I just need to know you're there for me, even without a solution to the problem."

The responses in this example invite cooperation. You are refusing to fight, and instead are reflecting your partner's feelings and stating what you would like without making demands. If your partner is willing to listen to your feelings without giving advice, you can show your appreciation by saying something like: "Thanks for listening; it feels good to know you care." If your partner continues on the advice-giving trail, you may want to respectfully remind the person: "I'd really like you to just listen to my feelings. That would really help me."

Recall the example above of your fifteen-year-old son saying, "Why can't I go to the party? Everyone else is going!"

Suppose you replied with, "It sounds like you're angry and think I'm being unfair because I won't let you go to the party." Let's continue with the way this situation might go.

Teen: "Yeah, you treat me like a baby!"

You: "You're feeling put down because you think I don't realize you're growing up?"

Teen: "You got it!"

You: "I do realize you're growing up, and at the same time I'm very worried about all those influences out there."

Teen: "So, you don't trust me."

You: "I can see where you might think that, but that's not it. It's just that I know how tough peer pressure can be and I love you so much. I just don't feel comfortable when I don't know the parents."

Teen: "I won't do anything wrong, I promise."

You: "I know you'll do your best, but I'm not comfortable with this. It's not just you; it's the other kids as well. My decision stands. If you're invited to a party where I know the parents and I'm sure it will be supervised, that would be a different story."

If the teen continues to be angry, you could simply tell him that he has a right to his feelings, but you're not willing to discuss it further. This is not an issue that requires continued discussion. You have respected him and communicated understanding of his feelings and desires. You gave him the conditions for attending a party. He now has a choice — if he wants to go to a party, he has to meet the guidelines you set. In this type of incident, where you have to make a decision based on your love of your child and your responsibility as a parent, consider the decision made and the issue closed.

Communication Skills Exercises to Build More Effective Relationships

The communication skills you're learning in this chapter can be used to help you build more effective relationships with your family members. The more respect, encouragement and effective communication that exists in your family, the less anger and stress you'll experience.

"Heart to Heart" Communication for Couples. In today's often frantic world, couples living together in intimate relationships commonly experience erosion in the quality time spent with one another. Once upon a time, during the dating period and the times before the kids arrived, there was ample time for couples to communicate and connect with one another. Not any more! There are never enough hours in the day. Distance leads to feeling uncared for, unloved, taken for granted, and misunderstood. Without regular communication little frustrations are unspoken, and are unattended to. They become bigger frustrations and finally result in anger. Distance in the relationship is a breeding ground for anger.

The "Heart to Heart" communication exercise described below is intended to build time in a couple's life for true intimate sharing on a regular basis (ideally at least once a week). This communication exercise is founded on the principle of mutual respect, and involves both the I-messages and reflective listening approaches discussed in this chapter.

Concepts at the foundation of the "Heart to Heart" model are:

A connection occurs only when the *Sender* communicates a clear and respectful message and the *Receiver* verifies that the message was accurately received. When both of these things happen, mutual understanding has been achieved.

An important concept to consider when thinking about communication is whether the communication is *level* or *vertical*.

Level. Picture a horizontal line of communication between two people who are at the same level, and who are therefore equal to one another. Level communication is effective communication; sending and receiving occur; a heart-to-heart connection is made.

Vertical. Picture a vertical line of communication, one person above and the other below, one talking down to the other. Vertical communication is ineffective communication. There is no real connection. Alienation, frustration, anger, and conflict are usually the result.

The "Heart to Heart" communication model is intended to reduce vertical communication and increase level communication, increasing intimacy in the couple relationship. The whole purpose of the heart-to-heart model is *connection* and *mutual understanding*. Notice that this model does not incorporate any problem solving. While problem solving is an important relationship skill and will be discussed in future chapters, there's a real benefit to having time together where only the connection matters.

The "Heart to Heart" Model Exercise. Ideally a couple would schedule a time each week for a "heart-to-heart" communication. However, if during the week one or both members of the couple are concerned about a problem, conflict, or issue, and it cannot or should not wait for the scheduled "heart-to-heart" meeting, by mutual consent a heart-to-heart communication may occur at any time. The model moves through the following steps:

1. Partner A shares with Partner B what she has been thinking and feeling lately, providing an update on her life and "internal world." Included in this sharing may be any experiences, appreciations, concerns, joys, sorrows, with emphasis on the relationship and the family. This is done in a level and respectful manner — "heart to heart" — using I-messages.

2. Partner B listens silently (from the heart) while Partner A is sharing. Only clarifying questions may be asked, in order to thoroughly understand what's being shared, such as "Are you saying _____?" No other comments — no criticism, no problem solving, no suggestions — may be made during the time that Partner A is sharing. Partner B may choose to write down very brief notes in order to later remember the topics that were shared.

3. Partner B, using reflective listening, tells Partner A only what he heard, using his own words in an empathic and level manner (heart to heart).

4. Partner A either verifies that the reflection was accurate or corrects any inaccuracies (in a level manner). If corrected, Partner B then reflects back until verification occurs.

5. The roles are reversed and the process proceeds again through steps 1 through 3 above.

6. The partners end the process following step 5 without any further discussion of the items that were shared. Whenever possible, a full day should pass prior to further communication on the items that were shared during the "Heart to Heart" exercise.

The Benefits of the Model. With this model, the person in the sharing role is reassured that the content of the sharing will be free of criticism or judgment. Consequently, the courage to share more of one's self, beliefs, feelings, concerns, hopes and dreams is enhanced. In addition, since the sharer (sender) is bound by the principle of respectful sharing, the content shared becomes much easier to listen to. This intimate sharing can only lead to further closeness and trust, increasing a sense of belongingness and value.

The person in the listening role (receiver) is aware that she will only reflect back what was heard, nothing more. Criticism and judgment have no place here. The listener's internal thoughts and feelings are focused on what the sender is sharing, instead of thinking of what to say in retort or retaliation — as is usually in the minds of listeners in everyday communication. With this focus, the listener begins to understand the partner in a deeper and more meaningful way. And the sender feels genuinely heard.

We suggest you share this model with your partner and invite him or her to participate. Couples who have integrated this model into their relationship consistently report a stronger, more respectful, and more intimate relationship. They're surprised when many of the concerns they identify when sharing seem to resolve themselves without a concerted problem solving effort. Furthermore, couples report that the model has helped immensely in preventing, reducing, and effectively expressing anger and the feelings associated with anger.

> *Mario and Alicia have been married for six years and their children are five and three. Like most couples with children, their life has become increasingly filled with responsibility, complexity, and stress. During their pre-child years, Mario and Alicia had plenty of opportunity for quality time together, to keep up on each other's lives and to stay in touch with each other's feelings. Now, these times are few and far between. Alicia is overwhelmed with her responsibilities as a mother of two young children with a part-time job, and feels that Mario takes her for granted. Mario is overwhelmed with work and unprepared for the stresses of family life. Neither feels close to the other any longer. The bulk of their communication focuses on the daily grind of working and running a family.*
>
> *This couple began learning the "Heart to Heart" communication model while in marriage counseling. They were amazed about how long it had been since they really connected with each other. Early on, Alicia was able to share with Mario her feelings about being a working mom, and how it felt to have such little acknowledgement of her important jobs. It was such a relief for her just to be heard by Mario and to see that he seemed to understand. Mario was*

able to share some of the details about his job and what made it so tough for him, as well as how hard it was to come home and face the family with so little energy left. It was a great comfort to him to have Alicia empathize with his position.

As time went on, this couple began incorporating the "Heart to Heart" exercise at home almost every week. As their intimacy and trust increased, they were able to share their appreciations for each other and the contributions and sacrifices each were making for the family. They noticed that by staying in closer touch with one another, by sharing, listening, and connecting, little frustrations seldom grew to big frustrations and to anger.

Applying the "Heart to Heart" Model to Your Relationship with Your Children. Okay, you've seen how you can use the "Heart to Heart" model with your partner, but what about communication with your kids — does the model work with them too? Yes, as you'll see.

A less formal and less structured version of the "Heart to Heart" communication model is appropriate in your relationship with your kids. Family life is so hectic these days, with everyone's busy schedules, it's important to check in with and connect to your kids on a regular basis. This is best done one to one. Depending on the needs of the situation you may choose to go through all three steps described below, or perhaps only steps 1 and 3. Remember the goal at this point is to connect and only to connect. The process could look something like this:

1. *Connect:* Start by approaching one of your children with a request to talk, "Rebecca, is this an okay time to check in with you?" If Rebecca's not receptive, it's important to accept her position and ask when would be a more convenient time.

2. *Share:* "Just wanted to give you an update on what's been on my mind lately." Or perhaps, "Want to let you in on how I've been feeling lately." You would then share with Rebecca in a

level manner, using I-messages what you have to share and without any expectation from her.

3. *Invite:* Either after you have connected (if you skip step 2) or after you have shared, invite your child to share. You may ask, "How have you been lately, Bec?" Or "What's been going on with you lately?" Or "How is life going for you these days?" If she doesn't want to share, you might ask, "What makes it so difficult?" If she doesn't open up at all, by accepting her wishes you will be gaining her respect and building trust. If this occurs, you may say something like, "That's fine with me. Just know that I'm here to talk things over any time you feel like it." If Rebecca shares with you, stay true to the model by reflecting back in your own words what you hear her saying, or by asking clarifying questions to better understand what she feels or means. Refrain from any judgment or any problem solving, unless she asks for your opinion. We know it will be tough to resist the urge to "help." You'll be glad you did, later.

Parents who regularly connect with their children in this way, heart to heart, consistently report a closer connection with their kids. Too often parents initiate a conversation with their children only when they have a problem and want to either "cross-examine" or lecture them. Not surprisingly when this is the pattern, kids will dread any parent-initiated conversation. Kids whose parents really connect with them in a heart-to-heart way actually report enjoying their parents' company! At the same time you're modeling for them how to effectively communicate and connect with others. Most important, when you take the time to connect with your kids for connection's sake, you are sending a very important message: "I value you. You're important to me."

The level communication skills you've learned in this chapter will go a long way in calming your family storms. After practicing these skills, your family will be ready to take the next step — problem solving. In chapter 8 you'll learn how to resolve issues with the adults in your life as well as with your kids. You'll also learn how to help your loved ones solve their problems.

MAJOR POINTS

- Anger in relationships is often fueled by misunderstandings and lack of good communication.

- Listening — "receiving" — involves really hearing how a person feels; doing your best to understand the emotions behind the words, tone of voice and body language.

- Listening begins with making a connection by inviting the other person to talk about his or her feelings.

- *Reflective listening* (restating what you understand the person to be saying and why) helps make it clear that you understand both his feelings and the content of his story.

- Reflective listening can help both when family members are upset and when they feel good about something.

- When communicating your feelings — "sending" — avoid "you-messages," which attack, blame or put down the other person: "You're a jerk! You make me so mad!"

- Express your feelings effectively with "I-messages," which convey that you take responsibility for your feelings: "When [something happens], I feel [angry, sad, frustrated . . .] because [how it affects you]."

- Adding an "I'd appreciate" statement, if your I-message goes unheeded, lets the person know what she can do to rectify the situation in the future.

- Whether or not to express your anger depends upon whether you think the expression will influence a positive change or make things worse.

- Some will respond positively to direct expression of anger, others will not. You may choose instead to express the feelings associated with anger, such as frustration, fear, or hurt.

- The more positive feelings you share as I-messages, the more encouraging you are and the greater your chances of gaining cooperation with the important people in your life.

- The "Heart to Heart" communication model can reduce "vertical communication," increase "level communication," and increase intimacy, through *connection* and *mutual understanding.*

- Couples can schedule a "heart to heart" session once a week, listening to each other without judgment, and sharing feelings in a respectful way.

- The "heart to heart" model works well with children also, on a regular basis, one-to-one, sharing feelings with mutual respect and without judgment.

8

Problem Solving
& Conflict Resolution

Sometimes life seems to reflect a line from an old Everly Brothers[8] song: "Problems, problems, problems all day long." Ah, for a problem-free life . . . Dream on! Besides, life would be pretty boring without some problems to solve, wouldn't it?

Problems and conflict are inevitable in relationships, but they can be lessened. And, sometimes your family members will even ask for help in solving their problems. In this chapter, you'll find some powerful tools to help you respond more effectively to some of the problems you might be facing in your own family life.

The listening and sending skills we discussed in the last chapter — reflective listening and I-messages — are very helpful in problem-solving discussions. In addition to these key communication skills, the problem-solving process involves recognizing *who owns the problem* and a method for generating solutions to problems called *exploring alternatives*.

WHO OWNS THE PROBLEM?

"Who owns the problem" simply means figuring out whose problem it really is, or who is responsible for solving it. If you take on the job of solving problems that actually belong to your partner, ex, or child, why should they be concerned about these problems? When you take over problems that belong to your children, you rob them of the opportunity to learn responsibility. Also, solving problems that belong to someone else is disrespectful, since it suggests that you believe the other person is not capable of taking care of the problem. At times, you may find that your attempt to "help" invites anger.

How do you determine who owns a problem? Look to see if your own rights are violated. If they aren't, then you don't own the problem. An exception to this would be situations involving a threat to someone's safety or property. With kids, you'll need to determine whether or not the child is mature enough to handle a particular problem. If the child is capable, and no one's safety or property is involved, the child owns the problem.

Deciding What to Do About a Problem When Another Family Member Owns It. When another family member discusses a problem she owns with you, reflective listening may be all that's needed — the person just wants to be heard. Sometimes the person will want your assistance in determining what to do about the problem. You can help by using a process called *exploring alternatives*, which you'll learn about shortly.

Assisting family members in generating solutions to their problems demonstrates you understand and are concerned about them. Such concern is usually appreciated and helps build a closer relationship, which naturally reduces anger. Of course, it's important that you find out if your family member actually *wants* your help in solving the problem. If so, your role is to listen and perhaps make suggestions, but not to impose your solutions.

There will be times when it's better for you to avoid becoming involved and let the family member figure out a solution without assistance. This doesn't mean you don't care. It simply means you have faith in the person to handle it, and that you recognize he will learn more by handling it himself.

EXAMPLES OF PROBLEM OWNERSHIP

You find out from your kids, ages seven and five, that your ex left them alone in the ex's house while attending to some errands. You own this problem because your children's safety is involved. You need to let your ex know that this is unacceptable.

◆

Your child continually interrupts when you are on the phone. You own this problem because the behavior interferes with your rights, and those of the other person on the phone. It's time to teach your child appropriate behavior during phone calls.

◆

Your child breaks one of his toys. Since this doesn't interfere with your rights, the child owns the problem. Again you may be empathetic, but it's still the child's problem. This time, you don't need to take action.

◆

Your partner complains about her ex's behavior. Since this doesn't interfere with your rights, your partner owns the problem. You very likely empathize with what your partner is experiencing, but solving the problem is her responsibility, not yours.

Think of problems that come up in your own family. Jot down a short list in your journal. Can you identify which ones actually belong to you? Consider whether it's really your responsibility to solve them. Which ones actually belong to a family member other than you?

Deciding What to Do About a Problem When You Own It. The exploring alternatives process described below applies to problems you own as well as those of other members of your family. You may also find I-messages to be a helpful tool for solving interpersonal problems that you own. Sometimes the I-message alone solves the problem — the person hears your feelings and decides to adjust behavior you find troublesome. But there will be times when negotiation is needed and an agreement made to solve the conflict. (With kids you may need to apply natural or logical consequences — see chapter 12). As you see, there's a bit of detective work in all of this!

PROBLEM SOLVING WITH EXPLORING ALTERNATIVES

Exploring alternatives is a process which can be applied to assisting a family member with a problem, or to negotiate a conflict when you own the problem. There are four steps to the process. Each step applies regardless of who owns the problem.[14, 40]

Step 1: Connect and Clarify. Use reflective listening and I-messages to make sure the problem is understood. Ask questions for clarification if necessary.

Step 2: Brainstorm Solutions. This is where alternatives are generated. Encourage a free flow of ideas, no matter how (strange, ridiculous, irrelevant, wacky, weird) they may seem to be. This is a time to get creative, and maybe even add a bit of humor to an otherwise serious discussion, raising both your spirits and adding energy to the problem solving effort. It's important to suspend judgment at this point — just let the ideas flow. (Evaluating ideas now can shut down the flow of creativity.) You can simply say, "What are some things you could do about this? Or "Let's think of everything we can, even if it sounds a little weird."

If the person has no ideas, or if you think you have an idea which would help, you can add your suggestion — if she's willing to hear one. "I have a couple of ideas. Would you like to hear them?" If you own the problem and are seeking to negotiate a solution, you can begin this step by asking, "What are some ways we could solve this?" Put your own suggestions in the pot as well.

If the other person starts to evaluate suggestions, you could say: "For now, why don't we just come up with all possibilities? When we've run out of ideas, we can figure out which ones might be best."

Step 3: Evaluate Solutions. In this step each idea is evaluated and a tentative solution developed. What are the pros and cons of each idea? Is there a combination of ideas that could be used? Which ideas are acceptable — to the family member if he owns the problem, or to both of you if you own the problem? If a family member owns the problem, the decision about what to do is up to him. If you have reservations about the chosen solution, give your reasons. But unless the solution is dangerous, leave the decision up to the person who owns the problem.

Step 4: Choose and Use a Solution. In this final step, the "problem-owner" agrees to test the solution for a period of time — such as a week (the "right" time period will depend on the nature of the problem). At that time, you can revisit the issue to see how it's going, and brainstorm again if it's not working.

When you own the problem, it's important that both you and the other family member make a commitment to use the chosen idea. Again, it's tentative and you'll want to revisit the issue to see how it's working after a brief test period.

There may be times when it's difficult to come up with solutions. Or you may not reach agreement on problems you own. In these situations, tabling the issue — to give both parties time to think it over — could be your best option. By tabling the issue when appropriate, you also gain by showing respect — that you will not force a solution upon your family member. If the problem continues to trouble you, however, be sure you don't avoid bringing it up again to seek fresh solutions.

The chart on page 118 summarizes the exploring alternatives process.

The encouragement process which we discussed in chapter 6 is especially important in exploring alternatives. The next section shows how to apply that process to your problem solving discussions.

The Value of Encouragement in Problem Solving Discussions. Accepting the person as is, instilling faith and confidence, building on strengths, accentuating the positive, and promoting responsibility — the skills of encouragement — are important for effective problem solving discussions. For example, when discussing a problem other family members own, some may be so discouraged they don't think there is a solution, so it's important to give encouragement. You could say: "I know it's tough, but I

PROBLEM SOLVING THROUGH EXPLORING ALTERNATIVES

Step	Assistance (When another owns the problem)	Negotiation (When you own the problem)
1. Connect and Clarify	"You feel ____ because ____	"When ____ I feel ____ because ____."
2. Brainstorm Solutions	What do you think you could do?	"How could we solve this problem? What are some ideas?"
3. Evaluate Solutions	About each idea ask: "What do you think will happen if you do this?"	Each party gives his/her reaction to each suggested solution. "What do you think about this idea?"
4. Choose and Use a Solution	"Which idea do you choose?" "Shall we check back in ___ days to see how it's going?"	"We've agreed to ____." "When should we check back to see how it's going?"

really think you can come up with a solution." If she's still stuck, you could make the issue less personal: "What if this happened to a good friend, what advice would you have?" If necessary, give your own ideas — if she wants to hear them.

When negotiating a problem you own, encouragement is especially valuable. Have faith both in the family member and in yourself that you'll come to agreement. Show your appreciation for cooperation. Expect the family member to be responsible for her part of the agreement and, of course, take full responsibility for your part

Providing Assistance When a Family Member Owns the Problem. When another family member owns the problem, you can invite discussion by simply asking if he wants to discuss what he can do about the challenge. This usually comes after you make a connection through reflective listening. Simply say something like: "Would you like to talk about what you can do about this?" or . . . "I'm here if you want to talk about it." Respect the person's decision. Some will jump at the chance; others will want to think about it themselves. For those who want to think about on their own, invite them to talk at another time if they wish. You could say: "If you ever want to talk about it, I'll be willing to listen."

Examples of Using Exploring Alternatives to Provide Assistance. In the last chapter, we gave you an example of a dialogue between your partner and you. Let's take another look at that conversation:

Suppose your partner is quieter than usual. You sense that something is wrong.

You: "You seem upset about something." (Connecting and clarifying with reflective listening.)

Partner: "I am. I'm sick and tired of working so hard and nobody appreciates it!"

You: "Something happen at work?" (Attempting to clarify.)

Partner: "Yes, we got our evaluations today and Kurtner was really displeased with my work. I was so embarrassed!"

You: "Sounds like that must have been a real blow, after all your hard work." (Clarifying with reflective listening.)

Partner: "It sure was. He didn't recognize any of the ideas I've had for increasing sales; just complained because the sales are down. Seems like he thinks it's my fault!"

You: "So you're feeling pretty angry because you were ignored and blamed." (Clarifying with reflective listening.)

Partner: "That's for sure! . . . Thanks for listening, hon. I'm sure I'll get over it."

Suppose your partner asked for some help, or you sensed your partner might want your assistance in figuring out a solution. You might say: "What have you thought you might do about this?" (Brainstorming.) The dialogue could then continue something like this:

Partner: "Well, I guess I could always quit!"

You: "Okay, anything else?" (Brainstorming.)

Partner: "Well, no. Do you have any ideas?"

You: "I'm not sure. Can you meet with him and talk about it? Or maybe you could talk to Bill about this, I seem to remember he had some trouble with his boss a while back." (Brainstorming.)

Partner: "Hey, that's right. I hadn't thought of Bill. Thanks, hon. I'll call him right now." (Evaluating, choosing and using a solution.)

Sometimes an idea just seems to jump from the air. At other times it's more challenging.

Another example from the last chapter: Your ten-year-old daughter, Melinda, says: "They chose the girls' softball team today and I didn't make it."

You: "You must be really sad about that." (Connecting and clarifying with reflective listening.)

Melinda (tears welling up): "Yeah, I mean I really practiced so hard."

You: "Sounds like you're really discouraged too, giving it all that effort." (Clarifying with reflective listening.)

Melinda (crying, sniffing and wiping her eyes and developing a scowl on her face): "Yeah . . . I'm, like, as good as Kim, and the coach picked her!"

You: (After being silent for a moment to show acceptance of Melinda's feelings.) "I'm sensing you're also angry at the coach?" (Clarifying.)

Melinda: "I don't know, maybe. I just don't know why she picked Kim instead of me."

You: "Sounds to me like you're confused about the decision. I can see how you would feel so strongly about this." (Reflecting and validating.)

Melinda: "Yeah, I really do. Well, okay. Thanks for listening Mom; it helps to talk about it."

Suppose Melinda also said, "I don't know what I'm going to do . . ." You could invite her to think about it by saying something like: "What would you like to do?" (Initiating brainstorming.)

Melinda: "I'd like to tell her what I think about her decision!"

You: "Okay, that's an idea. Any others?" (Brainstorming.)

Melinda: "I didn't mean that; I'm just mad, like you said."

You: "Is there something else you'd like to do?" (Brainstorming.)

Melinda: "I don't know."

You: "What other sports or activities might be fun for you?" (Brainstorming.)

Melinda: (Silent, apparently thinking.) "Well, I don't know. Maybe tennis."

You: "So tennis is one idea. Any others?" (Brainstorming.)

Melinda: "Maybe swimming. Sally said she's going to learn synchronized swimming at the Y this summer."

You: "Okay, you've got two ideas so far. Any others?" (Brainstorming.)

Melinda replies no and decides she wants to talk to Sally about the synchronized swimming. You invite her to tell you what she decides after she talks to Sally. (Choosing and using a solution, setting up a time to evaluate.)

COMMON MISTAKES OF PEOPLE IN CONFLICT

How effectively your family resolves conflicts is a critical factor in determining the magnitude of your family storm. In our years counseling families, we've found four common and "deadly" mistakes people make when involved in conflicts.

1. **Attempting to engage in problem solving when angry.** Since anger is often created to bolster dominance and power, to become more effective at fighting and winning, anger nearly always gets in the way of problem solving. Problem solving is about working things out collaboratively with another person — the opposite of fighting and winning. You'll find it very helpful to incorporate the anger-reducing skills we've described in this book — especially in chapters 2 and 3, (managing your "hot thoughts," purpose, "hot spots") — before making the effort to negotiate a conflict.

2. **Focusing on who's right and who's wrong.** This strategy is doomed to failure. It focuses on who's to blame, and turns the discussion into a competition, which has nothing to do with problem solving. This mistaken strategy nearly always leads to an intensification of anger, as each person attempts to defend himself and to blame the other. Problem solving is about learning from the present situation and working things out for the future. Psychiatrist Rudolf Dreikurs[20] offered an important concept: it's quite possible for a person to be "logically right and psychologically wrong." Robert L. Powers, psychologist, said it this way, "in an intimate family relationship, the more right you believe you are in a conflict, the more likely it is that you are making trouble."[46] This is the case whenever we communicate accurate facts, knowledge, or perspective in a way that puts the other person down. In a relationship the most important thing is not "being right," but "acting right" — with mutual respect.

3. **Believing that you must agree on all important matters.** For example, couples often operate on the romantic fantasy that when they get married, they "become one." There have been many romantic songs written with this basic premise. The notion of two becoming one is, of course, fiction. We indeed continue to be separate people, with separate histories, beliefs, and perspectives. It's far more accurate and useful to picture two individuals coming together in love and becoming three. Picture two circles overlapping and forming three distinct entities: one and two being the respective individuals, and the third being the newly formed relationship in the middle.

Our colleague and editor, psychologist Bob Alberti, puts it this way: "Why do wedding ceremonies often ask the couple to blow out their individual candles when they light the relationship candle? All three should continue to burn brightly!"

Here's an important new rule for couples to consider: *it's actually okay to have different opinions,* and they both can stand side by side. When accepted and embraced, differing perspectives actually add strength, balance, and flexibility to a relationship.

In conflicts between parents and kids, the same principle applies — you are separate individuals. You may be older, more experienced and know more than your kids, but believing they must always agree with you or do what you say is doomed to failure. As we've said before, with the sense of equality kids have today doesn't view their parents as superheroes. Obviously, they don't always agree with you. They may stand up for themselves in a number of ways, including open arguments with parents or behaviorally defying them. You and your kids don't always have to agree, but you can come to agreement!

Besides (are you sitting down?), kids often really do have good ideas. So, when you're negotiating with your child, make the effort to draw out his ideas — and listen to them reflectively. If you and the child don't arrive at an agreement, and you have to make the decision anyway, you can do so in a respectful way.

4. **Focusing on the past and ignoring the future.** Effective problem solving focuses on the future. The past is over; it can't be changed. The past incident is discussed only to understand better what isn't working, and is discussed using the respectful communication skills of I-messages and reflective listening. When the problem-solving effort is then guided by the question, "What can we do next time, so that things go better between us?" true problem solving takes place.

Negotiation: When You Own the Problem. When you own the problem and want to talk it over with the family member in order to negotiate, you can begin with something like this: "I'd like to talk with you about ____. Is this a good time?" If not, ask when would be a good time. Setting a time to discuss the problem could be your first cooperative agreement.

Once the two of you sit down to discuss the issue, you can begin by stating your feelings in an I-message. Be prepared to listen; your statement will probably provoke feelings from the other person.

PRINCIPLES OF CONFLICT RESOLUTION

When you're in a conflict, it's important to keep certain principles in mind.[22] First, realize that conflicts are often signs of disrespect — each person is focused on what she feels and wants, disregarding the other person's feelings and desires. People in conflict often treat each other disrespectfully with anger, name calling, or punitive silence. So the first step in resolving conflicts is to establish an atmosphere of mutual respect. You do that by showing respect to the other person's feelings and wants. When you show respect, others usually give respect in return.

People have conflicts about all kinds of issues, but the real issue is often not realized. For example, if you and your partner are fighting about money, the real issue may not be financial. Money may be the *topic* of the conflict, but the real *issue* could be things like who's right, who's in control, who's going to win, or who's superior. Once you realize what the real issue is, you're in a position to alter your point of view and look for ways to cooperate by giving up the desire to be "right."

Next, realize that there is *agreement* in a conflict — the parties have actually agreed to fight! So, to solve a conflict, the agreement must be changed. To change the agreement, decide what you are willing to do, not what the *other person* must do. Deciding what the other person has to do can lead to more conflict. Also, when you offer what you will do to cooperate, the other person will often be willing to do the same. Look for areas of agreement, no matter how slight.

Finally, encourage participation in decision making. Invite the other person to give ideas, using the process of exploring alternatives. Add your own ideas. Evaluate the ideas and reach an agreement on what you'll do to solve the conflict. Then put the agreement into practice for a short time and see if it's working. Plan a specific time to meet again to evaluate your progress.

Examples of Using Exploring Alternatives to Negotiate Conflicts. In chapter 7, we asked you consider the following situation: You're trying to teach the kids about budgeting. You give them an allowance and tell them it's to last the week. Your partner gives in when they ask for more money.

I-message: "When you give the kids money before allowance day, I really get angry (frustrated, worried) because I'm trying to teach them how to budget."

Knowing that your feelings are too intense to address the issue at the time, you state, "I'm too upset at this moment to discuss this with you. Can we arrange a time later to work it out?"

When you meet again:

You: "Thanks for sitting down and discussing the allowance issue with me. This is important to me, and I really feel strongly about it. Too often in my own childhood I was robbed of the opportunity to learn about how to manage things on my own. It's really important to me that we instill responsibility in our kids. Can we figure out how we can work together to help the kids learn about handling money?" (Connecting, clarifying and inviting brainstorming.)

Partner: "Sure. I didn't know how big a deal this was to you, and I wasn't that clear about the arrangement you and the kids had come up with. You know, I was away on that sales trip all last week."

You: "Right. I know I mentioned the allowances only briefly. I should have provided more details about the new system I worked out with the kids." (Go on to explain the allowance arrangement in full.)

Partner: "I'm concerned that we're not providing them enough to get them through the week."

(Together, by brainstorming, you and your partner discuss optional amounts and arrive at an amount that makes sense to both of you.)

Partner: "I'm still concerned about those times when our kids run out of money and need to buy something important."

You: "That's when it gets hard, I know, but it's also how our kids will learn about managing money, by experiencing the consequences of their choices." (Clarifying.)

Partner: "I understand. Can we look at ways they could have an opportunity to earn more if they need it, but still learn about responsibility?"

You: "What do you have in mind?"

Partner: "As we were talking I was thinking that perhaps we can provide them the chance to earn money by doing jobs above and beyond their usual chores. We can come up with a list of additional jobs and how much they would be worth, just in case the kids are motivated enough to want to work for extra money."

You: "I like the idea. They learn about money management, and have a way of earning more by working for it. Either way they are accepting responsibility. I like it!" (Evaluating and choosing a solution.)

Here's another situation we introduced earlier: Your ten-year-old leaves a mess in the kitchen, making it difficult for you to make dinner.

If you decided to express your anger directly, you might have said something like: "When I find the kitchen in a mess at dinner time, I feel angry because everything has to be cleaned up before I can make dinner." In addition to feeling angry, you probably also felt disrespected. If you decided it was best to express your disrespect rather than expressing your anger, you might have said something like this: "When I find the kitchen in a mess at dinner time, I feel disrespected because it seems unfair to be expected to be the cleanup person as well as the cook."

Using exploring alternatives, you could problem-solve with your ten-year-old.

You: "Adam, I have a problem I want to talk to you about. Is this a good time?" (Connecting)

(Adam says it's okay and you state your I-message of anger or disrespect.)

Adam: "Geez, Mom, why didn't you just ask me? I'd've cleaned it up!"

You: "Sounds like you're angry because I brought this up. But I feel we need to talk about it. I think giving reminders is disrespectful to both you and me." (Clarifying with reflective listening and an I-message.)

Adam: "What d'ya mean?"

You: "Well, I have a lot to do, and so do you. I wouldn't expect you to remind me of my responsibilities, and I feel the same way when it comes to things you're responsible for." (Clarifying.)

Adam: "But sometimes I do forget!"

You: "But you don't like it if I nag you." (Respecting and empathizing.)

Adam: "No, I sure don't! I guess I'll have to try harder to keep track."

You: "Good idea. I like it when you take responsibility for yourself." (Supporting with I-message.)

Adam: "Okay, Mom, I'm sorry I left the mess. I'll clean it up right now."

You: "I appreciate that Adam, but before you do, let's talk about how to prevent this problem in the future. Have you got some ideas?" (Clarifying with and I-message and introducing brainstorming.)

Adam: "I won't forget again, Mom, I promise."

You: "I know you mean that, son, but we all forget sometimes. What do you think you could do to help you remember?" (Clarifying with reflective listening and continuing brainstorming.)

Adam: "I don't know."

You: "I know it's hard, but let's just brainstorm. You know, give all the ideas we can think of, and then we can choose something." (Continuing to encourage brainstorming.)

Adam: "Well, maybe you could tell me ten or fifteen minutes before you're ready to make dinner and then I could go clean up."

You: "Okay, that's one idea. Any others?"

Adam: "No, not that I can think of."

You: "I have an idea. How about you clean up after yourself as you go. For example, after you eat your breakfast, throw out any trash and put things in the dishwasher. That way, things won't pile up. (Continuing brainstorming.)

Adam: "Okay, but what if I'm in a hurry and I don't have time?"

You: "Remember we're just brainstorming now, you know; anything we can think of. When we're done, we can choose an idea. Do you have any other ideas?

   (Let's say both of you have run out of ideas; now it's time to evaluate.)

You: "It looks like we have two ideas: I tell you ten or fifteen minutes before I'm ready to start dinner, and, you clean up as you go. You already said you don't like that idea and I think telling you ten or fifteen minutes before is like reminding you to clean the kitchen — you know, the thing I'm concerned about in the first place." (Evaluating proposed solutions.)

Adam: "So, what do we do? I mean, if I knew just when you were going to fix dinner, I could make sure I had things cleaned up, but it's not the same time every night."

You: "You're right. I'll tell you what, I'll be more consistent in when I make dinner and then you'll know by what time you'll need to clean up. What do you think?" (Choosing a solution.)

(Adam agrees and you set a time you'll start dinner.)

You: "Shall we talk about this in a few days and see how it's going? (Planning a time to evaluate decision.)

(You and Adam agree to give the agreement a three-day test period.)

If kids don't keep the agreements they make, you may have to decide what you will do with your side of the agreement. For example, if Adam kept forgetting, you could decide that you're not willing to cook until the kitchen is clean, and inform him of that in a follow-up discussion. Dinner would be delayed or not occur. (Of course, you'd need some snacks for yourself should this happen!) If you have a partner and/or more than one child, the solution would need to involve them as well and would best be addressed in the family meeting. (See chapter 9.)

In this chapter, we've shown you how you can help a family member solve a problem when the member owns it, and how to negotiate a solution to a problem you own. There's a lot of material here. You may want to make some notes in your journal before you go on, and you might want to practice these skills for a while before you try to tackle any more.

You can make your problem-solving discussions an on-going process by establishing family and marriage or couple meetings. The next chapter covers one of our favorite topics, and you'll find it a formidable ally in your efforts to calm the family storm at your house.

Major Points

♦ Problems and conflict are inevitable in relationships, but they can be lessened and resolved.

♦ Reflective listening and I-messages are very helpful in problem solving discussions.

♦ Helpful tools for problem solving also include recognizing who owns the problem and finding solutions by exploring alternatives.

♦ Encouragement — accepting the person, instilling confidence, building on strengths, accentuating the positive, promoting responsibility — is important for effective problem solving.

♦ If another family member owns the problem and wants to talk it over, you can listen and help her explore alternatives. The decision on what to do is up to her (unless it's dangerous).

♦ If you own the problem, you help brainstorm solutions and you have a major say in choosing the solution.

♦ Common mistakes in conflict resolution: problem solving when angry; focusing on who's right and who's wrong; believing you must agree on all important matters; focusing on the past; ignoring the future.

♦ Conflicts are often signs of disrespect: anger, name-calling, or punitive silence. The first step in resolving conflicts is to establish mutual respect.

♦ The issue people fight about may not be the real issue; it's the topic of the conflict. Real issues involve who's right, who's in control, who's going to win, who's superior.

♦ There is agreement in a conflict — the parties have agreed to fight! To change the agreement, decide what you are willing to do, not what the other person must do.

9

Family and Couple Meetings

"There's a meetin' here tonight, there's a meetin' here tonight . . ." Life is full of meetings — in church, business, organizations, politics — people gather together regularly to make plans and solve problems. What about holding meetings in the family?

We can hear you cry, "Not another meeting!" Take a deep breath, and spend a little time reading the material in this chapter. You'll learn about some of the important benefits of regularly scheduled meetings with the family. For instance, when family members know they have a definite time and place to bring up their concerns, to resolve issues, and to make plans, that assurance alone has the effect of reducing anger and conflict — another calming influence on the family storm.

FAMILY MEETINGS

Parents can introduce family meetings in a variety of ways.[14, 40] The idea can be informally introduced at a family gathering, such as a meal. "I (we) have been thinking we need a time when we can discuss problems in the family, talk about how to solve them, and plan family activities and fun. What do you think about having regular family meetings?" Be sure to invite each family member's opinions. In some families, it may be better to poll members individually. Not all members may want to take part.

LEADERSHIP SKILLS FOR FAMILY MEETINGS

Good group leadership skills will, ideally, be modeled by the chairperson or parent, and over time the kids will learn from your example and apply them whenever they serve as chair. As you notice this happening, it's helpful to "back off" and allow the kids more room to act as leaders.

◆ **Structuring:** To keep the meeting flowing and to stay focused on the topic being discussed, it's necessary to maintain some structure (roles, process, time limits and rules). It's natural for one topic to lead to another. When this happens, the chair or parent can bring the group back on topic by saying something such as, "It seems as though we've identified another concern — TV schedules. Let's finish with the bedtime issue and we can discuss TV later if there's time, or put it on next week's agenda."

◆ **Universalizing:** One of the most meaningful aspects of any meeting or group is the opportunity for the members to realize that others have similar feelings and/or concerns. In order to universalize a concern, the chair or parent might say, "Does anyone else feel the way Margie does?" or "It looks like you and Dad feel the same about this issue. Is that true?"

◆ **Making the rounds:** This skill is used when it's appropriate to get the pulse of the whole group on an issue. "Making the rounds" is simply giving each family member in turn a chance to share where she or he stands on the topic of conversation. Allow members the option of sharing an opinion or passing. The leader or parent can say, "Let's make the rounds on this issue to make sure everyone is heard. Who wants to start?"

Sometimes making the rounds calls for more specific questioning. We like the technique of "door openers." A door opener is an invitation to participate by asking a question or polling members to increase sharing and involvement. "Who has an idea on this?" or "Ben, you look like you have some feelings on this issue. Would you like to share?" or "Maria, we haven't heard from you on this; what do you think?" Door openers can also be used in structuring and promoting feedback (see below).

◆ **Bridging:** This skill involves moving the discussion from complaining and blaming to what we can do so things go better in the future. After some time spent reviewing a recent concern raised by Greg about the way the bathroom has been left lately, with Sue and Caitlin bickering over who is the sloppiest, Mom says, "Who has an idea of what we can agree to from now on to make the bathroom more livable for all of us?"

♦ **Promoting feedback:** Sometimes it's necessary to respond to a distracting or underlying issue affecting family members that presents a barrier to cooperation. Feedback can be given with an I-message. For example, "John, I feel frustrated with the frequent interruptions." Or, the chair or parent can also use a "door opener" by asking, "How are the rest of you feeling about this?" Underlying problems often involve issues like winning, being right, getting your way, being in control or getting even. If you notice underlying issues, bring them out in the open for discussion: "It seems to me that wanting to win has become more important than resolving this issue."

♦ **Promoting direct communication:** There are times when family members will speak for each other, "Valerie really wants to have the same bedtime as I have," or through a parent: "Tell Justin that I can't stand the way he leaves our room." Remind family members it's important for all of us to speak for ourselves and directly to the person with whom we wish to make a point. A chair or parent might say, "Let's let Valerie speak for herself." or "Cliff, please tell Justin how you feel about the room."

♦ **Brainstorming, evaluating, choosing and using solutions:** These skills, discussed in chapter 8, are also helpful in family meetings. The leader helps the family brainstorm ideas for solutions, delay evaluation until all ideas are given, summarize ideas and decisions and commit to carrying out agreed-upon decisions.

♦ **Promoting encouragement:** In the absence of encouragement, family meetings will fail. Who wants to attend a meeting filled with discouragement? You've probably had that experience at work! Family meetings can build self-esteem by focusing on valuing and accepting each other, emphasizing qualities and strengths, showing appreciation, accepting responsibility and demonstrating faith and confidence — "We can work it out." Family meetings can increase people-esteem by modeling respect, accepting and valuing differences in one another, respecting others' opinions and feelings. While it may sound appealing for family members to be alike, it's the differences that are the root of family strength and creativity![14, 40]

If some do agree to give it a go you can begin by meeting with those who are willing. For example, in some families, one parent may be willing; the other may see it as a waste of time. Chances are if the members who are willing do meet, reluctant members will join, especially when they find that the family decisions impact them as well.

While settling issues that disrupt family harmony is important, don't restrict the discussion to problems. This can put a negative tone on the meetings and cause them to degenerate. You can use the meetings to plan such everyday activities as the distribution of chores as well as special ways to have fun together.

Family meetings can be an important tool for building a democratic atmosphere in your family. The more issues you can leave to the family to decide, the more cooperation you will get from family members who feel they have a part in conducting family business. Everyone has an ownership stake in the decisions that are made in the meetings. Kids can help plan family vacations, for example, and will feel more committed to the activity by being a part of the decision-making process.

Whenever their ideas and feelings are heard, kids feel valued, but it will not be their prerogative to help decide some things, such as issues involving basic health and safety. Major life decisions, such as whether a parent takes a new job in another city, will impact the children's lives as much as they do yours, and you'll have to consider whether they're old enough to contribute to the family's decision-making process at those times.

The different roles in the family meeting should be rotated. With younger children, the parents will have to take greater leadership roles, serving as "chair" and "secretary" in the meetings. But as kids get older, they can assume these responsibilities as well, with coaching from the parents as needed.

As issues come up between meetings, family members can post these issues on the agenda for discussion at the next meeting. Some families post a list in a convenient place, such as on the refrigerator or family bulletin board, so members can write their issues for discussion at the next session. This method can also defuse conflict between family meetings. For example, if one of your children descends upon you in frustration and anger, complaining about a sibling, rather than deal with it at that moment you can say, "I'm sorry, why don't you write in on our family meeting list." In doing so, along with the satisfaction of knowing that their problem will be discussed in a few days, the child — you hope! — can let it go for now. Agreements from the previous meeting may be posted as well.

Most families find once a week the best frequency for family meetings. With young children, twice a week is better, because of their shorter attention spans. Time limits on the length of meetings are needed, lest they go on and on and people tire of the discussion. With older kids, an hour should be the longest. With younger kids twenty to thirty minutes is best. Also, when members know there are time limits, the meetings run more smoothly and stay on topic so that issues are resolved

The Structure of Family Meetings. Many families find that it's valuable to identify three roles for each family meeting, and to rotate these roles as appropriate, taking into account the children's abilities. The three key roles are: (1) the *leader*, who keeps the meeting going, incorporating the leaderships skills already described, (2) the *timekeeper*, who keeps track of time and, for example, lets the family know when ten minutes remain, and (3) the *secretary*, or note-taker, who summarizes the decisions made during the meeting.

A very important principle for family meetings is that any decision made during the meeting is in effect until the next family meeting. The mantra can be, "Let's do this until our next meeting and see how it goes." Since the family isn't "stuck" with the decision, this principle goes a long way to reduce resistance to new possibilities. It also invites creativity and cooperation. And it gives the plan you've decided upon a full week (or a few days, if your kids are younger) to see if it will work. You're encouraged to evaluate every new decision at the family meeting each week for several weeks after it goes into effect, and fine-tune or change it if it's not working.

While nobody wants highly formal sessions, family meetings work best if they are not too loosely run. A somewhat "business-like" atmosphere helps everyone to know they will be taken seriously, they won't be wasting their time, and important family work will be done. Here's a meeting structure that has been found to be effective:

1. Checking in. Everyone tells how things went for them this week.

2. Reading the notes of the previous meeting and reviewing how decisions were implemented.

3. Discussion of items left unresolved or decisions that may need to be changed.

4. Discussion of new business — items that have been put on the agenda/list this week.

   a. Problem solving.

   b. Planning family fun. (This helps create a positive feeling about the meetings and brings family members together.)

5. Summarizing the meeting — topics discussed and decisions reached. Members may also evaluate the meeting during the summary.

6. Sharing appreciations. Each family member shares something positive about the family as a whole, a particular family member, or how the meeting went.

Example of a Family Meeting. Here's an example of a "typical" meeting of a family who has held meetings for a couple of years. This meeting lasted forty-five minutes. The family consists of Mom, Dad, Stephanie (fourteen), and Andrew (ten). Stephanie is the chair for this meeting.

Stephanie: "Let's see . . . Dad, it's your turn to be secretary and Andrew is the time-keeper. Time for check-in; who wants to start first?" (Structuring with a door opener.)

(Family members share how they're doing and feeling lately. Andrew, who looks sad, mentions that a kid has been bothering him at school.)

Dad (empathetically): "When I was a kid, that happened to me in school. Have any of the rest of you felt intimidated by someone?" (Universalizing.)

(All say this has happened to them. Dad agrees to talk to Andrew about it later. Mom says she has been stressed at work lately. Dad is excited about coaching Andrew's soccer team. Stephanie is looking forward to going to a movie with her friends. Family members connect and empathize with each other with reflective listening.)

Stephanie: "Dad would you please read the notes from last meeting?"

(Dad reads the notes.)

Dad: "I guess we need to take another look at Labor Day plans and find out how the new chore list is going.

Stephanie: Okay, let's start with Labor Day. Anybody want to share?" (Structuring with a door opener.)

(Two family members want to go camping and two want to go to the beach and stay in a hotel. Andrew and Stephanie disagree intensely and begin calling each other "stupid.")

Dad: "It sounds like we have two different ideas about Labor Day and both have merit. Can we brainstorm ways to creatively solve this?" (Bridging, brainstorming.)

(After first getting all ideas out, including some humorous ones, such as swimming to Hawaii, the family has numerous options out on the table. There is a lively discussion. The idea that appeals to everyone is driving to the coast and camping at a beach park.)

Mom: "So let me see if I can clarify what we have decided. Over Labor Day, we will leave early Saturday morning for the coast and camp at a state beach park. I'll get the reservation. If this is to work, we all need to chip in and get the camping gear ready to go the weekend before. Will everybody help?" (Summarizing the agreements.)

(All agree, and Mom writes on the calendar the dates of the trip and the day the family will work on preparing the camping equipment. They decide who will do what. (Summarizing, obtaining commitments. The family then reviews the recent chore list, and with a few minor flaws, it seems to be going well.)

Mom: "I really appreciate how we have each taken responsibility to get the chores done well and on time. I hope you are proud of yourselves." (Promoting encouragement.)

Andrew: Yeah, I like working together and playing the music. It's a lot more fun that way. Mom, thanks for helping me with the vacuum cleaner. I didn't know all the stuff it could do." (Encouragement)

Stephanie: "On to new business. Who's got something new to deal with?" (Structuring with a door opener.)

Mom: "I'm concerned about how much you're on the phone lately, Steph. Some of my friends and co-workers have reported that they can't reach me in the evening because the line is busy." (I-message.)

Andrew: "Yeah, and whenever I ask her to get off the phone 'cause I want to use it, she says to shut up!"

Stephanie: "Shut up, Andrew!"

Dad: "Remember our rule, mutual respect." (Structuring.)

Stephanie: "Most of the time, friends are calling me, and I don't want to be rude and hang up on them. I have so many friends, I get called all the time."

Dad: "That's a very positive thing about you, Stephanie. You're the kind of person most everybody likes and wants to be around." (Encouragement.)

Mom: "Let's brainstorm ideas of how this problem can be solved. Remember that after the brainstorming, any solution we choose will only be in effect until our next meeting. We'll review our decision then. Anybody have ideas?" (Brainstorming.)

(A number of ideas are shared, including: (1) Stephanie getting her own phone and paying a share of the bill; (2) the family ordering call-waiting, so that when another call comes in Stephanie can see who's calling, and if it's important, get off of the phone; (3) moving the phone from Stephanie's to Andrew's room (Andrew's idea); (4) setting aside a designated hour each night when Stephanie can make or accept phone calls, and for Stephanie to let her friends know of this limit; (5) for Stephanie to be more aware of the problem and voluntarily work to keep calls shorter.)

(After much discussion, a combination of ideas 2 and 5 was decided upon, with the other ideas available as a back-up plan if needed. All agreed that the decision would be implemented for the next week to see how it goes, and at the next meeting the decision would be evaluated. Along with the decision, the other ideas were recorded in the meeting notes as back-up plans. Dad will order call waiting from the phone company; Stephanie will limit her calls to fifteen minutes each.)

Stephanie: "It's time to evaluate our meeting. How does everybody feel about it?" (Structuring, summarizing.)

(Family members share generally positive things. Dad uses an I-message to say he feels sad when the kids say cruel things to each other.)

Stephanie: "Appreciation time. Who wants to start?" (Structuring and encouragement.)

(Family members share their appreciations.)

Stephanie: "Okay, next meeting will be next Sunday — noon sharp, I'm going to the movies with Megan, after. Dad, you're the chair, I'm secretary, and Mom is time-keeper. Thanks everybody!"

COUPLE MEETINGS

Just as holding family meetings is a useful model for communicating, planning, and solving problems for families, the "couple meeting" is its parallel for couples.

Family meetings are designed to address problems and make plans that affect the entire family and involve the relationship between parents and kids, or kids and kids. They are not an appropriate venue for couples to resolve their conflicts with one another or to make plans that involve only the two of them. The *couple meeting* is a time, ideally set aside on a weekly basis, for couples to bring regularly scheduled quality time to their relationship. By addressing issues on a weekly basis, couples consistently report that they avoid the buildup of tension, frustration and anger that often occurs when issues are left unattended. In addition, the couple meeting provides a regular opportunity to plan fun activities with one another, and to encourage each other.

Although the conversation can be very informal, some structure can be helpful if you expect to make decisions at the meeting. One partner can act as facilitator (the job is simply to keep the discussion on target), the other can take notes. These roles are rotated each meeting. A time limit is established; we suggest sixty minutes as a maximum.

A structure like the following — similar to that described above for family meetings — has proven useful:

1. Check In, with each partner sharing her/his current "inner world" — thoughts, feelings, concerns, hopes — while the other partner listens and reflects what was heard.

2. Discuss any issues or concerns left over from the last couple meeting.

3. Identify together any new issues or concerns to address.

4. Apply the skills of communication and exploring alternatives that you've discussed for problem solving each issue.

5. Identify together any future plans that need to be discussed, again using your communication and problem-solving skills. Some couples find it useful to write a brief summary of any decisions or plans that are made. It can be helpful to refer back to these notes at future couple meetings to maintain continuity.

6. Share appreciations about each other and your relationship.

Some couples may wish to combine the weekly "heart to heart" exercise (described in chapter 7) with the weekly couple conference. If this is desired, the "heart to heart' exercise fits naturally within the first step of the structure listed above.

Example of a Couple Meeting. Here's an example of a meeting between Lara and David, married eleven years, with children ages eight and six. Lara and David have been holding meetings for about a year. This meeting lasted nearly an hour.

Lara checks in, sharing that she's excited about her new night class, is distressed about her many responsibilities at home, and is concerned about not feeling as close to David lately. David listens intently and following Lara's sharing, reflects back what he heard in his own words. Lara verifies that he "got it."

David checks in, sharing that he's feeling burdened at work. The project he's been working on has required him to work late too many evenings and he misses having quality time with the kids and with Lara. He also shares how good he feels about their six-year-old's positive adjustment to kindergarten following a "rough start." Lara reflects what she has heard and David corrects one minor misread, which Lara then reflects back more accurately.

Lara (looking at the notes from the previous meeting): "It seems to me that things are going better with the issue of you letting me know when you will be home late from work. I really appreciate your effort because it makes it so much easier for me to plan the evening routine with the kids." (Encouragement.)

David: "As we agreed last week, it helped to actually schedule a time in my day planner to call you every night at five o'clock if I'm going to be home later than six. Before I would get so wrapped up in work, calling you just didn't occur to me. It also helps that I'm now carrying my cell phone in the car and can call you when I'm on my way home."

Lara: "There is an issue that I want to discuss with you this week. It has to do with what I mentioned earlier about not feeling connected with you lately. We have so little time together with you working late and with my new evening class schedule. I'm hoping we can think of some ways to build in quality time during this challenging period." (Structuring.)

David: "You're right; we seem to be like ships passing in the night sometimes. But I didn't know you felt this way until now."

Lara: "There just have to be some ways we can build in time to stay in touch with each other. I always feel better and more supported when I'm closer to you." (I-message.)

David: "Why don't we brainstorm for a while?"
     (Lara agrees and they come up with a variety of ways to spend more quality time together: (1) reserving a few minutes every weekday evening after the kids are in bed and before they turn in for the night to catch up on each other's day; (2) scheduling a "date night" at least every other week and arranging for a babysitter; (3) planning a long weekend away, when the first opportunity presents itself in the next two months, arranging for the kids to stay with the grandparents; (4) talking on the phone during lunch a couple of days a week. After looking at each option they decide that all four have merit and decide to try all of them.)

Lara: "I feel so much better and want to start our appreciations off by letting you know just how much I appreciate these times, when we can connect and talk about our challenges, solve problems, and strengthen our relationship. I also appreciate you as a father. Even though you're so busy lately I notice how you work to stay involved with the kids. I know they appreciate it too. And I appreciate your support for my new school activities and the pressure that puts on everyone's schedule." (Encouragement.)

David: "Thanks hon, and I appreciate you for all you do for our family. I really respect how you continue to work for your degree by taking classes every term. I also appreciate the way you make our relationship a priority while you're doing so much else." (Encouragement.)

(David writes a brief note summarizing the decisions they have made as a reference for next meeting and places it in the couple meeting folder.)

In this chapter we've discussed how to use family and couple meetings to enhance relationships in your family and solve problems. When meetings are an on-going process they can defuse anger and provide more satisfying relationships, and prevent storms before they become too turbulent. Naturally, we've made our "examples" turn out well, although we know that doesn't always happen in the real world! Nevertheless, meetings such as these provide family members with assurance that they will have a chance to "be heard," and that their thoughts and feelings count.

The next chapter will focus on couple partnerships. Among other things, you'll learn twelve key principles for effective couple relationships that you can use to improve your communication and help lessen the anger in your own relationship.

Major Points

- Regularly scheduled meetings in the family give members a recognized forum in which to make plans and bring up issues.

- Topics for family meetings include problem solving, making plans, discussions on how to share chores, and planning family fun.

- Not all family issues are appropriate for children's input. If their ideas and feelings are heard, however, kids feel valued.

- Between meetings, family members need a way to post issues on the agenda for discussion at the next meeting.

- Rotate leadership roles for each family meeting, as age-appropriate: leader, time-keeper, and secretary or note-taker.

- Decisions should be evaluated for several weeks and fine-tuned or changed if not working.

- A weekly couple meeting gives partners a designated time to work on issues that do not involve the children, and to bring quality time — and fun — to their relationship.

10

"All's Fair in Love . . ."

Honey, can you pick up the kids? My boss wants me to stay late.

Can't, hon, got a client coming in at 3:30.

Well you'll just have to reschedule.

What do mean? This guy's a VIP; it just won't fly.

Are you saying he's more important than my boss?

Hey, it's not my fault your boss is a jerk!

Let's get back to the problem — how are we gonna get the kids home?

Don't know. That's your problem!

(Whoa, storm clouds forming!)

The demands of daily life today — work, kids, home, school, community activities, you name it — make it difficult for couples to connect and maintain a quality relationship. Families today are confronted by numerous and complex problems. Relationships — married or unmarried — have never been more confusing and complicated. In this chapter we'll show you a way to bring quality into your relationship despite the stresses you both face.

MARITAL AND COUPLE RELATIONSHIPS
IN TODAY'S COMPLEX WORLD

In chapter 6, we discussed how the democratic revolution has impacted intimate relationships. As a result, gender-based stereotypes that support inequality no longer apply, especially as they relate to power and control in the relationship. Due to the democratic revolution, women and men operate on an equality identity. Relationships are less well-defined than they were for earlier generations, and more complex to work out. The principle of mutual respect is essential if relationships are to thrive over the long term.

We have also stressed the importance of encouragement in couple relationships. And you'll recall our new "golden rule" for couples: do unto my partner as my partner wishes to have done unto him. Each partner and every couple are unique, and experience encouragement differently. If you assume that the same things that are encouraging to you are encouraging to your partner, you may miss the mark. Taking the time getting to know what encourages your partner is critical to a strong relationship.

In chapter 7, we presented a "heart to heart" communication model. Respectful and courageous sharing and empathic and sensitive listening are what defines true intimacy in a relationship. The "heart to heart" model provides important guidelines and a beginning structure to help make this happen.

In chapter 8 you learned some skills for problem solving and conflict resolution, and chapter 9 presented a structure for applying those skills in family and couple meetings.

Our modern lives are so filled with work and activity, it's easy to miss time with one another and attempt to find shortcuts in the process of touching base and working things out. This chapter offers a model for approaching the task of connecting, working out important issues in the relationship, making plans, and encouraging each other in the process.

You'll find that the twelve principles for couples discussed in this chapter consolidate the many points covered in earlier chapters, and offer some additional suggestions for strong, satisfying, and lasting partnerships.

TWELVE PRINCIPLES FOR EFFECTIVE COUPLE RELATIONSHIPS

These principles have grown out of our combined 50+ years of experience in counseling couples, and more than 60 years of collective experience as partners in our respective marriages — in both cases intact marriages with one marital partner. We think you'll find that these principles provide a basic foundation and direction for an effective couple relationship, while providing a lot of leeway for diversity and uniqueness.

With the explanation of each principle, you'll note we've included a description of the "anger factor," which briefly outlines how a weakness or deficit in that area can commonly lead to anger.

1. Make Your Relationship a Priority. In today's rapidly changing world, intimate relationships are more challenging and difficult to maintain. Kids, work, household tasks, friends, extended family, community activities, shopping, TV, etc., etc., all compete for time and energy. For any family with two parents, or two parent figures, this relationship sets the atmosphere for the entire family, so it's vital that the adult relationship be of the highest priority. When most couples think back to the "happy times" at the beginning of their relationship and ask themselves what was different about those times, one major difference was that at that time of courtship and discovery, each made the relationship a priority. As life progresses — as work, parenting, domestic chores, extended family, and the many competing outside activities impend on daily life and are added to the list of priorities — the relationship can inadvertently move down the list. No wonder estrangement and conflict creep in over time! We have found in counseling couples that moving the relationship to the top of the priority list can make all the difference.

Anger Factor: When the relationship is not a priority, feelings of worthlessness or devaluation may lead to anger.

2. Take Responsibility for Your Part in the Relationship. A common — and often lethal — approach to addressing issues in a marriage or adult partnership is the attempt to change the other person, and to blame one's partner if things are not going well. This approach is almost certainly destined to result in resistance, alienation, and an escalation of conflict. Let us emphasize the firm belief that we share with each couple we counsel:

> *There will be absolutely no positive change in your relationship, unless at least one of you — and hopefully both of you — stop making a project of the other and begin making a project of yourself.*

There is only one person you can change . . . yourself!

Anger Factor: Not taking responsibility can lead to blame-based relationships; this may lead to feelings of hurt or betrayal, and anger.

3. Maintain Mutual Respect and Social Equality. This is another fundamental principle. While in the distant past it was possible for an unequal relationship to work over time, this is no longer true. A relationship today can work over time only when each partner respects and views him or herself and the other as equals. This requires balance and, at times, re-balancing. This entire book rests on this principle, which was discussed in some detail in the section in chapter 6 titled, "The Democratic Revolution and Its Impact on Relationships."

Anger Factor: A lack of mutual respect may generate feelings of powerlessness or devaluation, leading to anger.

4. Support Individuality for Yourself and Your Partner. This principle is a natural extension of principle #3. Mutual respect implies that each person's growth and development as an individual is a high priority to both partners. One of the authors remembers a favorite sociology professor who stated that, "Marriage is an institution whose true purpose is to maximize the opportunity of being and becoming ourselves." This statement continues to ring true, and couples who adhere to it form relationships that are strong and lasting. In addition, this principle encourages couples to leave room in their relationship for differences of opinion. It's common for one or both members of a couple to believe that there is something wrong with the partner or the relationship if the other partner doesn't see things the same way. This is the basis for much anger and conflict in intimate relationships. You and your partner are each unique and will have different perspectives on many issues. An important rule for all relationships is that different perspectives can coexist and actually be a source of strength. Different viewpoints provide different options for couples. When combined together, different opinions can merge to provide a broader perspective and creative solutions. When valued, differences provide a foundation of strength in relationships.

Anger Factor: A lack of support for each person's individual development and differing points of view may invite feelings of frustration, worthlessness, hurt, powerlessness or devaluation, and anger. (Now there's a storm brewing!)

5. Have Fun Together. Most couples remember their early dating period as one of the happiest times in their life together. This of course is a time of excitement, discovery, the blossoming of romantic feelings, and having fun together. How common it is for the fun part of a relationship to be sacrificed as fun gives way to kids, work, home, finances, and other life demands. If there's no fun in a relationship, all that is left is work and stress. How is it possible to enjoy one another under those conditions? Fun can be maintained and brought back into any partnership. One of the authors and his partner, during the intensive parenting years, scheduled a "date night" every week. The fun of planning for the date alternated; the only goal was to enjoy being in each other's company, no matter what the activity was.

Anger Factor: When a relationship is devoid of fun, this can result in feelings of disappointment, fatigue, stress, hurt, or devaluation, leading to anger.

6. Develop a Balanced and Mutually Agreed Upon Division of Labor. Traditionally men were responsible for the family income and tasks outside the home, and women for childrearing and tasks within the home. This was an efficient gender-based system. As a result of the democratic revolution and related economic developments in our culture, this system is no longer appropriate — if it ever was. What's more, it isn't even efficient any more! In a respectful relationship, a balanced division of labor is important, so that one person is not over-burdened with work. At the same time, it's sensible for each party to assume primary responsibility for those tasks in which she/he is interested and able. This can change over time as circumstances change.

Incidentally, it's not so important whether the man or woman assumes responsibility for the traditionally masculine or feminine tasks. What is important is that division of labor works for the couple, and is worked out by the couple.

Anger Factor: A lack of balance in this area may generate feelings of fatigue, frustration, stress, hurt, devaluation, powerlessness, and anger.

7. Encourage One Another. Encouragement is the most important social skill, and an essential antidote for anger. We recommend you re-read the section of chapter 6 titled "A New Golden Rule For Couples," which emphasizes the importance of encouragement and an expansion of the "golden rule" to assure that what we intend to be encouraging actually is experienced as such by your partner.

Anger Factor: A lack of encouragement in a relationship can result in weakness, worthlessness, disappointment, stress, anxiety, hurt, or devaluation, leading to anger.

TWELVE PRINCIPLES FOR EFFECTIVE COUPLE RELATIONSHIPS

1. Make your relationship a priority.

2. Take responsibility for your part in the relationship.

3. Maintain mutual respect and social equality.

4. Support individuality for yourself and your partner.

5. Have fun together.

6. Develop a balanced and mutually agreed upon division of labor.

7. Encourage one another.

8. Communicate effectively.

9. Solve problems together.

10. Understand and correct your own belief system.

11. Understand, empathize with, and respond to your partner's belief system.

12. Express respectful affection and intimacy.

8. Communicate Effectively. Effective communication, as discussed in chapter 7, is a key to respectful relationships. "Level" and respectful communication helps prevent intense anger and is a primary anger management tool. Reflective listening, the use of I-messages, and "heart to heart" communication for couples, have been covered in previous chapters. These important skills integrate and increase a couple's connection and intimacy.

Anger Factor: A lack of good communication skills may result in feelings of worthlessness, frustration, hurt, and/or devaluation, and anger.

9. Solve Problems Together. How much anger exists in a relationship is often determined by how a couple solves conflict. Too often couples in conflict address differences by competing over who is right and who is wrong, and who is therefore to blame in the dispute. This is a focus that inevitably leads to conflict, anger, alienation, and the absence of any real problem solving — another formula for a family storm. This focus places all of the couple's energy on the past, which can't be changed, and too little energy on building a stronger relationship in the future. You'll recall that we discussed problem solving in detail in chapter 8. You may want to re-read the section titled "Common Mistakes of People in Conflict."

Anger Factor: A lack of problem solving skills may generate feelings of frustration, hurt, betrayal, powerlessness, or devaluation, leading to anger.

10. Understand and Correct Your Own Belief System. As the wise philosopher Socrates stated, "The unexamined life is not worth living." We believe that for couples to develop a strong relationship, it's important that each member of the couple know himself or herself well. Every human being possesses a unique belief system. This belief system determines how you each interpret and move through life and how you respond to every situation you face. Since the foundation of your beliefs was formed in early childhood, your beliefs are impacted by your childhood experiences, and are to some degree out of your conscious awareness. (They're also to some degree distorted and mistaken!) They can therefore interfere greatly with your relationships, and especially your intimate family relationships. Understanding and correcting your beliefs is therefore important in strengthening your partnership. Later in the chapter, we offer an exercise that will help you identify your beliefs and your "hot spots," and thus allow you to better manage potentially volatile situations.

Anger Factor: Not understanding yourself sufficiently can result in any of the challenge-based feelings listed in the "Feelings that Often Go With Anger" chart in chapter 2 — and thus lead to anger.

11. Understand, Empathize with, and Respond to Your Partner's Belief System. Understanding your partner's life experience and resultant belief system is an important principle to adopt in your relationship. There is a strong tendency to personalize conflict when it occurs in a significant relationship. When your partner behaves in a confusing, reactive, or cruel manner, you may conclude that the behavior is directed at you alone. The truth of the matter is that your behavior in the present is also impacted by conclusions you've drawn from experiences that occurred long ago. By understanding your partner's life and belief system, you'll be better able to replace confusion, bitterness, and anger with understanding and empathy. The section and exercise on belief systems later in this chapter is devoted to helping with this process.

Anger Factor: Not understanding your partner sufficiently can result in any of the challenge-based feelings listed in the "Feelings that Often Go With Anger" chart in chapter 2 — and thus lead to anger.

12. Express Respectful Affection and Intimacy. Experiencing love both verbally and physically is a vital human need. Research has shown that infants who are denied sufficient physical affection don't develop normally, are more prone to physical illness, and can actually die from a lack of loving contact. Adults meet this vital need through marriage or adult partnerships. Mutual, respectful, and sensitive physical and emotional affection forms the bonds of tenderness that allow couples to face each day knowing they're cared for. Sexual intimacy is but one expression of total intimacy. Other forms of physical intimacy — touching, holding and caressing — are perhaps even more vital. Physical intimacy is built upon a foundation of emotional intimacy, love, mutual respect, encouragement, and communication. Anger expressed in hurtful ways is a barrier to all forms of intimacy. The twelve principles listed in this section are tied together and each is affected by the others.

Anger Factor: A lack of affection and intimacy in a relationship can lead to sadness, worthlessness, disappointment, stress, fear, hurt, devaluation, guilt, and anger.

TAKE THE TWELVE PRINCIPLES INVENTORY

The Twelve Principles Inventory on page 157 provides a simple way to assess your current marriage or intimate partnership. You may choose to complete the inventory yourself, reflect upon your ratings, and then consider what you want to do to improve your relationship. You may use what you learn as a basis for discussion with your partner, or to help you decide what areas you want to focus on in your own behavior and role in the relationship. You might decide to share the inventory with your partner, agree that each of you will complete it, take time to discuss your ratings with each other, and together develop your mutual ideas for strengthening your relationship. The ideas you come up with can turn into plans, and progress can be discussed during subsequent "heart to heart" communication exercises or at your couple meetings. (You may want to photocopy the Inventory and put it in your journal.)

The Inventory asks you to think about the twelve principles and to rate your relationship on each. Any area rated as *weak* (score of 1 or 2) by one or both parties is clearly an area that is essential to work on. When an area is rated differently by each partner, it's important not to allow this to be a basis of conflict or competition. This is an opportunity to utilize your communication skills: respectfully sharing I-messages and sensitively listening reflectively. (To refresh yourself and/or your partner on these skills, review chapter 7.)

This exercise is an opportunity to recognize that the two of you are naturally different, and that both partners are impacted when either one experiences a weak spot in the relationship. To value the relationship means valuing each partner's perspective. The rule of thumb is to take seriously and work on any area that either partner rates as weak.

It's also important to notice the strengths in your relationship. We tend to be much more aware of what's not going well, and take for granted those areas that are going well. The Twelve Principles Inventory provides a concrete way to recognize the strengths in your relationship. Any area rated a 4 or 5 represents an area of strength in the relationship. This is a good time to celebrate your strengths and to encourage one another by sharing appreciations about how each of you contributes to this area of your relationship. It's also a time when you can commit to keeping those areas strong.

Here's an example of a couple who used the Inventory to strengthen their relationship.

Andrei and Rebecca had been married for eleven years, and had children nine, six, and two. They both noticed how frustrated and at times angry they had been recently, so they decided to assess their relationship with the Twelve Principles Inventory. Both scored their relationship high in mutual respect, support for individuality, communication, and problem solving, and low in the areas of making the relationship a priority, having fun together and knowledge of belief systems. Rebecca gave the balanced division of labor area a low rating, while Andrei rated that same area as strong. They were able to talk together with pride and gratitude about the many strengths in their relationship. The discussion of the weak areas was also useful. They both realized how little time they had spent in the past few years nurturing their relationship. They agreed to make the relationship a top priority and decided to schedule a "heart to heart," and to begin to schedule time away from the kids for fun alone together. They also decided to work together on the "Belief Systems Exercise for Couples" described in the next section. After several weeks, while sharing during a scheduled "heart to heart" experience, they agreed that the relationship had significantly improved; they both noticed feeling less frustrated and angry with each other.

The Twelve Principles Inventory is simple and easy to complete. It provides an excellent way for any couple to evaluate how their relationship is going and what they can work on to strengthen it. Consequently, as time passes and relationships go through their natural ups and downs, whenever times get tough, a couple can use it repeatedly to help themselves get back on track.

THE TWELVE PRINCIPLES INVENTORY FOR COUPLES

	WEAKNESS ◄——► STRENGTH				
1. Our relationship is a priority.	1	2	3	4	5
2. We take responsibility for our own role in the relationship (versus blaming the other).	1	2	3	4	5
3. There is mutual respect in our relationship. We each have equal value in the relationship.	1	2	3	4	5
4. Our individuality and individual development is supported in the relationship.	1	2	3	4	5
5. We have fun together.	1	2	3	4	5
6. We have a balanced and mutually agreed-upon division of labor.	1	2	3	4	5
7. We encourage one another.	1	2	3	4	5
8. We communicate effectively.	1	2	3	4	5
9. We effectively solve problems together.	1	2	3	4	5
10. I understand my own belief system and how it affects our relatonship.	1	2	3	4	5
11. My partner understands her/his own belief system and how it effects our relationship.	1	2	3	4	5
12. There is sufficient and respectful affection and intimacy in our relationship.	1	2	3	4	5

How A Couple's Beliefs Impact Their Relationship

Akasha and Malik were experiencing significant anger toward one another. They had been quarreling about many issues, including finances, household tasks, and parenting. This began soon after Akasha, out of financial necessity, returned to work for the first time since their daughter was born, some eleven years earlier. They were both surprised about the intensity of their fights and how the intensity seemed out of scale given the issues they were confronted with.

Does it seem that your anger is often out of proportion to the events that trigger it? Do you and your partner fight over minor issues? Maybe it's time to take a look at your personal histories. Experiences and beliefs from the past can be powerful influences on the present, and current relationships are often affected by our past experiences and the beliefs that were developed in our past. A current, apparently minor, situation or experience may have activated one of your "hot spots." As Danish philosopher Soren Kierkegaard (1813-1855) stated, "While life must be lived forwards, it can only be understood backwards."

There are four primary beliefs, formed in your childhood, that provide the frame of reference you take into all relationships. To better understand the hot spots that tend to play a role in your couple relationship, consider these four:

1. Your Beliefs About Life and the World Around You. The impression and image you developed as a child about what life and the world around you are like is a basic template which affects the way you see your world today. The atmosphere you were raised in, the climate or predominant "feeling tone" of your family of origin is the background from which these beliefs were formed. Hot spots are naturally activated in your family and your partnership whenever you find yourself re-experiencing an undesirable life situation from the past — or when you are losing one you found to be conducive to a happy life.

2. Your Beliefs About Gender and Relationships. The view you have internalized about female and male roles, and how intimate relationships work, has significant impact on your current relationships. This viewpoint from your early years is likely to be a major factor in creating your "hot spots." Each of us forms what psychologists Powers and Griffith[47] refer to as "gender guiding lines." These generalized — and often out-of-awareness — beliefs and expectations about men and women are drawn from your childhood impressions of gender models, especially parents and other important adult figures.

In addition, we each form beliefs about how relationships work, or a "relational image."[48] These beliefs are developed from impressions of how our parents' marriage or other significant relationships worked. Common hot spots in this area include times when your partner is behaving in ways that remind you of undesirable traits observed in a parent, or times when your partner falls short compared to a parent you admired. ("She's not as good a mother as Mom was.") Hot spots also include times when your marriage or relationship either repeats a negative aspect of your parents' relationship or falls short of those positive aspects you observed in their relationship and expect in yours. ("Mom and Dad never even argued; why do we fight all the time?")

3. Your Beliefs About Your Place in the World. The role you played in your family of origin led to your view of where you fit in the world among other people. Hot spots in this area include being relegated to a role similar to an undesirable role you held in childhood (e.g., the scapegoat), or not being treated in a manner consistent with a desirable childhood family role (e.g., "At home, I was the star!").

4. Your Value System. The values you have developed over the years, beginning in childhood, are areas of real sensitivity and can account for some of your hot spots. A common dynamic regarding values shared by both parents during childhood is that you'll tend to either adopt those values as your own, or reject them and adopt counter values as a "declaration of independence." If, for example, in your family of origin "orderliness" was stressed as a family value, you may either value having your home and your life well organized, or reject this value, and actually prefer clutter. Either way, whenever this issue arises in your relationships, it will be a hot spot for you, and may result in anger or other strong emotions.

Other common values people hold that account for hot spots include honesty, responsibility, achievement, appearance, or values related to more specific areas of life, such as athletics, politics, or religion.

Akasha and Malik, the couple introduced earlier, learned a lot about themselves in the course of couple counseling. Malik was raised by fairly traditional parents. His mother focused her life around the household and the children. Father was responsible for earning a living and making the "big decisions." Seldom was there any strife witnessed between the parents, and family life ran smoothly. Malik was the youngest child of three and his mother's favorite. She consistently over-indulged him and Malik was not expected to participate in any household chores. The atmosphere of his family was "calmness" and the values Malik's parents stressed were "orderliness" and "consistency," which he had adopted.

Based on the conclusions drawn from his family of origin, Malik was operating on the following beliefs: "Life should be calm, orderly and consistent. Women should manage the day-to-day activities of the household; men are responsible only for the economic support of the family. Relationships and family life should run smoothly. I deserve special treatment." It's easy to see how the change brought about by Akasha returning to work touched several "hot spots" for Malik.

Akasha's hot spots were also activated when she returned to work. Akasha was raised by her mother, a single parent who worked two jobs in order to support her family. To Akasha, because her mom worked so hard, she appeared to be tired and depressed much of the time and bitter about having the full weight of responsibility for the entire family. Akasha's father had abandoned the family when she was three years old. For Akasha, needing to return to work was, in a sense, replicating her mother's life, something she clearly wished to avoid. Malik's resistance to accepting more responsibility was naturally and painfully associated with her father's abandonment.

In couple counseling they not only learned better ways to communicate and solve problems in a level, respectful manner, but also learned about their "hot spots," increasing both their self-awareness and their empathy and under-standing toward one another.

When you and your partner are able to pinpoint your own and each other's hot spots, you are better able to catch yourself and make other choices before erupting into anger. You are able to recognize the issue not just for what it is, but also for what it was. Knowing your own and your partner's hot spots allows each of you to better keep the past in the past and the present in the present, allowing you to keep the issue before you in proper scale.

The "Belief Systems Exercise" on page 162 is recommended to help you and your partner understand your belief systems and pinpoint your hot spots. This is an excellent exercise for any couple who believe they have work to do in strengthening principle 10 or 11 of the "Twelve Principles Inventory." It will be helpful in increasing your awareness about your respective belief systems. Until you are able to be aware of your beliefs and their origins, it's very difficult to change them.

We recommend that you first work on this exercise privately, reflecting on your own family history. It will also be helpful if you write out responses in your journal for all of the sections in the exercise. If you and your partner both agree and are able to communicate respectfully about sensitive issues, it's a valuable exercise to share with one another. Many couples have reported a significant increase in understanding of themselves and each other, and identifying the patterns in the relationship, as a result of discussing this exercise together.

If you find that the issues and feelings that arise when answering the questions result in significant discomfort, it's a sign that you would benefit from personal counseling. If this is the case, we recommend that you address these issues with the guidance and support of a professional counselor rather than on your own. Likewise, if you discover that sharing the exercise with your significant other results in a lot of tension, or that communication breaks down, it's a sign that couple counseling is in order. We recommend that you suspend the exercise until you have obtained a professionally trained couples/marriage counselor to assist you in your communication with one another.

In Akasha and Malik's case, they were both able, for the first time, to understand why Akasha returning to work was difficult for both of them. This awareness allowed the couple to increase their understanding of themselves and their empathy for each other. Before this understanding, they were only able to experience the frustration and anger of their increasingly stressful lives.

This chapter has given you ideas on how you and your partner can use the Twelve Principles for Effective Couple Relationships to act toward each other in a less angry and more respectful manner. You've also discovered how your own and your partner's beliefs can create hot spots for your relationship. You have been introduced to an exercise to help you pinpoint your hot spots and, through increased awareness, to move beyond them.

In chapter 11, we turn our attention back to your relationship with your children. You'll learn about anger-free discipline. You'll discover why the common, traditional practices of reward and punishment are no longer effective and how to understand children's misbehavior. Chapter 12 will give you new discipline methods — natural and logical consequences — to respond more effectively to children's misbehavior.

BELIEF SYSTEMS EXERCISE

As you complete this exercise, review the section in this chapter titled "How A Couple's Beliefs Impact Their Relationship." First, complete each item on your own. Write your answers in your journal. If your partner agrees, have him or her do the same. Schedule a time to share with each other what each of you has written down. This is another excellent time to incorporate the communication skills described chapter 3 and this chapter. If answering these questions on your own or with your partner becomes too stressful, suspend the exercise and seek the services of a professional counselor.

A. Your Present Relationship Challenges

Write down the issues you are currently experiencing in your marriage or partnership.

B. Your Childhood Experiences

1. Describe the atmosphere, the climate, the feeling tone of the family you grew up in. (These impressions are most directly related to your view of life and the world around you.)

   Do you see any connection between the issues you've listed in item A and your description in item B.1? Any hot spots in this area?

2. During your childhood: What kind of a woman was your mother (or mother figure)? What kind of man was your father (or father figure)? What kind of relationship did your parents have?

   Do you see any connection between the issues you've listed in item A and your description in item B.2? Any hot spots in this area?

3. Describe the strengths and weaknesses of each of your siblings. What were yours? What role did each of your siblings play in the family? What was your role in the family?

   Do you see any connection between the issues you've listed in item A and your description in item B.3? Any hot spots in this area?

4. What values did your mother and father agree upon? (If raised by a single parent, list that parent's values.) How did your siblings adapt to these values? How did you? Which of these values have carried forward into the present?

   Do you see any connection between the issues you've listed in item A and description in item B.4? Any hot spots in this area?

MAJOR POINTS

◆ Mutual respect is essential if relationships are to thrive long term.

◆ Twelve Principles for Couples: (1) Make your relationship a priority, (2) Take responsibility for your part in the relationship, (3) Maintain mutual respect and social equality, (4) Support individuality for yourself and your partner, (5) Have fun together, (6) Develop a balanced and mutually agreed-upon division of labor, (7) Encourage one another, (8) Communicate effectively, (9) Solve problems together, (10) Understand and correct your own belief system, (11) Understand, empathize with and respond to your partner's belief system, (12) Express respectful affection and intimacy.

◆ Experiences and beliefs from the past — "hot spots" — are likely to impact the present. Watch carefully if anger increases for no obvious reason. This is a time to reflect on what issue from the past you are bringing into the present.

◆ When you and your partner can pinpoint your hot spots, you can catch yourself and make other choices before anger erupts.

11

Discipline Without Anger

"Your sons and your daughters are beyond your command."
— BOB DYLAN

That haunting lyric, from Bob Dylan's very popular song "The Times They Are a-Changin'," was written four decades ago.[16] If Dylan were writing that song today, he might well title it "The Times They Have Changed!" Today, Dylan's assertion that "Your sons and your daughters are beyond your command" may be truer than ever. It's certainly true that parents who insist on disciplining from the traditional coercive or controlling model find that their kids don't respond as well as they'd like.

There is hope, however. Cooperation is possible. Read on.

As you learned in chapter 6, today's kids are part of the "democratic revolution" in human relationships. Traditional methods of discipline don't work very well because they are often based on the old autocratic style. You can go to school for just about anything now from beautician to computer specialist, but parent training is a different story. There are no required courses in parenting (unless you get in trouble with the court), and many parents don't learn methods that follow the democratic tradition.

(Thankfully there are some good parenting education programs and books like this one to assist parents in the challenge of parenting. We've offered a selection of materials we like in Appendix D.

DISCIPLINE: WHAT IT IS AND WHAT IT ISN'T

The root word of discipline is *disciple*. A disciple is a follower of a respected leader. In the case of parent-child relationships, the child is the follower of the parent, who ideally models respect and cooperative social living.

Discipline also refers to a profession or course of study. So, in effect, your kids are your students. You as the teacher provide the discipline to enhance your kids' knowledge and skills. Most importantly, your kids are studying what it takes to live effectively with others — something all humans must do, since we are, by nature, social beings. From you they learn the give and take of life: cooperation.

Discipline is not punishment. Punishment is a form of discipline — often an ineffective form in today's world.

THE PITFALLS OF PUNISHMENT

From *spanking* (which teaches kids that the way you handle problems is through violence) to *withdrawing privileges* (which usually have little or no relationship to the misbehavior) to *restriction or grounding* (which parallels incarceration in our criminal justice system and breeds resentment), punishment today fails. Kids who are punished often punish back, or become sneaky and deceptive in an effort to avoid the punishment.

Punishment is usually administered by frustrated, angry parents. Anger often scares kids, increases rebellion and revenge, and teaches them they don't have to cooperate unless you're mad at them (assuming they decide to cooperate even then, and being angry with them is no guarantee.) Any cooperation you get from punishment is often short-lived.

Then there are parents who rely on rewards. But rewards have their pitfalls too.

REWARDS ARE OFTEN UNREWARDING

Some parents misinterpret basic psychology and use "rewards" — tangible payoffs — instead of punishment, or in addition to punishment to "discipline" their kids. But what do rewards teach kids? Parents who rely on rewards are giving this message: "You should expect to be *paid* for good behavior." Does society work this way? There are rewards in society, of course; you get paid for your work. (Probably not enough, but paid nonetheless!) But there are many things you're expected to do just because you're part of a family or community. Think about it: who pays you to do the things that are expected of you as a parent?

Rewards don't always produce the desired result. Kids today, operating on an "equality identity," see rewards as something they are entitled to. Besides expecting payment for cooperation or good grades (when learning should be the real reward), the rewards often have to increase in value as the children get older. And some kids rebel more when parents try to "bribe" them. Kids interested in power see rewards as an attempt to control them, which they are! When rewards fail, parents often revert to punishment and the anger cycle continues.

"So, Docs," you may be asking, "if punishment and reward are out, what can I do to motivate and discipline my kids? Obviously I can't let kids do whatever they want. What do I do?"

The answer lies in understanding why kids misbehave in the first place, and that's our theme in this chapter. In the next, we explore alternatives to reward and punishment — natural and logical consequences — based on the democratic, respectful parenting style and understanding the purpose of children's behavior.

UNDERSTANDING KIDS' MISBEHAVIOR

Human beings are *interdependent* social creatures: we live in groups among our fellow human beings. From birth, we try to figure out how to fit into our primary group, our family. We strive to find a place of significance. In other words, as kids, we attempt to develop a sense of belonging. Kids try to belong in a variety of ways. Children and teens who find they are successful when they behave in ways their parents like are mostly cooperative kids. When kids don't feel a sense of belonging by being cooperative, however, they discover they can belong through misbehavior. For example, parents may not pay attention when a child is behaving, but if the child misbehaves, the child gets the attention. It doesn't take much for the child to conclude, "If misbehavior is what it takes to fit in around here, I'll misbehave!"

Dr. Rudolf Dreikurs[19] discovered that children's misbehavior may be viewed in terms of four categories of children's goals for their actions. Let's take a look.

THE FOUR GOALS OF MISBEHAVIOR

When kids feel they can't belong through useful contribution, they get discouraged and misbehavior is their way of expressing this discouragement. Kids can seek attention, power, revenge, or they may display inadequacy.

Attention. While all kids need attention, the question becomes "How much and what kind?" Even kids who do good deeds simply to get attention lack a spirit of cooperation; they will stop performing if they don't receive the attention on demand. ("Mommy, see my picture!" "Mommy's busy right now darlin'. I'll look at your picture as soon as I'm through with . . .") These same kids, if they don't immediately get attention for their positive acts, will slip into misbehavior to get the attention. The parents' job is to teach these kids that while everyone deserves some attention, demanding it or misbehaving are not the ways to go about it. That's why it's important to pay attention to kids' positive behavior *when they are not demanding or expecting it.* ("Tommy, I see you're really working hard on your school project and you seem to be enjoying it too!")

Power. Kids also need a sense of power. Everyone wants to feel they are in charge of at least some aspects of their lives. Parents can empower children by first refusing to let the kids overpower them. When we fight or give in to kids' bids for power, we are actually reinforcing them. Withdrawing from the power contest by refusing to fight or give in lets them know this isn't the way to seek power. Offering choices and letting kids experience the consequences of their choices gives them a sense of power, but lets you remain in charge of the situation. "Brenda, I'll wash only what I find in the hamper," is much more empowering to the child — and to you — than constantly nagging her to put her dirty clothes in the hamper, or fighting with her about it, or picking up after her. If she chooses not to put her clothes in the hamper, she wears dirty clothes. Can you handle that? (More on choices and consequences in chapter 12.)

You also empower kids by enlisting their help in areas where they are willing to help. "Josh, I'm having trouble with . . . Would you be willing to help me?" Josh learns that his contribution to the family is important, too.

Revenge. Getting even, or revenge, can result when the child feels hurt, whether or not you intentionally set out to hurt the child. You encourage the hurt child by refusing to hurt back and working on building a positive relationship. You can also help the child feel a sense of justice and fairness by doing your best to be fair, without being manipulated into accepting misbehavior with the accusation of "you're unfair."

Displaying Inadequacy. This may happen when a child loses faith in her ability. This may occur in school subjects, peer relationships, sports, family responsibilities — almost any activity important to the parents in which the child feels she can't measure up. Parents can encourage such a child by examining their own standards (are you expecting too much?), commenting on the slightest effort or progress, and pointing out areas where the child can feel competent.

You can see that to encourage the child to change his behavior, it's important to change your own, often by doing the opposite of what is expected. If you continue in your same pattern of response to the child's goal — doing what the child expects — you reinforce the goal and thus the undesirable behavior. Only when the child feels he can belong in a positive way will he begin to give up the misbehavior.

These four goals represent levels of discouragement. Least discouraged are the attention seekers, most discouraged are those who give up and display inadequacy. Kids can seek different goals in different circumstances depending on their level of discouragement in any given situation.

The goals of attention, power and revenge relate to anger. When your child seeks attention, you may experience annoyance — a mild form of anger. Your reponse will likely move up to anger and provocation with children who are "power seekers." And you'll probably feel hurt and anger in response to kids who "get even." A child's display of inadequacy usually doesn't relate to anger unless the goal is associated with past angry interactions — which eventually lead the child to give up. You're no longer angry at the child; you've given up too.

Okay — attention, power, revenge, displaying inadequacy — the four goals of misbehavior. So how do I know which goal my kid's after?

DISCOVERING THE GOAL YOUR CHILD IS SEEKING

In order to understand which goal of misbehavior your child may be seeking in any situation, *identify your feelings* and *your child's reaction to what you do* about the misbehavior. This interaction is directly related to the goal the child is seeking. Chart 1 on page 170, "The Four Goals of Children's Misbehavior," shows the pattern, as well as general steps in redirecting the goal and behavior.

Most parents first learn to identify their child's goal of misbehavior after the incident has passed. To identify the goal, ask yourself: (1) "What, specifically, did my child do?" (2) "How did I feel?" (3) "What did I do?" (4) "How did my child respond?" Using the chart, you can identify the goal based on your answers

CHART 1: THE FOUR GOALS OF CHILDREN'S MISBEHAVIOR

Child's Goal	Your Feeling	Your Reaction	Child's Response	Redirecting
Attention	Annoyed	Remind and coax.	Stops temporarily or chooses another attention getting behavior.	Ignore behavior when possible or give attention in ways child doesn't expect. Give child positive attention when s/he's not expecting it.
Power	Angry, provoked	Fight or give in.	If fight, child fights back. If give in, child quits as s/he has won.	Don't fight or give in. Withdraw from power contest. Let child experience consequences. Help child use power constructively.
Revenge	Hurt, then anger to punish	Punish. Get even.	Punishes back by intensifying misbehavior or choosing a different weapon.	Don't feel hurt or angry, or punish. Build relationship.
Displaying Inadequacy	Despair (feel like giving up)	Give up.	No improvement as no action on parent's part.	Encourage slightest effort and progress. Find areas where child will feel successful.

to questions 2, 3 and 4. Then ask yourself: "What could I have done, or what could I do the next time?"

With practice, you can learn to identify the goal and choose a response while the misbehavior is happening. After you've calmed yourself, ask yourself: (1) "What am I feeling?" (2) "What does my child expect me to do?" (3) "What is his/her goal?" (4) "What can I do instead?" In question 2 — "What does my child expect me to do?" — you know from your experience what the child's response will be if you do what's expected. Combining your experience with how you're feeling gives you a good clue to the goal of the misbehavior.

Okay, you've learned how to identify your child's goal for her misbehavior. The next step is to plan a response that's different from what she expects you to do. Listen carefully to your self-talk to help gain control of your emotions and behavior.

Your Self-Talk and Your Child's Goal of Misbehavior

As you have learned, your self-talk — including the irrational "hot" thoughts you create — relates to your purposes, emotions and behavior. Let's examine your reactions to your kids when they pursue each goal of misbehavior and how you can change what you think, feel and do.[37]

Attention. When your child seeks inappropriate attention, you probably tell yourself something such as, "He should stop bothering me. I'm busy and I have a right to finish what I'm doing without him interrupting me." Since attention-getting is usually a minor irritation, a demanding statement ("shoulding") is probably all you would tell yourself about the situation.

Your belief, "He should stop bothering me . . ." will produce annoyance and will lead you to make an effort to stop the misbehavior through reminding and coaxing: "George, stop that! How many times . . ." "Sally, come on. It's almost time to leave! Will you please hurry up? I've got enough to do without having to constantly tell you to get going." Of course, any compliance from the child under these circumstances is usually short-lived.

He's got his attention "fix." It only lasts a little while; he'll come back for another soon.

You might consider what could happen if you were to change your self-talk to a "cool" thought, something like this: "While *I wish* he would stop bothering me, there's no reason why he *should*. He thinks he 'needs' attention whenever he wants it — that this is the only way he can belong. This is a discouraged belief and I'll not further reinforce him by reminding and coaxing. Instead, I'll ignore him now (or give him a choice) and give him attention later when he's not demanding it. I'll 'catch him being good.'" Your new purpose encourages the child's self-reliance. This belief will also eliminate the annoyance and replace it with a feeling of determination, which will allow you to respond in ways the child doesn't expect.

Power. When kids are after power, it's quite a different matter. When your child seeks power, you feel your authority as a parent is challenged and you might think, "You're defying me and I can't stand it! It's awful when you don't do what I say (or try to get me to give in to your attempts to overpower me). You must obey me or you're a bad kid and I'm a terrible parent!" Obviously these types of "hot" thoughts will generate anger at your child — and yourself — leading you to try to establish control or win (or protect, if you feel your rights are violated or the child's safety is involved). You will then proceed to fight with the child: "I said no! Now stop that whining right now!" Or if you feel defeated, you give in to the child's demands: "All right, you can have a cookie, but just this one time."

If, instead, you create a "cool" thought about the situation, your anger will rapidly diminish. You could tell yourself: "I really *don't like* it when you defy me, but *I can stand it*. It's not a catastrophe, only frustrating and inconvenient. You're behaving badly, but you're not a totally bad child, and I'm not a terrible parent, just because you defy me. Kids do test limits, that's how they learn. You believe you have to be the boss and that's a discouraged viewpoint. It doesn't help you learn cooperation. I'll not add to your discouragement by fighting or giving in. Instead I'll help you learn by letting you experience the consequences of your behavior and look for positive ways to help you feel powerful." (You might actually tell yourself only part of all that, but you get the idea!)

You now have a new purpose: gaining control of yourself, the situation, and winning the child's cooperation. This kind of self-talk will also produce determination, and possibly regret that the child has to experience the consequences. Your new purpose and feelings will lead you to more encouraging responses. "I'm sorry, but dinner will be served soon, so you can't have a cookie." If your child throws a tantrum, you can walk away, or offer a choice to cooperate or take a time-out. (See chapter 12.) If the tantrum continues, you can remove her to her room to have a tantrum by herself.

Revenge. When a child seeks revenge, parents feel hurt. They initially believe they must have done something terribly wrong or the child would not treat them so. But this idea doesn't last very long as they switch to anger-generating beliefs, telling themselves the child is horrible and they didn't deserve this treatment and the child must be punished. The belief can go something like this: "This is awful, you hurt me! I must be a terrible parent or you wouldn't have done this . . . Hey, wait a minute, I haven't done anything to you that deserves this. This is awful! You're just a mean kid who deserves punishment for such terrible behavior! I can't stand this and I'll show you that you can't treat me this way!" You're hurt and angry and you get even by punishing the child: "Just for that, you stay home and clean your room today."

But you can change your thoughts, purpose and feelings when your child seeks revenge. Hard as it is, you can develop "cool" thoughts by telling yourself something like this: "For some reason you want to hurt me. This is very unpleasant but it's not awful and I can stand it, even though I really don't like it. While your behavior is mean, you're not a totally mean kid. You must be very discouraged and hurt or you wouldn't treat me so. How unpleasant for you! I'll not further discourage and hurt you by getting even. Instead I'll look for ways to improve our relationship and to see if I'm doing anything you might find hurtful." With this belief, your new purpose becomes demonstrating compassion and seeking fairness. You generate new feelings of regret, empathy and determination, which allow you to carry out your plan for improving the relationship and seeking fairness.

Displaying Inadequacy. This goal reflects a child's high level of discouragement. When children are this discouraged, they tend to do whatever it takes to keep the spotlight off of themselves. They give up trying, because they believe they will fail and further humiliate themselves. Their goal and related behavior are efforts to protect themselves. They hope others will give up as they have.

When your child persistently does this, you may tend to agree with her assessment of her "inability." You may tell yourself something such as, "This is awful. I should be able to help you, but I can't. I've tried everything I know to help you. You are just unable, and I'm incompetent as a parent. You'll never improve." This belief allows you to give up. You generate despair to fortify your belief and end up doing nothing. "You just can't do it, so I won't expect anything out of you."

Changing this belief requires that you take a realistic view of the situation. Unless the child is seriously disabled, it's her *belief* in her ability that's lacking rather than her *actual* ability. It's important to convince yourself of that before you'll be able to help. You could tell yourself: "You are very discouraged and believe you can't do it. It's very frustrating that I haven't been able to help you so far, but that's because I've chosen not to believe in you, or myself. I'm changing that view now. I choose to believe in you and me, and will do my best to help you believe in yourself by finding areas where you can feel successful, and noticing the slightest effort or progress in the area where you feel unable."

This new constructive belief will spur you on to look for the tiniest spark of interest, potential, motivation, development or ability. You'll have faith and confidence in your child and yourself and will be determined to do what you can.

When faced with this situation, don't concentrate on the area where your child feels inadequate; this will just influence her to feel more inadequate. Instead, look for areas where she can succeed. When you do notice effort and improvement in the area of her "disability," point it out *without* any messages; avoid saying "you can do it if you put your mind to it." The child will see such a statement as a demand and will be further discouraged. Instead, focus on the child's effort, progress and accomplishment: "You're really trying," "You're making progress," "I hope you can take pride in your accomplishment."

Notice that with each new belief, regardless of the goal, a common new feeling arises with your positive self-talk — *determination.* You need this feeling to carry out encouraging responses to your children's misbehavior.

Chart 2, "Points of Conflict and Collaboration . . ." sums up what occurs in the belief process of both parent and child with each goal. Notice that with attention, power, and revenge — the misbehavior goals that commonly result in parental annoyance, anger and hurt — there is obvious conflict between parent and child. Only with displaying inadequacy is there collaboration; the parent agrees that the child is unable and "can't do it." Only when you change your beliefs, purposes, feelings and behavior, can there be progress in helping the child change his.

CHART 2: POINTS OF CONFLICT (AND COLLABORATION) BETWEEN PARENT AND CHILD

Child's Belief	Child's Goal	Parent's Belief
You should pay attention to me when I want it.	Attention	I should have the right to not be bothered when I'm busy.
I must be the boss.	Power	I must be the boss.
You hurt me. You must be punished.	Revenge	You hurt me. You must be punished.
I can't do it.	Displaying inadequacy	You can't do it.

In this chapter you've discovered why kids behave the way they do, and you're beginning to understand what you can do about it. You've seen how your beliefs (your "hot" thoughts), purposes, and emotions have reinforced your child's misbehavior. You've learned how you can change your beliefs, purposes, emotions and behavior to encourage the child to behave more cooperatively.

In the next chapter, you'll discover how choices and consequences can help with positive, anger-free discipline. A focus on choices and consequences can help kids accept responsibility for their behavior so that everybody wins. Think of how that may help calm the "storms" at your house!

MAJOR POINTS

- Our kids are part of the "democratic revolution" in human relationships. Traditional autocratic methods of discipline don't work very well.

- Effective discipline does not include punishment, which is most often ineffective.

- Punishment is usually administered by frustrated, angry parents. Any cooperation derived from punishment is often short-lived.

- Parents who rely on rewards are giving this message: "You should expect to be paid for good behavior."

- Instead of the desired result, kids may see rewards as something they are entitled to.

- Kids may attempt to achieve a sense of belonging through misbehavior, if they find cooperation doesn't work.

- Misbehavior has purpose: attention, power, revenge, or displaying inadequacy.

- Redirect your child's goal and misbehavior by examining your own belief, purpose and behavior. Change "hot thoughts" to "cool thoughts" and develop a positive purpose.[14]

12

Children's Choices and Consequences

Kids are always making choices. What to wear, what to play, who to play with, who their "best friend" is this week. They even choose whether or not to comply with your wishes. Since your children are making choices anyway, why not learn to use this ability to help your kids take responsibility for their behavior? That's a choice you could live with!

In chapter 11, we discussed the pitfalls of punishment and the problems with rewards. We explained the goals of misbehavior. Now that you understand the problems with traditional discipline methods, we'll turn our discussion of discipline to methods that fit with the democratic revolution.

GIVE 'EM CHOICES!

The more choices you offer, the more opportunities your kids have to learn to make good decisions. Also, giving choices allows you to refrain from using anger as discipline. Give your child a choice — within the limits of her age and abilities — and a chance to experience the consequences of the choice. Consequences can be positive or negative depending on the choice the child makes. Most kids test limits and experience the negative consequences of breaking the limits. But the consequence doesn't have to be *punitive*, it can be just the *result* of the choice.

For example, suppose your child wants to invite a friend for a sleepover. You agree, as long as the kids are willing to go to bed on time and quiet down when the lights are out. He agrees but doesn't follow through. You don't have to be angry and demand quiet. Instead, you can offer him and his friend another choice: to be quiet or to be separated for the rest of the night. Then calmly act on the choice. If they continue to make noise, move one of them to another part of the house to sleep. They can decide who goes where by flipping a coin or any other method they choose. But there is no bargaining; once their behavior shows they've decided to be separated, it happens. There are no second chances.

There are two types of consequences: *natural* and *logical*.[19, 14, 40] Let's take a look at some examples that will explain both types.

Natural Consequences

A *natural consequence* results when we allow the laws of nature to take their course, or comes from experiencing the "natural flow of events . . . without any interference from the parents."[19]

- If a child doesn't wear a raincoat when rain is predicted, he'll probably get wet.

- If a child skips a meal, she'll probably be hungry before the next meal.

- If kids stay up late, they'll probably be tired in the morning.

- If you tell your kids that you're only willing to wash the clothes you find in the hamper and they decide not to put their clothes in the hamper by wash day, they end up with dirty clothes.

- If a child is rude to a friend, the friend may not want to play with her.

- If your ten-year-old thinks it's cool to walk around with untied shoes, even though you've mentioned to him that he might fall (as if he isn't old enough to know that), and you decide it's his problem, and he trips and falls, he may decide it's not so cool.

◆ If your teen has plans to meet friends on Saturday morning and forgets to set her alarm clock and misses the fun . . .

Well, see what we mean by natural consequences?

Of course, we can't let kids experience natural consequences that are dangerous, but we can be brave enough to allow them to experience ones that are not — like those we just mentioned. If we decide to stay out of the situation, refraining from constant reminders, such as "It looks like a storm is coming; be sure to take your raincoat," and let them learn by experience, they will most likely learn, and become more self-reliant in the process. Natural consequences will help build your children's "psychological muscle."

> One of the authors effectively used natural consequences when his son was nine years old. Jason developed a habit of forgetting his lunch money even though it was given to him in the morning at the breakfast table. On days that he forgot, the school would phone one of us, at home or at work, and the lucky parent would dutifully transport the lunch money to school. Not surprisingly, the pattern continued. My wife and I realized that our behavior was a part of the problem, that we were supporting Jason's irresponsible behavior and giving him undue attention with our rescuing behavior. So, we decided to use natural consequences — no more parents taking the lunch money to school.
>
> The next time the school called, we followed through, explaining to the school official that this had become a pattern and that Jason was not learning to be responsible for his behavior. We informed the school that we would no longer help him to be irresponsible and dependent. We explained that letting Jason experience the natural consequence of his behavior — no lunch that day — would encourage him to become more self-sufficient.

Guess what? Jason did go without a meal that day, but it was the last time he went hungry at school. His memory suddenly improved!

Think of consequences that either occur in nature or that happen without you needing to be involved. You can let your child experience results that stem from nature — or the "natural flow of events" — and learn from that experience. While you wouldn't want to let your daughter ride her bike without a helmet, you might be brave enough to stop reminding her to take her books to school and let her deal with the teacher.

But what if there is no opportunity for nature to do the teaching, or nothing flows from the natural order of events, or the natural consequence for a particular misbehavior is dangerous? In other words, what do you do when natural consequences don't apply? This is where logical consequences come into play.

LOGICAL CONSEQUENCES

Logical consequences are created by the parent, sometimes through discussion with the child, or with the family at a family meeting. To be effective, they must be seen as logical by the child. In other words, the *consequence fits the misbehavior* — while the child doesn't like the results, they will make sense to her. Examples:

Your four-year-old dawdles when it's time for you to drive him to preschool. You say, "It's time to go. Do you want to get in the car on your own or shall I help you?" You act on his decision. If he doesn't get in the car, you pick him up and put him in the car.

You give your eight-year-old a choice of cereals for breakfast. She chooses one kind, pours on the milk, then changes her mind. You say, "I'm sorry, but you chose Bran Bubbles this morning, so that's what you'll be eating. Tomorrow you can

choose another kind." The point is, once the milk is poured, the decision is made. Your intent is to teach your child to plan ahead, not to waste food, and to accept the consequences of her decisions.

You give your eleven-year-old an allowance, with an understanding the money is to last him a week. He decides to spend it all in one day, and asks for more money to go to the movies. You say, "I'll be glad to give your allowance again next week, on Saturday."

You have an agreement with your teen that she can use the family car as long as she's willing to buy gas when she uses the car. You find the tank nearly empty when you're heading for work. When she later asks to use the car to go see a friend, you say, "No, I'm sorry. I found the gas tank nearly empty. You can try again tomorrow to see if you're ready to keep the agreement."

When children's behavior indicates they've chosen to experience the consequences of their decisions, you may hear griping, complaints and promises to behave better — anything to get out of experiencing the consequences. Don't respond — this is not the time for comments, including reflective listening. Commenting will just reinforce the child's goal of attention, power or revenge. Just go about your business. Use the "on-the-spot" anger management techniques we talked about in chapter 3 to keep yourself from responding.

Your attitude and intention are extremely important when applying natural or logical consequences. If your intent is to use *consequences* as a substitute for punishment, or in a punitive way, they will be mostly ineffective. But, if you use them simply as *an opportunity for your child to learn to make good decisions*, then your chances of success are much greater.

Consequences differ from punishment in a number of ways. The chart on page 183 illustrates the difference.

USING TIME-OUT AS A LOGICAL CONSEQUENCE

Time-out can be an effective logical consequence if used appropriately. The problem is many parents use time-out for practically everything — a kid belches, he goes to time-out! Also, some parents use time-out in a punitive way. The child is punished by being "banished" until she straightens out. Or he's supposed to think about how bad he's acting and get control of himself.

Time-out should be used only when the child's behavior is disruptive and other methods you've used — such as I-messages or reflective listening — fail to solve the problem, or make it worse. Whenever possible, it's better for *you* to take a time-out by removing yourself from the disturbing child. This provides no conflict in trying to remove the child — you simply take yourself out of the situation, providing no reinforcement for the child's goal of attention, power or revenge.

Temper tantrums are a good example. Most tantrums are designed to get you to give in or to punish you (power or revenge). If you take yourself out of the situation, the purpose is not achieved — no audience, no performance. When it's not possible to take yourself out of the situation — e.g., the child may harm others or property — then a time-out can be designed.

Discuss time-outs with a child in advance so that she knows what to expect should she decide to create a disturbance or throw a fit.

Most important, the time-out should be a time to feel better, not worse. We improve our behavior when we feel better about ourselves. This is true whether the child takes the time-out or you do.

> *Eight-year-old Dewayne threw temper tantrums when he didn't get what he wanted. If dad walked away, he found that*

Differences Between Punishment and Logical Consequences[14, 40]

	Punishment	Example	Logical Consequences	Example
1	Focuses on power of personal authority.	You're driving and kids are misbehaving in back seat. "You two knock it off right now!"	Focus on cooperation.	Pull over to side of road. "I'm sorry but I can't drive with all this noise. When you settle down, we'll continue."
2	Rarely related to misbehavior.	Borrows something from you and loses it. No TV.	Logically related to misbehavior.	Replaces item from allowance.
3	Often implies child is bad for making bad choice.	Spills food on the floor. "You're so clumsy. How many times have I told you to carry the dish with both hands!"	Separate the deed from the doer: bad choice, not bad child.	"Whoops, you spilled, please clean it up."
4	Focuses on the past.	Wants to invite a friend over to play. "No, you can't have Billy over. Last time you guys kept running through the house and almost broke a lamp in the living room."	Focus on the present.	You can have Billy over as long as the two of you are willing to run outside and not in the house. If you decide to run in the house, I'll know it's time for Billy to go home."
5	Voice and or accusing. Disrespects child.	Glaring at child with hostile tone. "You have a choice..."	Voice and nonverbal behavior firm but friendly. Shows respect for child.	"You may . . . or you may . . . you decide."
6	Makes demands.	Playing music loud. "Turn down that music right now!"	Give choices.	"I'm sorry but the music is too loud. You may turn it down, use earphones or turn it off. You decide."

Dewayne would get angrier and throw various objects. Dad decided to talk this over with Dewayne during a calm time. "Dewayne," said Dad, "sometimes you get so angry that it's impossible for us to be together. So, when you do this I'll know you need some time-out and I'll ask you to go to your room until you feel better. While you're in your room, I'll be in the living room by myself so I can feel better too. When you're feeling better, you can come out of your room if you want to."

The next day, Dewayne threw a good one when dad turned down his request to ride his bike to a friend's house. Dad calmly said, "I see you've decided to take some time-out in your room. I'll see you when you're feeling better." Dewayne balked, so Dad said. "Would you like to go to your room on your own, or shall I help you?" Dewayne said nothing and stayed in the family room. Dad calmly, but firmly, took Dewayne's hand and led him down the hall to his room.

The next time Dewayne threw a tantrum, all Dad said was, "I see you've decided to take a time-out." This time, Dewayne stomped off to his room. As time went on, Dewayne had fewer tantrums. He learned that they didn't work!

If Dewayne came out of his room too soon — obviously not yet feeling better and willing to cooperate, Dad could say, "I see you're still not feeling better," and escort Dewayne back to his room if need be. Dad could then say, "I'll check on you in a few minutes to see if you're feeling better and ready to come out of your room."

If a child wants, she could have things in her room that help her feel better — certain toys, books, etc. You could discuss this with the child. "When you're really angry, what helps you feel better?"[43]

CONSEQUENCES AND THE TYPICAL DAILY ROUTINE

Most parents encounter stormy challenges with their kids, from getting up in the morning to going to bed at night. In this section, we're going to deal with the typical problems parents report with daily routine.

Parents are often confronted with a child's anger, disrespect, irresponsibility, or conflict. We've found that parents who can focus their attention on improving things during a specific portion of the day — e.g., the morning — frequently experience a "carryover" effect to the rest of the day and to family relationships as a whole. To understand this, it will help to examine some issues that commonly occur at particular times of the family's day.

Morning Madness. "Carl, get out of that bed right now!" "Carrie, hurry up and get dressed!" "Tommy, eat your breakfast! We have to leave for school in a few minutes." Sound familiar? Morning routine in many homes is morning madness! But it doesn't have to be. Applying the principles of choices and consequences can help.

Let the child own the problem. Kids as young as five are capable of learning to use an alarm clock. Tell the child you think he's old enough to assume this responsibility. Teach him how to set it and let him choose where he wants to place the clock in his room — what location will work best for him.

Five-year-olds can also choose what to wear (within the limits you set) and dress themselves.

For kids who dawdle in the morning, structure the routine so breakfast is served after they're dressed and ready to go to school. If they're not ready in time for breakfast, they may experience the natural consequences of being hungry before lunch. Missing a few breakfasts won't kill them, and the natural consequences of being hungry will probably teach them to hurry up if they want to eat. Also, kids as young as four are able to learn to choose their own cereal and pour on the milk. This contribution frees you for other morning chores.

With young kids who still won't dress even if they miss breakfast because they don't have time, you can offer the choice of dressing by the time you're ready to leave, or dressing in the car on the way to school. (Try not to laugh out loud as the child tries to put on a shirt within the confines of a seat belt or safety restraint!) It won't take too long for them to learn, if you can be consistent about the consequences.

Announce your plans for changes in the morning routine in advance — the night before you initiate changes. Talk with them in a respectful way. "Mandy, we have a problem with you being dressed in time to leave for school in the morning. So, starting tomorrow, you have a choice. You can be dressed in time for breakfast, or you can skip breakfast. If you're still not dressed when it's time to leave, you can dress in the car. I'll know by your behavior what you've decided. I won't remind you in the morning." Then, the next morning, if Mandy chooses to dawdle, don't remind her. When it's time to go, say, "Do you want me to take your clothes to the car, or do you want to do it? You might want to put your coat over your pajamas, it's cold out there." Then act on her decision based on her behavior.

With younger children, you'll want to go over the choices again the first few mornings until the new routine gets established. From then on, don't remind them; trust them to be responsible and remember.

After-School Antics. Too much TV-watching, forgetting chores, arguing and fighting — oh, what fun you can have when your kids come home from school! TV's not all bad. You can use it to help you teach kids anger management (see chapter 14). Too much TV, however, can be used as a substitute for other activities, such as interacting with family and peers. Too much computer time serves the same purpose. Limit kids' use of the TV, computer, and other electronic devices (except for homework, of course).

At a family meeting, discuss and agree on how much TV and computer time is acceptable. You will have one proposal, the kids may have another. Compromise may be needed. Make sure the rule is for the whole family. If you restrict TV or computer time for the kids and flop down in your easy chair or plant yourself in front of the monitor for hours on end, what message are you sending to the kids?

When the kids reach the end of their TV or computer time, you can say, "The time we agreed on is up. Do you want to turn off the (TV/computer) or shall I?" Ignore any complaints. The next time, don't say a word — just turn it off.

Chores can be a real challenge because most parents assign chores without any input from the kids. Family meetings can be a big help with chore decisions. At a meeting, work together to list all the chores that need to be done and to decide a way to share them. Of course, who does what depends to some extent on age. Young kids can help set or clear the table, bring in the mail, help bring in the groceries, put dirty clothes in the hamper and pick up their toys. As kids get older, there are many things they can help out with, such as carrying out the trash (but don't always give the garbage to the kids — share the job), helping prepare meals, loading the dishwasher, putting away clean dishes, watering the lawn, shoveling snow, washing their own clothes or helping with the washing and hanging up, changing their own sheets, mowing the lawn. Teens who get their driver's licenses can help with errands.[13]

What do you do when the chores are "forgotten"? You own this problem because it interferes with the functioning of the household. The first rule is, don't remind — this actually makes you responsible for the chore, and encourages the child to be dependent on the reminder. Instead, decide in the family meeting when each chore will be completed and the consequences if the chore is not done. For example, if it's agreed that chores are to be done before the child heads out to play or another activity, and the child "forgets," you can say: "You can go as soon as you finish your chores." "But Mom! I promised Nita I'd be there by four o'clock!" "You might want to give her a call."

If forgetting chores is a frequent occurrence, discuss it at the family meeting. If the kids' behavior shows they're not willing to do their chores, there's no reason why you should continue to do your chores that involve providing certain services for them, such as rides to activities they want to be involved in. The logical consequence of failing to cooperate and contribute is losing the cooperation of others when it comes to what you want. Don't make this a threat or revenge; it's just a statement of fact. "We have an agreement. You do your chores, and I do the driving. If you don't do the chores, I don't do the driving. I won't be driving you to the skate park until you show me you're willing to keep your agreements."

Kids' arguments and fights can drive parents crazy. If the conflict is between your child and a friend who's visiting, the solution can be fairly simple. They can be given a choice of getting along, or the friend goes home. Fights between siblings can be a bit more complicated. We'll discuss those conflicts in chapter 13.

Homework Hassles. A real attention grabber or a way to defeat parents and thus meet the goals of power and revenge — involves problems with school, grades and homework. Parents remind, prod and fight with kids about homework. It makes one wonder who's responsible for doing the homework — who owns the problem? You went to school years ago; now it's the kids' turn.

An exception would be if it's possible that your child has a learning problem that makes studying and learning difficult. If you believe this is a possibility, speak to your child's teacher or counselor. Most schools are able to help you arrange for testing, assessment, and any specialized services needed to help your child succeed in school.

One way to handle homework hassles is to give kids a choice about when — not whether! — they do their homework, such as before or after supper. If the child chooses to do it before supper and doesn't do it, he's actually chosen to do it after supper that day. "I'm gonna watch the 'Mr. Dithers' show now, Mom." "It looks like today you chose to do your homework after supper."

Of course, you can be available in case one of your kids has a question. If she has a question every five minutes, however, you could be involved in an attention-getting game. Check your feelings. Are you getting a bit annoyed? Are you pretty confident she can find the answers without you? If so, tell her you're sure she can handle the task and ignore further questions.

Some families find setting a *family study time* helps. The parents do their "homework" at that time too, which could involve paying the bills, writing emails or letters, doing work brought home from the job, etc.

With some kids, homework, school and grades can become a real battle for power. You can give them all the choices in the world about when to do their homework and they still won't do it. You end up feeling frustrated and angry and trying to force them do their homework. When this happens, it's best to back out of the power contest. Admit to the youngster that you can't make him do his homework, so from now on you'll leave that decision up to him. The problem is now between him and the school. If he decides he wants to do the work and needs some help, you'll be glad to assist.

This is a difficult choice for most parents, but when there are lots of fights over homework — either openly or through the child's stubbornness — not only is it ineffective to try to force the child to improve the homework situation, it puts a real strain on the relationship. Your only hope is to stay out of it. If there's no fight, and the relationship improves, the child may decide to study.

If the school complains to you, respectfully share that you are doing all you can to support your child's education, and that when you take too much responsibility you undermine your child's responsibility and end up in a power contest. Tell them that you fully support the school in applying whatever consequences they deem appropriate.

Don't let the school try to force you into bribing, punishing or fighting with your child about homework. This is often the way some school people try to shift onto the parents their own failures to motivate children.

The same is true for grades and behavior at school. Many parents reward or punish in an effort to improve grades. With some kids this works, but at what price? What are you teaching the kids about responsibility and cooperation? Who are the grades for?

Concerning their behavior at school: what does the educator expect you to do — come and sit in the class with the child? You wouldn't ask the educator to come and sit in your home when you're struggling with your child's misbehavior. It works both ways. Problems at school are between the school and the students.

Do keep in mind, of course, that children have a shorter perspective on time. If they are to take responsibility for not doing their homework, they must understand the long-range consequences. A few missed assignments won't hurt anybody, but a child who is allowed to get farther and farther behind in school may not realize that the consequences can be life-long. A conference with the teacher(s) or the school counselor or school psychologist is in order for the child to get the information and support she needs to think about the future consequences of her behavior. It also may be useful to consider arranging tutoring assistance to help your child learn smarter study habits and test-taking strategies. This kind of outside support helps you to stay out of power struggles with your children about school. It's very easy — too easy — to get caught in the power struggle trap, and it can undermine a child's desire to learn and succeed.

Dinnertime Turmoil. "Harry, you're 15 minutes late! You know dinner's served by 6:00." "Lauren, how many times do I have to tell you to wash your hands? Just look at the dirt!" "Billy, no 'yuks' tonight; eat your vegetables!" "Tina and Toby, stop kicking each other under the table or you can just go to bed without your supper!"

Typical dinner conversation at your house? Let's see how choices and consequences can work for these challenges. (You can discuss the new mealtime rules at a family meeting.)

If your child knows when dinner is served and he's late, remove his plate and assume he's decided not to eat. Breakfast will be served in the morning. Don't serve any snacks. Snacks are for those who eat their meals, not a substitute for meals. He owns the problem; let the natural consequence of being hungry do the teaching.

The same goes for kids who keep forgetting to wash their hands. If your schedule is not as regular as you'd probably like it to be, then give a 10 or 15 minute notice of when it will be served. This will give the kids time to wash up.

For picky eaters, assume they'll eat what they want of what's on the plate. Don't cater to them. If they won't eat certain foods, don't try to coax them or force them. If they don't get enough for dinner, again, they'll be hungry by breakfast. Don't use dessert as an attempt to bribe them. Trying to lecture, coax or bribe kids just feeds the power contest, not the child. You can gain more cooperation and prevent some of this problem by involving the kids in meal planning at the family meeting.

Fooling around or fighting at the table means they're not interested in eating. Remove their plates and say, "When you guys settle down, I'll know you're ready to continue eating." When they settle, return the plates. Then if they start up again, simply remove their plates and say, "It looks like you're finished eating. See you at breakfast." If they misbehave at a following meal, don't say a word, just remove the plates.

Bedtime Bedlam. "Kelly, get to bed right now!" "Okay, Aaron, just one more story." What else do your kids do to try to stay up as late as possible? You can approach this problem by discussing bedtime with the kids earlier in the day. Of course, kids of different ages will have different bedtimes — a five-year-old will have an earlier bedtime than a ten-year-old sibling. But, there's usually room for negotiation, even with young kids.

When bedtime comes, it's time for them to go to their rooms. If you read your younger kids a story at bedtime, make it the last thing in their getting-ready-for-bed routine.

When you discuss bedtime with your child, you can say, "When we say 'goodnight,' that means we'll see each other in the morning." After the child is in bed, refrain from responding to pleas for additional attention (unless the child is ill, of course).

THINGS TO CONSIDER WHEN USING CONSEQUENCES

Following is a list of requirements for effective use of natural and logical consequences.

◆ **Identify the child's goal of misbehavior.** Natural consequences work with any goal of misbehavior because you step aside and let them happen. Logical consequences, on the other hand, require some involvement with the child, and are most effective when a child's goal is attention. Attention-getting involves minor conflict between parent and child.

With *power*-seeking kids, logical consequences can turn into a major conflict, trying to apply the consequence even though there was a clear choice. The best logical consequences for power-seeking kids involve negotiating agreements and consequences in advance, individually or at family meetings. You can ask: "What do you think should happen next time if . . .?" When you're negotiating a consequence, use the principles of "exploring alternatives" discussed in chapter 8.

Be sure to work out a consequence that applies the principles discussed in this chapter. This negotiating approach is effective because children appreciate that the present issue is being handled by considering future consequences, and they are involved in developing the consequence; they have "buy-in." Working together to agree on the consequences in advance is especially effective with teens, who tend to rebel against consequences — however logical — that they had no hand in determining.

Stating what you will do or not do can also be an effective consequence when dealing with power. That way you're not trying to force the child into anything.

Here's an example: You've told your kids that if they want something from the grocery store to write it on a list you keep posted on the refrigerator. You've also informed them of what days you go to the store. Your son forgets to list his favorite treat. You come home from the store without the item. Later in the day, he's looking for his snack and when he can't find it, he asks you where it is. You tell him that you didn't get it because you didn't see it on the list. He asks you to return to the store and get the treat. You say, "I'm not willing to make another trip. I'll be going to the store again on Wednesday. If you write it on the list, I'll be glad to remember to get it."

You'll also gain more cooperation when you "turn the power around." That is, you use their desire for power in a positive way through asking for their help (on things where they're willing to help).

For kids who pursue revenge, logical consequences are seen as punishment and promote more revenge behavior. It's best to avoid conflict, and work on improving the relationship first. Kids who display *inadequacy* are very discouraged, and require much encouragement, so logical consequences don't apply. Besides, their behavior is seldom disruptive.

◆ **Consider who owns the problem.** If your child owns the problem, natural consequences can often apply. If the child skips breakfast, it's her problem — the natural consequences of hunger may influence her decision the next day. If your child gets angry and breaks one of his toys, that's his problem. He experiences the consequences of not having the toy to play with. If you replace the toy, you've assumed ownership of the problem and there's no lesson learned except, "I can be irresponsible and (Mom or Dad) will take care of it."

When you own the problem, you can use logical consequences. For example, if your child breaks something that belongs to someone else, the logical consequence relates to how she will pay for the item.

◆ **Don't talk too much.** Most parents talk too much when there are discipline challenges. When they do, they fall right into the kids' trap — this is what kids expect parents to do. And do they listen? Too much talk reinforces kids' misbehavior goals.

While a certain amount of talk is necessary to give the child a choice, choose your words carefully and be as brief as possible. "You may settle down and watch the program with us or leave the room." If the kids continue to disturb you, they've made their decision. "I see you've decided to leave, you can come back when you're ready to watch the program." If they return and still fool around, you can say, "I see you really don't want to watch the program. You may try again tomorrow." Then don't talk about it anymore. Telling them they may "try again" (at a certain time) assures them of another opportunity to cooperate. Consequences are not a life sentence.

Of course, if they do the same thing the next time, they've decided to accept the consequences. You don't have to state the choice again. *This is the way we train kids not to listen — we keep repeating.* All you have to say the next time is, "I see you've decided not to watch the program with us. You can try again on Thursday." Increase the time with each occurrence of the misbehavior.

Keep your tone firm, but also respectful. Watch your body language and your intention. Remember, effective consequences require the attitude of letting kids learn from experience, not trying to "teach them a lesson."

If the child keeps getting out of bed and coming to where you are, you can still pretend he's not there and go about your business; he'll get the message. If necessary, gain your privacy by going to your own bedroom and closing the door (as long as you believe your child will be safe). After a few nights of not being able to get your attention or engage you in a power contest about bedtime, the child will probably give up trying.

For kids who are especially stubborn and don't respond to agreements about bedtime, there's a natural consequence that can do the teaching — if parents will let it occur. Kids who don't get enough sleep, just like adults, are tired the next day. Let the child own the problem. You can say to the child, "I can't make you go to bed, so you decide when you want to go to bed." Of course when morning comes, the kid will need to get up to go to school — perhaps in her pajamas and dressing in the car (with seat belt securely fastened)!

In this chapter you've learned how to use natural and logical consequences to discipline without anger. Many a family storm has been calmed — or even prevented — when the children learned that they can choose the consequences of their own actions!

In the next chapter, we'll discuss how to handle kids' anger toward you and toward each other.

MAJOR POINTS

- The more choices you give, the more opportunities kids have to learn to make good decisions.

- Give kids choices — within the limits of age and abilities — and allow them to experience the consequences — positive or negative, depending on the choices they make.

- There are two types of consequences: natural and logical.

- A natural consequence results when we allow the laws of nature to take their course, or comes from experiencing the "natural flow of events" . . . without interference from us.

- Logical consequences are created by parents when a natural consequence is dangerous, or there is no natural consequence for a particular misbehavior.

- To be effective, the consequence must fit the misbehavior. The child may not like the results, but they make sense to the child.

- Don't respond to children's griping, complaints and promises to behave better. Use "on the spot" anger management techniques to keep yourself from responding.

- Use consequences as an opportunity for your child to learn to make good decisions, not as a substitute for punishment, or in a punitive way.

- Logical consequences focus on cooperation, are logically related to the misbehavior, separate the deed from the doer, focus on the present, show respect for the child, and give choices.

- When using consequences, identify the child's goal of misbehavior, consider who owns the problem, and don't talk too much.

13

When Kids Get Angry

I don't care what you say, Mom. I'm not going to do it!
You're so mean, Dad. I just hate you!
Say that one more time, Ali, and I'll hit ya!
Norman, get out of my room right now!

Do you have a "Stormin' Norman" or "Hurricane Ali" in your house? Lightning strikes in the family storm often come from the kids. Wonder where they learn to behave so angrily? And, how can you teach them to be less angry — or to handle their anger more respectfully? Stay tuned.

In this chapter, we'll give you some ideas on how to handle the kids' anger toward you and toward each other, sibling and peer conflicts, and tattling. In chapter 14, we'll discuss ways to help kids manage their anger.

HANDLING KIDS' ANGER TOWARD YOU

When your Norman or Ali is angry at you, you have several choices. *Avoid your first impulse!* If you do what your child expects you to do, you'll only reinforce the misbehavior. Give yourself some time to think by telling yourself to stop, using calming phrases, counting to ten. Use the "Stop, Think, and Act" technique. After you tell yourself to *stop, think* about what your child wants. What is her goal? Use the questions listed in chapter 11: "What am I feeling?" etc. This helps you to identify the child's goal and to choose your course of *action*. For example, you may decide to ignore the outburst, or to use reflective listening. Use the approach that you think will work with your child.

Parents and kids usually establish a pattern between the child's misbehavior goal and the parent's response. For example, a child's favorite goal might be power, and the parent's common response is to yell and threaten, which actually helps the child feel powerful. If the parent decides to withdraw from the behavior and not react, the behavior will likely get worse before it gets better. The child will work extra hard getting the parent to react in the typical way so that his goal will be achieved.

When the child learns he can no longer achieve his goal though misbehavior, the behavior will eventually improve. If you begin making new choices in response to your child's anger, and want to see more positive behavior result, it is important that you stick to your resolve. He will test you for a while!

You can "take a time-out in your mind" by forcing yourself to think of something else. You can also talk out loud about something else, such as planning your shopping list ("That reminds me, I've got to get eggs at the store later") or what you have to do next ("Well, I'd better mow the lawn before it gets too hot"). These are forms of ignoring, which is a type of logical consequence. When the child chooses to bug you or get angry, she discovers the consequence is that she is ignored — she doesn't get the attention she's after. Be sure to replace the attention you take away by paying attention to the child when she's not demanding or expecting it. "I see you're really enjoying that book. Want to tell me about it?"

Kids are pragmatic. If it doesn't work, they'll give it up and try something else. It's only we adults who keep doing the same thing over and over, thinking somehow it will eventually work with kids!

You may have to take a physical time-out and move away from the child. If the child is too young, a physical time-out may not be safe. In that case, if the behavior is quite disruptive (such as a temper tantrum), you may have to remove the child to a time-out area, perhaps her room. Follow the suggestions discussed in chapter 12 ("Using Time-out As a Logical Consequence") for using time-out.

If you decide to use reflective listening, you may find that the child does not calm down at first. When the child does calm down, you'll be able to discuss his angry feelings and possibly work something out. If the child doesn't calm down, you could say. "It looks like we're both pretty upset right now. Maybe we can talk about it later when we've both calmed down." Then remove yourself from the "field of engagement." If the issue still needs to be discussed, bring it up later when the storm passes.

You can also have a discussion with your kids — at non-conflict times — on how to express anger appropriately. For example, you can teach them how to use I-messages. (The next chapter addresses how to teach anger management skills to your kids.)

Arguments and Fights Between Siblings and Stepsiblings

Sibs are going to disagree — and occasionally fight — even in the best of families! And who's the referee? That would be you, right? Well, not necessarily . . .

While a certain amount of conflict between siblings is natural and to be expected, there's nothing that bothers most parents more than cruelty between siblings or stepsiblings. This accounts for how strongly parents feel when they witness sibling conflict and how many, if not most, parents tend to overreact. In our experience, it is the parents' overreaction that moves families from an acceptable level of sibling conflict to a pattern of frequent and often painful disruptions to family life.

Several of the concepts we've discussed in previous chapters apply to understanding the dynamics of sibling conflict. You may wish to review the material on the democratic revolution (chapter 6), the goals of misbehavior (chapter 11), coercive and pampering or permissive parenting styles (chapter 6), and hot spots (chapters 3 and 5). Let's add one more important factor to the list: the nature of relationships between older and younger siblings.

OLDER VS. YOUNGER SIBLINGS

Younger siblings tend to see themselves as underdogs. They usually feel inferior to their older brothers and sisters. They have less life experience and are less developed, less knowledgeable, less capable, smaller and weaker. What's more, they usually have fewer opportunities and privileges in the family. Consequently, young ones look for ways to overcome this position of inferiority to their older rivals.

Junior siblings over the centuries have discovered that one of the cleverest and most creative ways to bridge the power gap is to create a situation in which the parents will intervene and take their side against the older sib. It's pretty easy, actually. It begins with the younger sibling conducting "research" on the older, in order to discover what things really "bug" the older one. Armed with this intelligence, the younger sib can easily devise ways and means of annoying the "enemy." When the older sister or brother responds — usually by verbally or physically objecting in some way — the younger child makes enough noise (crying, protesting, yelling) that the parents feel obliged to rescue the poor, innocent "victim."

At this point, parents naturally side with the "poor, helpless" younger child (pampering parenting style) and blame the older one, who seems to have the unfair advantage and who should "know better." At this stage of the drama, parents typically conduct a brief investigation, pronounce the older child guilty, and administer punishment (coercive parenting style). The cycle is complete: the younger sibling has attained the goal of attention from his parents and has gained power and revenge at the expense of the older sib. The parents are baffled that the sibling "warfare" continues — in some families every day.

As these battles continue, they may become a pattern:

sniping → response → crying → rescue → punishment → gloating.

With this all-too-common pattern, the older child usually begins to feel unfairly treated by both the parents and the younger sibling. The older sibling has his own motive for keeping the conflict going — to defeat his parents and punish the younger one.

"Hot Spots" and Overreaction to Sibling Conflict

In our experience, parents have a variety of reasons, psychologically speaking, to overreact to sibling conflict. Let's take a look at some of the common parent "hot spots" that can be activated when kids engage in sibling conflict.

- **Family alliances.** A parent who is more closely bonded with one child, for whatever reason, will naturally want to side with and protect that child.

- **Biological alliances.** In stepfamily situations, it's common for parents to align with and take the side of their biological child when conflicts occur between that child and a stepchild. (Occasionally, the opposite occurs: the parent may discipline "her" child.)

- **Birth order identification.** A parent who, for example, was a younger or youngest child can over-identify with the plight of the younger child, and therefore wish to protect that child.

- **Gender identification.** A parent may align with a child of the same gender (e.g., mothers with daughters).

- **Lack of protection in childhood.** Parents who remember their own childhood times of "abuse" by siblings can easily get "hooked" by issues of sibling conflict.

- **Rescuer of the underdog.** All of us tend to want to protect powerless people from intimidation. Parents who (rightly or wrongly) see one child as "weaker" may — like Superman — adopt the socially approved role of defender of the powerless.

Think about these issues in terms of your own situation. Do you identify with any of these "hot spots"? If so, maybe it's time to re-balance your family relationships. You can accomplish this in at least two ways: by beginning to see the favored family member more objectively; by working to strengthen a relationship with a child or stepchild where the relationship is not so naturally aligned.

> *Raymond, whose boys are twelve and eight, found himself consistently getting into power struggles with his older son, Scott. He was frequently angry with Scott for his cruelty to the younger Devin. He saw Scott as a bully and Devin as an innocent victim of Scott's bullying behavior. When Dad brought the boys in for family counseling, he was invited to explore his own role in the family turmoil. The counselor gathered information about Raymond's family background, and as it turns out, he was the youngest child of three children. He got along with his older sister, but always felt picked on by his much older brother. He also felt neglected by both of his parents. As he explored his own background, Raymond began to understand his resentment toward his older son, and his tendency to sympathize with Devin. He also understood that his over-involvement in their conflicts was an effort to prove that he was an involved parent (unlike his parents) and not a neglectful one. Like many people in our society, Raymond admitted a bit of the "superhero" in himself. These insights helped him to realize that his identification with his younger son and anger toward his older son were to some degree based on events and beliefs from his own history. He was then ready to work on re-balancing his relationships with Scott and Devin.*

Since parental over-involvement is so central to the dynamics of sibling conflict, parents who wish to have a positive impact on sibling skirmishes will want to look for ways to apply the principle of "less is more." That is, to *let the kids work it out by themselves* whenever possible — to intervene only when necessary and then to take a neutral position that puts the kids in the same boat.

LETTING THE KIDS WORK IT OUT

It's important for parents to avoid playing detective. Despite our best intentions, it's usually not helpful to find out "who did what to whom," or to judge who's guilty and who should be punished and how. This has the potential for increasing the conflict between sibs and making your relationship with the "guilty one" worse.

By now, you won't be surprised to hear us suggest that the first question for parents to ask themselves is, *"Who owns the problem?"* When siblings are arguing or scuffling with one another — unless someone is in danger of serious harm — it's *their* problem. The problem belongs to the children, since they are the ones who created it, and therefore they have the responsibility for solving it. When you as the parent step in to take responsibility for the problem, you're robbing the children of a chance to learn to solve it on their own. Furthermore, you're playing right into the hands of the child(ren) who may be attempting to meet the goals of attention, power, and revenge through this behavior. The most effective response is no response at all. Walk off the stage, and you'll disrupt the sibling conflict drama by not playing your part to help the children meet their goals of misbehavior.

Most parents are shocked when they discover that, by resisting all temptation to get involved, and by giving their children the responsibility to resolve the conflict, the kids actually work out most of their disputes on their own and peace is restored. When you allow this to happen, you are encouraging and empowering your children and increasing their confidence. This also strengthens the relationship between the siblings, since they are able to work through a difficult experience together and achieve a shared success.

Don't be surprised, however, when you decide to give the kids responsibility for their disputes, that things get worse before they get better! Consider our discussion of older versus younger siblings, for example. It shouldn't be surprising that, when parents disengage from the struggle, the younger child will feel as if she's being abandoned by the parents. "What happened to my protectors? Where are the big people who are supposed to show sympathy for my plight *(attention)*, and to give me the weapon to knock the bully down to size *(power and revenge)*?"

Hang in there, Mom and Dad. She'll soon learn that she's getting nowhere with this tactic. This is a "teachable moment" for presenting an alternative way to gain your attention and support, however. Give each child some extra encouragement, as an antidote to their feelings of inferiority or abandonment. Spend some special time with each of your kids. Set aside time to be with just that child, doing something the child considers fun.

We've suggested that you stay out of kids' fights and arguments, but there may be times when you have to step in. Let's consider what situations require your involvement and the best way to intervene.

WHEN AND HOW TO STEP IN

If a dispute involves a third entity, such as a toy, or other object the kids are fighting over, or a house guest, there is a logical consequence that will apply. First, offer a choice, "Kids, if you want to play with that toy today, you'll have to play with it cooperatively." Or, "You can either play cooperatively with Tim (the visiting friend) or I will have to take him back to his house." This response places the responsibility directly on the kids, where it belongs in this situation. It avoids taking sides or playing into the other dynamics involved in sibling conflict. If the kids continue the conflict, simply take the toy or object away, or let Tim know he will have to go home. You must, of course, be prepared to follow through with the consequence.

When a situation escalates to the point that your rights are being violated, however (e.g., the noise factor prevents you from doing what you need to do, or safety or property is at risk), then you own the problem. When you own the problem, the responsibility to effectively — and respectfully — intervene is yours. You have a number of choices for responding to such a situation. You'll need to balance protecting your rights with the safety issues. Remember the dangers of parent over-involvement, and avoid playing into the children's goals of misbehavior.

If the conflict is just a nuisance, and safety is not a concern, you can interrupt the skirmish by sending an I-message: "I'm not able to concentrate on my paperwork with all this noise," and give the kids a choice to either end the fighting or to take the fight somewhere that won't be disruptive to what you're doing.

> On a family vacation in the mountains years ago, the young sons of one of the authors were fighting vigorously late one evening. The family was in a small rented trailer, it was cold outside, and the kids were wearing their pajamas. The boys were given a choice to either end the fight or take it outside. It continued. The parents kindly but firmly escorted the kids outside into the frigid weather and informed them that when they were through fighting they could knock on the door and would be allowed back in the trailer. The conflict lasted about three minutes longer, followed by a gentle knock on the door. There was not a single episode of fighting the remainder of the trip.

If safety is involved, however, and you're truly concerned about your kids' physical well-being, or about property being destroyed, an active and protective approach is necessary. The most effective approach is solely to deal with the safety/property issues. You can do this simply by offering a choice: "Kids, this can't continue. Someone or something is going to get hurt. Either end the fighting or you'll need to separate until you are willing get along."

Be prepared for one or both kids to make a deliberate effort to pull you in by appealing to your sympathies, blaming the other, or trying to get you to punish the other. This is a time to restrain yourself and merely address the fact that the fighting must stop. If you interfere by becoming investigator, judge, jury and executioner, you'll become a key factor in meeting the goals of their misbehavior. You can certainly address the concern with the complaining parties by reminding them that they can place the complaint on the family meeting agenda, and you can all discuss it together at the next family meeting. If this occurs it'll provide a wonderful opportunity to teach the kids about anger, anger management, and the value to them of the family meeting.

There are situations in which anger, jealousy, and conflict between siblings become a pattern and are beyond normal, healthy behavior. This is a time that professional counseling may be necessary. When dealing with a pattern of sibling conflict, the following guidelines are offered to help you decide when to seek outside assistance:

◆ You've addressed the issues raised above, including your "hot spots," that might contribute to the pattern;

◆ You've accounted for any over-reaction on your part;

◆ You've been disengaging where possible (i.e., letting the kids own the problem);

◆ You've intervened only to address safety, property, or your rights; and

◆ You have allowed time, at least several weeks, to see if conflicts decline as a result of taking a different approach.

If counseling appears needed, we strongly suggest that you seek a qualified counseling professional — one who's well-trained and experienced in working with kids and families. Among the professions in which you're likely to find a licensed, trained, and qualified person are psychologists, marriage and family therapists, clinical social workers, and licensed professional counselors. (See Appendix A.) Look for someone who will involve the whole family in the counseling (not just one child or the parents), and who will address everyone's role in maintaining these conflicts. It would be a mistake to have counseling only for the child who seems to be most responsible for the conflict. This will only add to this child's feelings of being blamed, targeted, and alienated from the family.

If sibling conflict gets to the point of violence, it is imperative to do all that it takes as a parent to keep everyone safe. This may mean contacting the police department if immediate intervention is necessary as well as accessing professional counseling services just as soon as possible.

> *Sean and Nancy entered family counseling because of constant fighting between Justin (eight) and Sheridan (six). The pattern was that whenever the children's fights resulted in screaming, crying, or what sounded like a physical tussle, one or both parents would come running. Not surprisingly, the older Justin was nearly always blamed. Justin's response was to protest that Sheridan initiated the conflict by entering his room uninvited, taking his stuff, calling him names, or teasing him in numerous ways. The parents' logic was that Justin should know better, since he's older, and since Justin was larger and a boy, he held an unfair advantage over his smaller sister. The parents, after giving Justin a stern lecture, usually placed him on "restriction" or took privileges away.*
>
> *This pattern repeated itself nearly every day. The counselor discussed the situation with the children, and discovered that Sheridan indeed enjoyed the drama, the sympathy and attention. She felt powerful getting Justin in trouble. Justin admitted to the counselor that he resented all of his family for participating in Sheridan's ploy. He had actually come to the point of feeling he must "defend his honor" and defeat his unjust parents by hurting his sister.*
>
> *The counselor was able to educate Nancy and Sean about what was going on, and to teach them how to take a less*

active and more neutral position in the sibling battles. The parents told the children that from now on their fights would be their responsibility. If they became too distracting or dangerous, the parents would ask them to either take the conflict to a less disruptive location, or would have both children retreat to their bedrooms until they were calm enough to come out and get along with one another. The counselor prepared them for the possibility that the fighting might worsen before getting better. This is indeed what happened, as they noticed Sheridan dramatically attempting to get her parents involved as they had been in the past. Sean and Nancy persisted, however, and after several weeks, noticed the children fighting less frequently. More often than not, the kids were able to settle their differences without any parental intervention.

Sometimes the conflicts between kids are not so obvious. What do you do when one of the kids makes it a habit to tattle on another one?

TATTLING

Tattling is nearly always another way for kids to gain attention, sympathy, or special status. The goal is usually power or revenge over the other sibling. Usually the tattler is a younger child who tells the parents about alleged misbehavior by the older child. The younger child thus attempts to compensate for feelings of inferiority by tarnishing the image of the older sibling. It can also work the other way around.

By playing into the hands of the tattler, parents feed these dynamics. In most cases of tattling, the tattler owns the problem; consequently, it's important to respond in a way that encourages the child to solve the problem. Here are three ways you can respond that are respectful without becoming over-involved.

- **Use reflective listening.** "Sounds like you are feeling concerned about your brother." This is both responsive to the child's feelings and if you stop here, doesn't play into the child's goal.

◆ **Explore alternatives with the tattler.** "How is this a problem for you? What do you think you can do about this?"

◆ **Tell the tattler to bring it up at the family meeting.** He can place the concern on the family meeting agenda. This provides a solution, but again isn't making the mistake of over-stepping your responsibility.

> *Nine-year-old Dean regularly told Mom what his younger sister, Julie, was up to. He was filled with stories of Julie's use of "bad" language, and other examples of doing things she shouldn't, or not doing what she should. Mom didn't observe these behaviors herself, but she would listen to Dean's reports with great interest, and frequently confronted Julie with what Dean had told her. This created conflict and tension in her relationship with Julie, and seemed also to add to Julie's resentment toward her brother. Mom was beginning to feel that it was not healthy for her to be involved in this way, but didn't know what else to do. A parenting class leader discussed the situation with Mom and made these three suggestions: (1) None of the concerns were owned by Mom (they did not interfere in her rights directly and the concerns Dean reported involved neither safety nor property); (2) Mom could communicate empathy to Dean about his concerns, demonstrate faith in his ability to address them directly with Julie, and invite him to place his concerns on the family meeting agenda; (3) Mom should no longer confront Julie on the strength of Dean's tattling. Mom was actually relieved to be out of the investigator and interrogator role. She noticed that at first Dean was frustrated with this response and attempted to get her involved again. Within a few days, however, he quit coming to Mom with his reports and complaints. Before long, his relationship with his sister*

improved. Mom also noticed that eventually her own relationship with Julie became stronger and more cooperative.

If the child is bringing to your attention safety issues or illegal behavior on the part of the sibling, then you own the problem and have a responsibility to address it. In this case, it would be important to thank the child for bringing the information to your attention, acknowledge that it must have been difficult to do so, and proceed to find out what the facts are.

Addressing the involved child about your concern is a sensitive matter. If you want to know what the facts are, it's important to not confront the child in an accusatory way. You could approach him privately with an I-message, inviting him to connect and problem solve with you. It could sound something like this: "Scott, I've learned something about you that has me worried. I don't know if it's true, but it involves your safety, so I want to find out exactly what's going on. Whatever it is, please know that I love you, and we will work it out together. Is this an okay time to talk it over, or can we agree to discuss it this evening?" If the problem is a serious one — involving chronic dishonesty, alcohol or illegal substances, criminal activity, actions that violate the rights or safety of others — it's time to seek professional counseling help for both your child and your family.

FIGHTS WITH FRIENDS OR WITH KIDS IN THE NEIGHBORHOOD

It can be painful for parents to experience their children's struggles with friends. It's important to remember once again, as long as the conflicts aren't violent, damaging to property or interfering with your rights, it's your child's problem. You can offer empathy through reflective listening and act as a sounding board by offering an invitation to talk. "It sounds like you're frustrated with Jim. Want to talk about it?" If your child takes you up on it, help him explore the total situation, including his role in the conflict, and to problem-solve by looking at various alternatives. Help him see that the only parts of the situation he can change are his own choices and his own actions. There are some constructive choices that are in his hands, and that you can help him to consider, including deciding to apologize, deciding to forgive, talking things over and working things out, taking a break from the friendship, or ending the friendship for now. It's also important that you be the voice of reason, to help him see that if he chooses to get even, he'll tend to escalate the conflict and add to the hurt going both ways. Ask a question such as, "What do you think would happen next if you did that?"

Derek came storming in after school, clearly distraught about something. He went immediately to his room — unusual behavior for him. His mother observed this and decided to give him some time to cool off. After awhile, she knocked on his door and he agreed to let her in. She said, "I can tell you're upset about something. Want to talk?" He was resistant at first, but Mom remained patient. Derek began to share an incident at school. It seems that Mario — someone he considered to be a friend — had accused Derek of talking behind his back and then shoved him. Derek retaliated by shoving back. A hall monitor broke up the brief scuffle.

Mom gently asked questions to better understand the situation, and Derek told her that he hadn't said anything negative to anyone about Mario. He felt "filled with anger" because he was falsely accused and shoved. He wanted to "make him pay." Mom empathized, validated Derek's feelings, and asked him to imagine what would happen if he followed through on his solution by "making Mario pay." She asked what else he could do to address this difficult and challenging situation. The conversation ended at this point, as Derek asked his Mom for some time alone.

Derek re-joined the family for dinner, said very little at the table, and asked to be excused early. Later that evening, Mom made a point of checking in with him again about the incident at school. Derek shared that he had thought about it and called Mario. He told her that he'd apologized for his part in their conflict, and assured Mario that he hadn't said anything bad about him. Mario had apologized in return, and they made plans to get together after school later in the week.

If the fight your son or daughter is having with a friend has gotten to the point of being a safety risk, this becomes your problem, and it's important to be proactive. If the conflict is occurring with a friend or neighbor, it may be time to get the parents and kids together for a meeting. By shedding light on the conflict and bringing it thoroughly out in the open, de-escalation is more likely. If you arrange such a meeting, be sure it is noted that both parties are responsible for what happened. "It takes two," and blaming either one will not help you reach a solution. Keep the focus on the future and not the past. The differences between the two kids have reached the stage of being dangerous, so a plan needs to be developed to prevent further conflict and possible harm. Avoid the temptation to take anyone's side — it will be tough not to defend your child — and seek common ground with all of the participants in arriving at a solution.

If the conflict is at school, it may be time to bring in the school authorities (principal, vice-principal, school counselor). Again, the goal is to bring the situation out into the open, and to keep the focus not on who's to blame, but on the future safety of both youngsters. Some schools have mediation programs that can help work out the differences between students when they have escalated to this degree. This may be a helpful resource.

If the conflict has escalated to violence or a serious risk of violence, you may have to contact your local police or sheriff's department. This is a logical consequence for a situation involving this degree of concern. It's important to remind yourself when doing something this serious that you're not betraying your son or daughter, but offering love and protection, and perhaps preventing a difficult situation from becoming far worse. Professional counseling is called for here, as well.

Keep in mind that it is not uncommon, in these days when dangerous weapons are all-too-readily available to young people, for interpersonal conflict to result in serious violence. Bringing it into the open and nipping it in the bud can be the best preventive measures.

In this chapter, we've addressed the challenging situations of sibling conflict, tattling, and conflicts between your kids and their friends. Conflicts between siblings and stepsiblings can be fueled by parental interference — reinforcing kids' goals of attention, power and revenge. Parents who have difficulty staying out of kids' conflicts often have "hot spots" of their own about kids fighting, perhaps resulting from their own experience as children. When parents decide to let the kids own the problem, and to get involved only when safety issues are present, they find the kids learn how to get along with others better and more quickly.

In the next chapter, we'll discuss how to teach kids anger management skills. You'll find that you can help your children learn to use the techniques you've learned in this book, and that might just prevent a few family storms before they begin.

MAJOR POINTS

◆ When your child is angry at you: don't do what the child expects; Stop, Think and Act; consider your child's goal; force yourself to think of something else; ignore the behavior; use reflective listening and problem solving; move away from the child; remove the child to a time-out area.

◆ Don't overreact to sibling conflicts. Your attention may be the reason they continue!

◆ Parental hot spots are often activated by sibling conflict: family alliances; biological alliances; birth order identification; gender identification; lack of protection in childhood.

◆ Let kids work it out by themselves whenever possible. Intervene only when necessary for safety, and then take a neutral position.

◆ Ask, who owns the problem? When siblings argue or scuffle, it's their problem. They created it, and they own the responsibility to solve it.

◆ If a dispute involves a toy or other object, or a house guest, a logical consequence will apply. Stop fighting over the object, or lose use of it. The house guest can go home.

◆ If your rights are being violated, or safety or property is at risk, you own the problem and the solution is up to you.

◆ When a child tattles, you can: use reflective listening, explore alternatives with the tattler or tell the tattler to bring it up at the family meeting. If safety or illegal behavior is involved, you own the problem and have a responsibility to address it.

14

Anger Management for Kids

Parents report that one of the toughest challenges they face is witnessing anger in their own kids. Their feelings are intensified each time the morning paper or evening TV news reports another high-profile incident, in which one or more youngsters have spun out of control and acted in shockingly violent ways in their homes, schools, and communities.

TEACHING KIDS ABOUT ANGER AND ANGER MANAGEMENT
You may doubt it at times, but parents really are the most influential people in the lives of their children, and whether you know it or not, you are teaching every moment. Kids closely observe their parents and look to them for examples of how to interact and solve problems with others. Since parents are their kids' most important teachers, and anger is such an important issue, it's essential to look for opportunities to effectively teach your children about anger and anger management. In previous chapters, we've discussed how to respond when your kids are angry with you and how to handle sibling conflicts. This chapter will show you how you can teach your kids to better understand and manage their own anger.

MODEL EFFECTIVE ANGER MANAGEMENT

Every concept and idea in this book applies to effectively modeling anger management. As mentioned previously, your children will learn far more from your behavior than from anything you tell them to do or forbid them to do. They will observe your behavior toward your spouse, friends, and other family members, as well as your behavior when you're with them. Anger, when often expressed by parents and observed by their children, becomes natural and familiar to the child and a learned way for dealing with life's disappointments, stressors, and conflicts.

Teen anger and violence expert Ken Wong[62] states: "Parents need to be role models for positive anger interactions. When they model negative interactions their kids will follow suit." Anger specialist Joni Ballinger,[6] who works with younger children and their parents, agrees: "In effectively helping children with their anger, first and foremost it is vital for parents to be aware of their own anger. Children will initially be frightened of their parent's anger but will eventually replicate it." We suggest you review and commit to the many concepts and ideas for dealing with anger that have been proposed in this book, including:

1. Strategies to help yourself internally with your own anger, as discussed in chapters 2, 3, 4 and 5:

- Making the anger decision: taking charge of your anger

- Interrupting anger on the spot

- Knowing your "storm warnings": anger triggers and hot spots

- Changing your hot thoughts and purposes to cool thoughts and positive purposes

- The five-step process: situation; inner processes; rethink; cool thoughts; new behavior

- The anger journal.

2. Strategies to effectively build family relationships and solve problems as discussed in chapters 6, 7, 8, 9, 11, 12 and 13:

◆ Encouragement skills

◆ Communication skills, including reflective listening and I messages

◆ Problem solving with exploring alternatives

◆ The family meeting

◆ Understanding and effectively responding to goals of misbehavior

◆ Choices, natural and logical consequences

◆ Handling kids anger toward you.

Let's see how a mother applied the above strategies to take charge of her anger and, as a result, to help her kids take charge of their anger in the bargain.

> *Marguerite is the single mom of Jared (eight) and Jamie (six). She has found that the stress involved in raising two children alone has been taking its toll lately, especially since she has been working additional hours in her job to catch up financially. She has noticed growing frustration with the many tasks related to her roles as mom and employee. One result: she has been short-tempered with the children. She also noticed that both Jared and Jamie have been angrier lately — with her and with each other.*
>
> *Marguerite decided to take charge of her own anger and become a different kind of role model. She started by using the "Stop, Think, and Act" technique. When she noticed herself feeling frustrated, followed soon by anger, she stopped and began breathing deeply. Then she thought about the situation for a moment. Most of the time, she quickly concluded that the issue was just not that important, and that she would be able to deal with it more effectively later. This allowed her to walk*

away. At other times, she was able to think of a response that would be more respectful and effective. When she did act, instead of showing her exasperation by yelling or threatening the kids, she began to use I-messages: "I'm feeling really frustrated about what is going on right now, and I would appreciate it if we could pause a moment and work this out together."

She also decided to keep a journal about what was going on in her life lately, and through this process came to realize that she was most vulnerable to stress right after work, when the kids were eager to see her and she was the most drained from her work day. She realized that her kids' persistent rambunctious behavior at this time was an anger trigger for her. She reflected upon what the kids were experiencing at this time and realized their "goal of misbehavior" probably involved both attention and power — in effect they were demanding she pay attention to them. She realized that she hadn't been very available to them lately, and so it was understandable that they would be craving her attention.

When she recognized this pattern, Marguerite sat down with Jared and Jamie and did some problem solving with them. She started by sharing how stressful life had been for her lately and apologizing for her frustration and anger. The kids obviously appreciated her honesty, and both apologized for being difficult themselves. They all agreed that they wanted things to go better than they had been of late. Together they looked at alternatives and decided that after mom spends a half an hour or so with them as soon as she gets home from work, she would then have a half-hour to herself, resting before facing the evening tasks. They worked out a chart of chores that included jobs Jamie and Jared will do to help make dinner preparations easier on work nights. Finally, they also agreed to make the weekends better by planning some fun activities, and spending quality time doing things that they all enjoyed.

LISTEN, REALLY LISTEN

Anger and violence expert Ken Wong, M. S. W.[62] notes that, "Kids need a sounding board when they are angry, a relationship where they can understand all that is involved in how angry they feel. This involves both really listening and educating and not judging and blaming. When parents don't listen when their children are angry, their anger escalates." According to Mr. Wong, "It is important for parents to avoid seeing their children's anger as a sign of their personal failure, but rather as a normal part of being a kid. It is essential for parents to resist the temptation to want to fix the anger in their children. Emotions cannot be fixed; they can only be heard, acknowledged, and understood."

Of course, there are exceptions to this. If the anger is directed toward you, for example, and you're feeling angry or hurt, the child may be seeking power or revenge. Listening at this time may increase the conflict. This would be a time to take some time out and use the "Stop, Think and Act" technique (as Marguerite did in the example above) to keep yourself calm. Ignoring the angry outburst can be a good alternative if your experience with your child tells you that trying to listen at that time can make things worse. Or you could acknowledge the child's anger with reflective listening and offer a time to talk later, if need be. "I can see you're very angry with me. When you calm down, if you want to, we can talk about it." You'll recall that chapter 13 presented various ways to respond when your child is angry with you.

TEACH KIDS ABOUT ANGER

Kids are curious and want to learn. They have a surprisingly large capacity to understand issues that parents may believe are beyond them. In fact, parents often underestimate what kids are capable of understanding. The following are themes consistent with the principles of this book that we have found children are able to grasp. While the earlier children are exposed to this basic "emotional and relationship education" the better, it's important to keep in mind where your children are developmentally when choosing which of the ideas to share, and how to share them. These themes can be built into your everyday life with your kids, and shared during those "teachable moments" when anger is still an issue but the angry feelings have subsided. Teachable moments are not moments when you or your kids are feeling angry! Wait until later that day, the next day, or perhaps at a family meeting to introduce, teach, or reinforce any of the following important themes:

- Anger is a natural human emotion. Everyone feels angry at times. This is normal.

- Anger, if expressed in hurtful ways, causes problems in relationships.

- Human beings are endowed with a wonderful quality called choice. Adults and kids alike are able to choose how to express anger. This can be hard, but like everything else, if we practice, we can get better at it.

- Anger can be expressed in ways that are healthy for everyone. The energy anger provides can actually help us to solve problems together.

- Anger is connected to lots of things: our situation, our beliefs and goals, and our related challenge-based feelings (e.g., tired, disappointed, stress, fear, hurt, powerless). The more aware we are of these things, the easier it is to choose healthy ways of expressing anger.

- There are four common goals that all kids at times try to meet that accounts for their misbehavior: (1) attention, (2) power, (3) revenge, and (4) displaying inadequacy (see chapter 11). When kids seek power and revenge, anger is a common emotion that helps them reach their goal. Power and revenge, while tempting, don't solve problems, but actually cause more conflicts in relationships. It's possible to solve problems with mutual respect, in ways where power and revenge aren't needed. For this to work, it's important for parents and kids alike to do their part in respecting one another, both when things are going well and when there are differences.

TEACH KIDS TO EFFECTIVELY MANAGE THEIR ANGER

There are a number of anger management skills that kids can learn and that can actually be fun for them. Consider your child's age and ability to grasp concepts when choosing how and which strategies to teach. Remember to wait until you and your child are both "emotionally receptive" before offering these ideas. If you or your kids are emotionally distressed, wait. Choose a later time when everyone is calm.

Develop a "What Bugs Me the Most" List. This is associated with the points we made about "hot spots," "anger buttons," and "anger triggers" in chapters 3 and 4. It's important for kids to realize that, like everybody else, things happen to them or people do things that will really bug them. It can be fun to write these down and actually "get into" the annoyance and frustration that your child feels when these things happen. Help your daughter or son realize that these are the areas where they are most likely to feel mad, behave angrily, and make matters worse.

Teach Your Kids About Hot Thoughts and Cool Thoughts. It's important for children to realize that whenever they are angry they are engaged in self-talk that can lead to — and increase — their anger, as we discussed in chapters 2, 3 and 4. You can help them to identify their hot thoughts, to become aware of the goals or purposes that they are seeking to meet when they're angry, and to develop cool thoughts. This will raise their awareness and help them begin to take more responsibility for themselves versus seeing themselves as victims of their own emotions and of the actions of other people.

For example, you could ask your child, "How do you feel when you tell yourself that something or someone is awful or terrible, or horrible?" "Would it feel different if you told yourself that you don't like this, but it's not really *awful*, just *frustrating?*" "When you get really angry with someone, what do you want to do?" "What would happen if you got even with the person?" "What could you do instead?"

Help Your Child to Create Cool Images. Most children are able to form images or pictures in their minds. It's very helpful for kids (and adults alike) to identify one or more "cool images" that, for them, have a calming influence. Examples might be: a teddy bear, the ocean, a best friend, or a sunset. Whenever your child is encountering something on his "what bugs me the most" list, and is beginning to feel angry, he can calm the intense feelings by picturing this image in his mind. He can also choose to take a personal time out and visualize the image, draw the image, or describe it in other ways (write a poem, make music . . .).

Educate About the Feelings Associated with Anger. The chart, "Feelings That Often Go With Anger" in chapter 2 shows six clusters of feelings. Each cluster in the chart shows faces that typify how a person looks when she experiences a feeling in that emotional cluster. For each area your child describes above on her "what bugs me the most" list, you can help the child to identify the feelings she has most often when facing the issue. Help your child learn to share and communicate these feelings that go with her anger.

Teach "On the Spot" Alternatives to Acting Out Anger. Teach your kids that instead of feeling mad and saying and doing things that hurt other people, they can choose to do any (or all) of the following:

- Use the Stop, Think, and Act method (chapter 3)
- Picture a stop sign, and tell themselves to stop acting on their anger
- Count to ten
- Take a personal time out

- Picture a "cool image," draw the image, or depict it in their own way

- Share the emotion that goes with the anger, using an I-message (e.g., "I feel frustrated when I'm interrupted while I'm trying to do my homework")

- Add the issue to the family meeting agenda if the challenge the child is facing is related to something or someone in the family. This gives the child a sense of addressing the issue, knowing it will be discussed later, and suspending the need to address it now (see the family meeting section in chapter 9).

- It's important to connect at the child's level. Anger specialist Joni Ballinger[6] has developed a couple of effective techniques to help younger children manage their anger. One is the "turtle technique." When your child is feeling acutely angry, invite the child to "pull into his safe shell," like a turtle. In his safe shell, his job is to become calm. When he is calm, he's ready to pop back out of his shell, rejoin family life and if he decides to, work to solve the problem. Ms. Ballinger also finds that it's very effective to have children imagine a person they're angry with as a favorite cartoon character (e.g., Tweety Bird, Bugs Bunny, Sponge Bob), and imagine the person looking like, talking like, and acting like this character. This technique is fun and helps young children calm down so that they can begin to solve the problem.

Use TV as a Teaching Tool. Have you noticed how frequently television shows or movies contain scenes where the characters are acting out their anger in harmful ways? In fact, anger often is glorified on film, or made to appear humorous. When you're watching television with your child or children, such scenes offer teachable moments about anger and other issues related to values, emotions, and relationships. Of course, you don't want to overdo it and ruin the entertainment value of the program, but discussing a show (after the program) with your kids can be very instructive.

This works best if you ask questions to engage your child before offering your own thoughts.

For example, you and your two children are watching a comedy, where the main character in the show, Kim, gets angry because her best friend canceled an outing at the last moment. The main character blurts out a revengeful comment to her friend on the phone, hangs up on her, tears up her friend's picture, and then throws her cell phone against the wall. See if you can get your child(ren) talking about the show. Don't make it an "exam," but you might ask questions like these to get the conversation started:

"How do you feel about how Kim handled the situation?"

"Did she make things better or worse? Why do you think so?"

"How do you suppose her friend felt being treated that way?"

"What do you think was going on with her?"

"What other thoughts do you think she had?" (e.g., hot thoughts)

"In addition to anger, what else do you think she was feeling?" (e.g., disappointed, devalued, hurt)

"In this situation, what might her goal have been?" (e.g., revenge)

"What else could Kim have done to handle the situation better?"

After your child responds to each question, share your own ideas in a friendly and respectful way. While your children may not agree with you on every point, realize that you're helping them think about the issue in a way that's relevant and fun.

Use Role Playing and Puppets. Role playing is another effective tool for teaching anger management. The kids can role play "what if" incidents where they may be invited to be angry. They can act out the situations using alternative non-angry responses. For example, "What if a friend calls you a name? How could you respond differently?" Play out the scene. Sometimes you can model behavior by playing the role of your child using a different approach to the name-calling friend.

With young children, puppets are a good teaching tool. You can set up scenes using the puppets to act out the scene. For example, one puppet gets angry with another. How can the second puppet respond? As in role playing, you can set up the scene so that your child plays the angry puppet and you play the puppet who responds, modeling an alternative approach.

Discuss Anger Management in Family Meetings. As discussed in chapter 9, family meetings are for planning and problem solving. But they can also offer teachable moments about many issues, including anger. Here's how one family used the family meeting to deal with anger issues.

> *Jason and Molly are parents of three children: Timothy is eleven; Tabitha is eight; and Alicia is five. This family had the usual amount of challenges with anger. Jason and Molly clearly cared for each other and believed it was important to teach and support their kids in every way possible. They decided to bring up the issue of anger at a family meeting and began a conversation in which each shared their ideas about what anger is all about and how it affects themselves and others. They all agreed that anger is "normal," but can be harmful when it leads to cruel or disrespectful behavior. Timothy was able to admit that he gets scared when Dad is angry and yells. Each family member agreed to write up a "what bugs me the most" list for the next meeting. (Tabitha and Molly offered to help Alicia write her list.)*
>
> *At the next family meeting, they had a lot of fun going over everybody's list and were surprised to learn about some of the issues that were shared. At the meeting a week later, Jason*

began a conversation about ways family members could better deal with themselves and others when they're angry. He and Molly shared some ideas they had picked up at a seminar (led by one of the authors). They discussed the "Stop, Think, and Act" model and several specific ideas that had been helpful. Among the strategies they talked about were counting to ten, taking a personal time out, identifying their associated feelings, such as stress, disappointment, and fear, and expressing those in I-messages.

In later discussions, each family member was invited to create a cool image he or she could picture to help calm down when angry. Each shared his/her cool image, and everyone was especially impressed with Alicia's vision of lying on her bed, napping with the family cat. Several times over the subsequent weeks, after watching a movie together, the parents asked the kids to discuss scenes involving anger and conflict. To their surprise the kids picked up on the issues involved and were able to identify other ways that the incidents could have been better handled.

Not surprisingly, the storms in this family began to be fewer and less fierce.

This chapter has helped you to learn some ways you can teach your kids about anger and how to deal with it effectively. The behavior you model is probably the most powerful teaching method you posses. In addition to modeling, your kids, depending on age and maturity level, are capable of learning many of the strategies in this book. TV and movies offer powerful tools for teaching about anger, also. The family meeting is a good forum for teaching specific anger management skills.

In the next chapter we'll address special situations in family life: angry divorces, single parents and stepfamilies. If your family storm involves one or more of these elements, you'll learn how to apply the skills you've learned to the many challenges you face.

*Helping Your Sons with Their Anger

Due to gender based cultural influences that date back thousands of years, there are special challenges you may face in helping your son(s) with their emotions, especially anger. Youth and Family Counselor David Weed, M.A., a specialist in working with boys, offers this counsel:

Due to the lessons and messages boys pick up throughout their growing years — through family, cultural, and religious traditions, through extensive media and internet exposure, and through seemingly innocent activities such as the playground, boys learn to hide their emotional experiences from others, disregard physical pain, and solve conflicts either through violence or indifference. Boys are constantly assaulted with the message that feeling and sharing emotions is weak, that they need to be persistently strong in the face of pain, that they must have an answer to every crisis or problem, and that they need to figure things out "on their own." Because of this, it is often difficult for boys to identify what they are feeling, and embarrassing for them to share those feelings with others. Boys are given messages by parents, coaches, and through the media that being sad or afraid is showing weakness — but that showing anger is strong "manly", and "acceptable." Consequently, boys become limited and inflexible in their emotional expression, and too quick to express anger in harmful ways.

According to Mr. Weed, parents can provide corrective and balancing messages and practical guidance to their sons that will help them with their emotions, including anger. He gives parents the following suggestions:

◆ Provide viewpoints that promote the possibility that boys and men can be flexible, expressive, respectful, and sensitive.

◆ Give your son(s) undivided attention and love every day.

◆ Remember that boys often express themselves best while doing an activity. Have a talk while driving in the car, or taking a walk or when engaging in a physical activity.

◆ Don't expect your son(s) to share when you're ready. Give boys time and space to process their emotions on their own before sharing them. Invite, don't force.

◆ Look for the emotions connected to your son's anger and aggression, including emotions such as frustration, embarrassment, inadequacy, and fear. Provide a clear message that these emotions are a signs of being human and not a sign of being weak.

◆ Never shame your boys when they express themselves emotionally. Emotions are to be heard and never judged or fixed.

◆ Model, Model, Model effective and respectful management and expression of emotions and anger.

*David Weed, M.A., LMHC, Youth and Family Counselor, Youth Eastside Services, Bellevue, WA, personal correspondence 4/29/04

*Helping Your Daughters with Their Anger

Due to gender based cultural influences that date back thousands of years, there are special challenges you may face in helping your daughter(s) with their emotions, especially anger. Youth and Family Counselor Heidi Arizala, M.S.W., a specialist in working with girls, puts it this way:

Messages and models provided to girls in our culture have the effect of disallowing girls to express very normal feelings without them feeling bad or like they are letting everyone down. From a very early age, girls are trained in our culture to be nurturing and relationship oriented along with the expectation that they be "good girls" — behave appropriately, not be too loud, be dainty, pretty, and sweet. Consequently, girls learn ways to avoid direct conflicts so as to remain feminine and not jeopardize their relationships. It is not surprising then that girls have a difficult time dealing with emotions such as anger. Our daughters tend to struggle whenever they are feeling angry. They often deny their anger and then when things get tough and they directly communicate their anger, they often do so in a very passive way or in an awkward and overly aggressive way. Girls easily feel guilty about feeling angry and expressing their anger. These gender-based limits inhibit girls from being as strong, capable, and flexible as they are capable of being . . . and it is exactly these qualities that girls will need in order to be resilient enough to succeed in today's challenging world.

According to Ms. Arizala, parents can provide corrective and balancing messages and practical guidance to their daughters to help them with their emotions, including anger. She offers the following suggestions for parents:

◆ It is important that as a parent you learn to express your own feelings in a very sincere and direct manner. This will give your daughter(s) the modeling and the tools to do the same in her own life.

◆ Where anger is concerned, it is particularly important for you to explain to your daughter(s) that it is okay (even good) to be angry. Offer her your assistance to help her develop new ways she can manage and communicate her anger.

◆ Help your daughter(s) see that resolving conflict is okay and will strengthen relationships with friends rather than threaten these valued relationships.

◆ Understand that her feelings and experiences are very significant to her. Respect her feelings even if you don't understand them.

◆ You may also want to use situations on TV, in movies, or magazine articles to begin a conversation with your daughter(s) about expressing and working through anger and conflict.

◆ Listen, Listen, Listen.

*Heidi Arizala, M.S.W., LICSW, Youth and Family Counselor, Youth Eastside Services, Bellevue, Washington, personal correspondence, 4/29/04

MAJOR POINTS

◆ Parents are the most influential people in the lives of their children, and are constantly teaching them how to interact and solve problems with others.

◆ Anger modeled by parents and observed by their children becomes natural and familiar, the method of choice for dealing with life's disappointments, stressors, and conflicts.

◆ Angry kids need a sounding board, a relationship with someone who really listens and educates, and does not judge or blame, so they can understand and handle their feelings.

◆ Teach kids about anger. E.g., Anger is a natural human emotion; anger expressed in hurtful ways causes problems in relationships; adults and kids alike are able to choose how to express anger; anger can be expressed in ways that are healthy for everyone.

◆ Use a variety of ways to teach kids to effectively manage anger: "What bugs me the most" lists; hot thoughts and cool thoughts; cool images; "on the spot" alternatives to acting out anger; TV as a teaching tool; role-playing and puppets; family meetings.

15

Angry Divorces, Single Parents, Stepfamilies

The divorce rate is 50%.

There are more single parents than ever before.

Stepfamilies often must respond to complex problems and intense feelings.

Each situation is unique and is accompanied by its own challenges, including the challenge of anger.

While we believe that every concept and strategy offered in this book applies to virtually every family situation, certain changes, challenges and circumstances that occur in families require special attention.

Children today experience a wide variety of living situations. Among them:

◆ living with both parents in one household,

◆ living in a primary household with visitation with the "non-custodial" parent,

◆ shared custody, where children split time evenly between households,

- living with a single parent and having little or no contact with a second parent,

- living with non-biological parents, including adoptive or foster parents or other family members,

- living with a biological parent and an adult partner,

- living in blended or stepfamilies.

Each situation is unique and is accompanied by its own challenges, including the challenge of anger.

Divorce rates continue to be high — at or near fifty percent — impacting parents and children alike. Divorce itself often leads to family turmoil and anger. There are more single parents than ever before, raising children along with the mountain of responsibilities that all adults have in making a life for themselves in a not-always-supportive world. Parents with children from previous relationships are finding each other and forming new families. These blended families or stepfamilies are responding to multiple challenges and intense feelings.

Entire books have been written on these special issues and circumstances, as each one is significant and complex. This chapter isn't intended to be the last word for understanding these important topics, but will serve as an introduction and a connection of these special situations and circumstances to the concepts already presented in this book.

The following topics will be addressed:

- Divorce: The Ultimate Adjustment

- The Challenge of Single Parenting

- Stepfamilies: Yours, Mine, and Ours

DIVORCE: THE ULTIMATE ADJUSTMENT

Not surprisingly, families going through or living with divorce find anger a common challenge. Divorce is known to be equal to the most stressful experiences anyone can go through and recent research suggests that divorce is even more stressful for families than the death of a parent. In our experience counseling families, divorce is a challenge requiring the ultimate adjustment.

Divorce affects everyone in the family, and is a situation ripe for "hot thoughts," "hot spots," and the challenged-based feelings we have discussed that are associated with anger: sadness, worthlessness, disappointment, stress, fear, hurt, guilt, and powerlessness. Divorce is a time when problems associated with anger can be especially prominent. In this section, we'll touch on anger within and between divorcing parents, as well as anger that kids are likely to experience when living with divorce.

DIVORCE AND ANGER WITHIN PARENTS AND BETWEEN PARENTS

When you're living with divorce, anger and the feelings associated with anger are compounded by a wide range of divorce-related issues. Among the special concerns that may impact anger in divorced families are: legal aspects of the divorce; custody and visitation; finances; emotional adjustment to, and recovery from, the divorce; child support; alimony or spousal support; relationships with both extended families; and more. Intense anger is a common experience for anyone involved in a divorce, and can surface long after the original separation and legal divorce.

In most divorced family situations, there is some contact — from occasional to regular — between the divorced ex-partners. Whether the relationship is non-existent, strained yet unavoidable, or generally friendly and therefore tolerable, all of the ideas and skills offered in this book apply to the anger that will often surface. A principle we've constantly been reminded of during the course of our careers is that children benefit tremendously when their divorced parents find a way to work out their relationship in a respectful and cooperative way. (We're clearly aware that there are circumstances — such as spousal or child abuse, or drug and alcohol addiction — where a severance of all contact with the former partner is the best, safest, and most effective option.)

If you have gone through (or are going through) a divorce, you'll find the following material will help you effectively address your anger and related personal and relationship challenges. Here's help for recovering from your divorce, and creating a more harmonious family environment for your children.

RECOVERING FROM DIVORCE

Taking time to recover from your divorce, getting a support network, journaling, examining your belief system, keeping your conflicts in check and addressing them in respectful ways, moving on, examining your choices for handling your ex-spouse's anger, and considering professional help — all are things you can do to recover from your divorce.

Realize that It Takes Time to Recover from Divorce. Divorce is a complicated loss — not unlike the experience of losing a spouse through death. At the same time, it's even more complicated, since the person you've lost remains in your life, creating continual practical and emotional challenges. This is not a time to expect yourself to "get over it." Famed divorce therapist Bruce Fisher's research suggests that it often takes two years or more of work on your "divorce process" to rebuild your life and be ready to go on to successful singleness or new relationships. While you want to begin the process of moving forward in your life, this is also a time to be kind and patient with yourself, to realize that the process is gradual and developmental. To some degree, the divorce will forevermore be a part of your life story, a story that will include challenge, pain, and growth.

Create and Strengthen Your Support Network. This is a time when it's vitally important to have a solid and reliable support system. But it can also be a time when you may not feel like reaching out, when — as a result of diminished financial resources and/or emotional energy — it's easier to remain isolated.

Overcoming this tendency and connecting with people you trust and can share with serves several purposes. First, it makes your ex-spouse less important. You are much more likely to stew over every little thing your ex-spouse does, or doesn't do, if he/she remains the primary person in your life, concretely or symbolically. Similarly your kids become too important if you deny yourself your own support system. While it's important for kids to be a major priority, when they become the primary relationship by which you measure your own worth, you can easily overburden the relationship and overreact to everything that they do or don't do. This is a time to maintain connection to friends, family, support groups, or to consider counseling. Having a person or people in your life with whom you can share anything and everything you're thinking or feeling related to this difficult transition is of key importance to managing your life and your anger.

Do keep in mind, however, that shortly after a divorce is not the time to establish a new serious romantic relationship. You have lots of work to do putting your own life back together first. Friendships and "transitional relationships" are helpful, but intense emotional commitments should wait until you're really ready — probably a year or more.

Use Your Journal. It can be helpful when going through the divorce recovery process to work through your anger by journaling. It may also be helpful to actually write letters to your former spouse, but *without mailing them.* Through this activity, you're creating a direct channel for expression of your thoughts and feelings. Yet you are doing so without creating further conflict.

Examine Your Belief System. The section in chapter 10 on beliefs and hot spots clearly applies to a person working through life following divorce. The more aware you become of your beliefs and how they impact your relationships, including your relationship with your ex-spouse, the less you will be under your ex's "spell" and the more choices you will have.

Keep Conflicts in Check. Divorce is a time when every little thing your ex-spouse does, or doesn't do, can be irritating. If you react to every irritation, your ex will often match or exceed your level of intensity, leading to constant animosity and conflict. Having a high degree of turmoil in the relationship with your ex can only compound the difficulty your children may have adjusting to the divorce. This is a time to address the significant issues, and choose to not allow the smaller issues to grow out of proportion.

Address Conflicts in a Respectful Way. Use "I-messages." Say, "I feel frustrated when you bring the kids home late, because it makes it hard to plan the rest of the day," and not, "You stupid idiot; you're always late!" (Even if some of your friends agree with you that your ex is an idiot, this won't help!)

Work on Moving Toward the Future — Yours and Your Children's. While it's important to accept that working through divorce is a process and takes time, it's also possible to get stuck. The period of sadness and resentment following a divorce can become a kind of familiar comfort and the role of victim or martyr a way of finding significance. This is a formula for prolonged misery. You have a choice whether to dwell on your misery and remain stuck, or liberate yourself by beginning to move forward. We suggest that you take some time examining not just your ex-spouse's role in the divorce, but your own as well. It's a rare couple in which both partners played an exactly equal role in the break up of the marriage, but it's also rare to find a couple in which one partner was solely responsible. By examining your role, your own personal growth will be enhanced and you'll avoid repeating patterns that don't work if you can see that divorce is also a learning opportunity .

Consider the Many Choices You Have for Handling Your Ex-Spouse's Anger. You have the choice to match your ex's anger with your own. You could choose to create a family storm and the misery that comes with it for all concerned, including your children. You also have the choice to use the various methods of interrupting your anger on the spot (chapter 3). You can choose to take a personal time out: "I'm not going to talk with you until you're willing to discuss this more calmly." Or you may elect to use the basic skills discussed in chapter 7, including reflective listening: "It sounds like you're feeling angry about what happened at the soccer game." You could decide to engage in problem solving (chapter 8): "Would you like to schedule some time so that we can discuss this and prevent it from happening in the future?"

You'll find that the more you handle your relationship with your ex-spouse with mutual respect, the more likely it is that he/she will return the favor. In addition, you'll develop more self-respect along the way, create a healthier family environment, and be a positive model for your kids.

Consider Professional Help. Remember that divorce is one of the most stressful life events that people go through. Support groups for people going through divorce can be very helpful. Learning that you're not alone, that others share the same experiences, is of tremendous value. If you're finding that nothing seems to help, individual counseling may be in order. Divorce touches on such a wide variety of personal and practical issues, and can be such an intense emotional experience, that divorce-related stress can lead to serious mental health and/or substance abuse problems. Only a counseling professional is trained to help with these more serious issues. You'll find suggestions for finding a qualified professional in Appendix A.

Stephanie and Eric were both very bitter about their divorce. They each blamed the other and both felt like victims, especially as the complicated legal and financial issues began taking their toll. Eric, who moved out of the family home, at first attempted to act as though this was but another life challenge to get over, and coped by immersing himself in his work. Stephanie focused her life on her children, and had very little contact with friends or family.

Alone and without social support, their stress and discouragement mounted. Each focused anger and resentment on the other, and saw every contact as an opportunity to get even. They were both truly stuck in their misery. Eric's boss, who was very concerned about Eric's obvious deteriorating behavior, referred him to the company's employee assistance office where, for the first time, he was able to talk openly about the divorce and its effect on him and his family. The employee assistance counselor helped Eric understand that divorce was more than a common challenge, and that he needed much more support in his life to help him through it. As a result of the counseling, Eric realized the damage he and Stephanie were doing to their family by continuing to interact with such animosity.

During a brief visit with Stephanie, Eric was able to convince her that she also needed help in her life in order for all of them to get through this difficult period. Stephanie found a divorce support group and realized in the first meeting that she wasn't alone — that what she was going through was a normal reaction to the ultimate challenge of divorce. She learned in the group the importance of having more support in her life and began reaching out to friends and family. She also learned to make better choices when interacting with Eric. While life isn't perfect for this family, they now have the support in their lives necessary to help them move forward toward a brighter future.

DIVORCE RECOVERY FOR KIDS

Much of the pain and anger that comes from divorce is related to the suffering you witness in your kids. Typically, divorced parents blame each other for this pain. Responding effectively to the needs of your kids will help reduce anger all around.

Realize that your experience of the divorce is very different from your kids' experience. First of all, the entire situation was out of their control. They didn't choose their parents, nor did they choose the divorce. Second, while most divorcing or divorced parents have lost respect for their ex-spouses, kids want and need to look up to *both* of their parents. Also, realize that kids are resilient. While divorce has some lasting impact on most people, your kids will recover their strength, confidence, and optimism with some help from you. Here are some ways you can facilitate their recovery.

Avoid Criticizing, Blaming, or Condemning Your Ex-Spouse in Front of Your Children. Peter Kaperick, MSW,[32] youth and family counselor and divorce expert, states that the important thing for a parent to keep in mind is that, whenever possible, children are much better off with both parents as supportive people in their lives. Maintaining this as the goal can help parents living with divorce to make the right choices when faced with a variety of challenges.

MAKE YOUR CHILDREN'S SAFETY YOUR NUMBER ONE PRIORITY

If you sincerely believe that the safety of your children is at risk as a result of your ex-spouse's behavior (or potential behavior), you must take legal action. Situations where children are being neglected or abused, or where a parent or other key adult figure is abusing alcohol or drugs are times to involve the child protective services department in your community and to consider legal support. If you are struggling with your own mental health to the point where you're not able to adequately care for your children, seek the support of family members, professionals, and the relevant health or public safety agencies in the community.

Children know they are "part mom" and "part dad" — their identity is tied to both parents. Criticism directed at the other parent can harm the child's self-esteem and sense of optimism about her own future. In addition, it's hard for kids to care about both parents when the parents are continuously mad at each other. The kids may feel compelled to develop loyalties, to take sides.

According to Mr. Kaperick, "Younger children will tend to believe you and reject the other parent, while older kids will resist your effort to destroy their relationship with the other parent and resent you for attempting to do so."[32] Both parents know a lot of things about the other spouse that the kids are better off not knowing — this is the parents' "stuff," and should not be shared with the kids. This is where the importance of a support system comes in. The parents need their own "sounding boards" to discuss their issues with their ex-spouse, so they aren't imposing their stuff onto their kids.

Mr. Kaperick suggests that if parents refrain from influencing their children's view of the other parent, most kids will realistically sort out their impressions over time. He states, "Typically there are periods of both idealizing and rejecting of the other parent. This is natural and it's important to allow time for the children to work through any disappointment they may feel and to gradually develop a realistic image. If you haven't overdone the criticism, the children will feel free to turn to you for support in working through their disappointment. If this is unavoidable, and you have to explain to the children why you are taking certain action as a result of their other parent's irresponsibility or dysfunctional behavior, do so with the greatest care. Choose descriptions of the other parent that are sensitive to the image they hold of that parent. They will more quickly sort out their own opinions and feelings toward their other parent, and do so more realistically if you refrain from imposing your own."[32]

Don't Use Your Children as Messengers Between You and Your Former Spouse. The less the children feel a part of the battle between their parents, the better. Children naturally resent this burden and will often feel angry toward both parents for being placed in this situation.

Reassure Your Children that They Are Loved, that the Divorce Is Not Their Fault, and that They Have Value. Many children assume that they're to blame for their parents' divorce. Therefore, it's vital to explain to your children that the divorce was only the result of problems between their parents and had nothing to do with them, their behavior, or anything they could have done differently. Be alert also to your children's feelings of inadequacy that can come from living with divorce. Kids can easily conclude that they're being rejected or devalued since they're not living with both parents. It's important to correct this and any other negative story they may be telling themselves. It's also possible that professional counseling assistance may be in order, to help them correct any mistaken beliefs that arise from the divorce.

Support Your Children in Maintaining a Relationship With Both Parents. Spending quality time with both parents is an important variable in children's positive adjustment to divorce. Unless safety issues are involved, do everything within your power to accommodate your children in spending time with their other parent. Work out directly with your ex-spouse, not with the kids, any difficulties you have related to the visit. Realize that it's common for kids to go through a period of erratic behavior just following a visit with their other parent. It's difficult to adjust to two different households that consist of totally different people and entirely different ways of doing things. While it's important to remain attentive, don't automatically assume that this is the result of an unhealthy environment.

Focus Your Attention on Where You Have Influence. It's too much to expect that you can directly influence the children's relationship with your ex-spouse, or the environment they're in when they are with him or her. To attempt to control these areas of their lives is certain to increase your frustration and your ex-spouse's resentment. Rather, place your energy on your own relationship with your kids and the environment you are creating. While it's an adjustment living in different environments and relating to different people, this experience can also be a real asset to them as they develop. In their future, flexibility and resilience will certainly be required.

Resist the Temptation to Make It Up to Them. It's common for parents to feel some guilt during the post-divorce period. It's also common for parents to feel sorry for their children for the loss, pain, or suffering they have gone through in the divorce. Along with the desire not to add to their difficulty, parents can feel obligated to somehow make it up to them. This is a mistake. "Making up for what kids have gone through" can easily lead to the pampering or permissive style of parenting described in chapter 6. Such over-indulgence undermines a child's development of internal strength, resilience, and caring for others. This approach doesn't provide the firmness the parent needs in order to be an effective leader in the family.

You can risk allowing your children to feel unhappy. It's normal and natural for all of us — including our children — to feel unhappy at times, especially when divorce is such a major factor in our lives. Attempting to "make it up" to the children is also draining for parents at a time when they are going through a lot of stress themselves. The whole family benefits much more if each family member shares some of the load by assuming age-appropriate responsibility for herself or himself, and responsibility to the family as a whole.

Understand Your Children's Desire to Live With Both Parents. Kids naturally want to live with both of their parents. Younger kids will often hold on to the fantasy that their parents will get back together, even long after a legal divorce. Some parents find it difficult to be honest with their kids when this is just not a possibility. It'll hurt younger kids to hear that no matter what, the parents aren't getting back together. Knowing this, however, will help them to move along the path of adjusting to their circumstance instead of staying stuck by keeping their fantasy alive. Parents who are reluctant to speak the truth to their children on this matter may actually delay their adjustment. At the same time it's important to handle this conversation with sensitivity and to employ your best communication skills, including reflective listening and empathizing with their normal feelings of disappointment and anger.

Following a divorce, some kids will also declare that they want to live with the other parent. Do your best to stay cool. After you calm down, it's important to take this seriously and find out what's behind it. This is very common, and it may come up more than once. It's important not to take it personally, or to see this idea as rejection, defeat, or disloyalty to you. The child may simply be angry with you and saying this to get even. Or it may be that the child really misses the other parent. This is another time for your best expression of empathy. If you can accept and validate the child's feelings, you'll keep communication open and she'll be more likely to understand the realistic choices.

Don't Let the Kids Act as Your Caretaker. Resist the temptation to let the kids take care of you. Build a support system among your friends, adult family members, divorce recovery group contacts, and helping professionals. Let your kids be kids.

Pay Your Child Support If You Are the Non-Custodial Parent. The loss of income facing many children after divorce puts them at a financial disadvantage that can have a negative effect on the rest of their lives. Your reliable support will go a long way to help them through the divorce. Their respect for you will rise at a time when they need to believe in you. Child support is the best investment you can make in your children's future — and your own.

Maintain Stability and Routine. Divorce is a time of major changes for children, and it's important to give them solid ground wherever you can to buffer the instability they experience from their parents' breakup. Stability in their residence, school life, family and peer relationships, activities, and daily routines are all helpful. It isn't always possible to maintain these factors, as divorce sometimes includes the need to relocate. In these instances, you'll want to make every effort to help the children to establish support systems and routines in the new home and community right away.

Get Professional Help If Needed. Many kids receive and benefit from talking to a professional counselor when living through or adjusting to a divorce in the family. This can be a relief to parents as well, not to have to carry the entire burden during this challenging time. Be sure to seek the services of a counselor who has special expertise with children in divorced families.

> *Yolanda and Andre had been divorced for eighteen months. Rachel and Joshua, their twelve- and eight-year-olds, were still very distraught about the divorce and all of the changes in their lives. Yolanda continued to be preoccupied with how Andre parented the kids when they went to visit him every week. She grilled the kids about their experience with their Dad, and was openly critical of Andre, both with the children and in phone conversations with him. She noticed and was concerned that Rachel had been distant and critical of her recently, and Joshua had become increasingly unhappy and agitated. As Yolanda witnessed her children's pain, she attempted to make it up to them by giving them whatever they wanted, and by not expecting too much of them around the house. This began taking a toll on Yolanda, who began to resent both the work she had to do and the children's lack of consideration for her or the needs of the household.*
>
> *One day, following an angry argument between Yolanda and Rachel, everyone broke down in tears and started talking about all they had been through since the divorce. Wisely, Yolanda recognized this as a sign that outside help was needed. She arranged for them all to participate in family counseling. Through the counseling she learned about how much Joshua blamed himself for the divorce, and how much*

Rachel resented her for so often belittling her father. She learned that it was much more important to the children's development to be supported in their relationship with both parents. Yolanda also learned that her guilt was feeding her over-indulgence of the kids and how much healthier it would be to give them responsibility and expect them to do their part at home. She discovered that she needed more of a life outside the family, and began to socialize more with friends. Overall, Yolanda came to realize that her focus should switch to where she has influence — away from her kids' relationship with their father, to the relationships in her own home.

THE CHALLENGE OF SINGLE PARENTING

Today we see all sorts of single-parent families, headed by mothers, fathers, grandparents, or other family members. While single parents and single-parent families are scorned by some, the facts show that single parents are capable of raising healthy and happy kids. At the same time, being a single parent carries with it special challenges. In this section we'll address some of the distortions that exist about single-parent families, describe the special challenges that single parents and their families face, and suggest ways for single parents to respond to the variety of challenges that come with being the only parent in the household.

Life in a single-parent household, common as it is these days, can be quite stressful for the adult and the children. Single parents may feel overwhelmed by the responsibility of juggling their many tasks, including caring for the children, maintaining a job, keeping up with the bills, and household chores. Single-parent family life may also be complicated by issues not faced by the "traditional" two-parent family. Among these issues are visitation and custody problems, a single paycheck and the financial hardship that may come from a limited income, continuing conflict between the parents, less opportunity for parents and children to spend time together, disruption of extended family relationships, and complications caused by the single parent's dating relationships. It's no surprise that single parents and their families may also be challenged by problems associated with anger!

Distortions abound concerning single parents and single-parent families. These distortions result in single parents and their families being negatively stereotyped and, despite their numbers, thought of as an inferior minority. As you're well aware, the issue of "the family" and "family values" has become a political hot potato in recent national elections. The heated rhetoric has led some politicians to suggest that the only healthy family is one where children are being raised by a mother and a father. The term "broken homes" is still used to describe single-parent families. What a discouraging and distorted message! Here are the facts:

◆ There are 11.9 million single parents in the US.[56]

◆ Twenty-eight percent (twenty million) of all children in the US under eighteen live with one parent.[57]

◆ Eighty-four percent of children who live with one parent live with their mother.[57]

◆ The percentage of children who live with two parents has been declining among all racial and ethnic groups.[56]

◆ The number of single mothers (nearly ten million) has remained constant, while the number of single fathers grew twenty-five percent in three years to over two million in 1998. Men comprise one-sixth of the nation's single parents.[57]

◆ Of children living with one parent: thirty-eight percent lived with a divorced parent; thirty-five percent with a never-married parent; nineteen percent with a separated parent; four percent with a widowed parent; four percent with a parent whose spouse lived elsewhere because of business or some other reason.[11]

◆ In the twenty-five year period 1973-1998, the number of single-parent families more than doubled. According to U.S. Census

Bureau estimates, fifty-nine percent of United States children will live in a single-parent home at least once during their minor years. That is a majority.[56]

♦ Many well-researched studies document positive outcomes in single-parent families. "Single parenting develops the parent's independence and ability to handle a variety of situations."[50]

♦ "Children benefit from increased levels of responsibility."[3]

♦ "Parental — and child — health outcomes were related to larger networks of social support and good communication within the single-parent family."[28]

♦ A 1994 study by University of Michigan researchers of over six-thousand adults had surprisingly positive conclusions for children of divorce. Statistically, it turned out that adult children raised in a single-parent family due to a divorce were just as likely to be happily married as someone who grew up in a two-parent home.[12]

EFFECTIVE SINGLE PARENTING

It's difficult and challenging to be a parent today, and it's even more difficult to raise children alone. Therefore, it's important for single parents to keep in mind that all parents feel overwhelmed at times, and many parents lack the parenting skills necessary to do an effective job. Whether the single-parent household is headed by a mother, a father, an aunt, or a grandparent, raising children alone is an enormous task. *Effective and respectful parenting has less to do with the number of parents in the home and more to do with the quality of parenting.* One quality parent will have a more positive impact raising kids than a dozen unskilled parents.

Please note that we are aware that many single-parent families are impacted by a prior divorce and the ongoing issues of divorce, discussed in the previous section of this chapter. If you are a single parent whose life is complicated by factors related to divorce, we invite you to view this material on divorce and single parenting as connected.

You will notice that many of the suggestions we make are related to the importance of single parents empowering themselves and their kids. According to youth and family counselor and single parenting expert Lynne Haudenschield, M. Ed.,[29] "The greatest challenge for a single-parent family is to develop a sense of personal power, dignity, and confidence in a society that disenfranchises and disempowers them. To me this is the key in helping single parents and their children." Lynne should know; she was a single parent herself. She tells a touching and all-too-common story of a time in college when she and her two children lived in "Griffin Woods," the community's government subsidized housing for low-income families:[29]

> *It was at this time that my children and I forever joined with the struggles of the less fortunate. The housing development consisted of a mixture of students and low-income families, mostly single-parent families. Some of the people were rough, uneducated, abusive, and addicted to alcohol or drugs. Living in that housing development was not as physically difficult as the emotional implications of the stigma associated with living there and being a single-parent family. In my human development class the professor would often talk about the unfortunate children living in poverty and with only one parent. I thought to myself, "That's us." Despite the fact that we were somewhat different, that feeling of inferiority penetrated our defenses. One day while working as a guidance counselor intern, a veteran guidance counselor said to me, "Can you believe that anyone that cared about their children would live in Griffin Woods?" I lied, "No, it's hard to believe." Again this was all about me and my family, and I actually agreed with him!*

Single parenting can easily give rise to all of the challenged-based feelings that are associated with anger (described in our

"Feelings That Often Go with Anger" chart on page 25). The suggestions that follow are intended to bring greater dignity, balance, and support to the life of the single parent. We hope this section may serve as an antidote to the myths of doom and gloom that society tends to dump on single parents.

Review Your Attitude Toward Your Family. Adults and children do better when single parenthood is perceived as a viable option and not as a pathological situation. It's important to realize that this is not a "broken home." This is a whole family, a complete family, a family that has value just as it is. Focus on the benefits of single parenting, such as having less conflict and tension in the home, and the opportunity for kids to accept more responsibility. Many single parents treasure their autonomy and independence and feel hopeful about the future.

Accept Yourself as the Leader of the Family. Leadership is essential for any effective group, organization, or family. As the primary leader in the family, you'll have more impact on your children than you would have if you were sharing the responsibility with another parent. This entire book is filled with ideas and effective skills for you to employ that will help you as your family's leader. In order to sharpen your knowledge and skills, it can be helpful to take parenting classes as well. (See Appendix C.)

Realize that You Are *One* Parent. Many single parents we have counseled think they must be more than they are, that they somehow must be both mother and father — expecting more of themselves than any single parent could possibly accomplish. This impossible expectation is an unnecessary burden. You are one parent, one parent is all you can be, and one parent can do a fine job raising kids. Furthermore, unrealistic expectations can prevent you from engaging in the kind of self-care you need, and from obtaining the kind of support you need, for your family to become cooperative, strong and healthy.

Stop Feeling Sorry for Your Family. Again, the negative stereotypes surrounding single-parent families and the guilt that often follows, can make it too easy for single parents to feel sorry for their kids and believe that they must make it up to them. This is a setup for misery. Feeling sorry and making it up invariably lead to ineffective parenting: insufficient firmness; over-indulgence; the tendency for your kids to feel sorry for themselves; and parental exhaustion that comes from over-compensating. It also prevents your kids from developing their "psychological muscles" — the self-sufficiency to respond to life's challenges. The families we have worked with where feeling sorry is a dynamic are filled with anger.

Realize that Your Kids Are Fortunate. Another way to think about your situation is that your kids are fortunate. If you take the time to compare the quality of life your kids enjoy compared to many families around the world, you will discover how fortunate they actually are. They live in a family, and they have a parent who cares and is doing the best job possible to contribute to their life and to their future. You have nothing to make up for, only a job to do — the job of helping your kids prepare for life as responsible, caring, and confident persons.

Take Care of Yourself. Single parents have less opportunity to have a break from parental responsibility. Thus it's essential that single parents take time for doing things that are restorative. Many single parents report that they already feel guilty about having too little time to spend with their kids. Carving out time for themselves increases this guilt. This position deserves reconsideration.

The truth is that by not taking the time to do the things that give you energy and vitality you're undermining and compromising the time that you're able to spend with the kids. Quality time counts. There can be little quality in the time you spend with your kids if you are depleted, discouraged, frustrated, exhausted, and angry. An analogy from a different area of life applies here.

Consider the instructions we're all given at the beginning of every flight by our flight attendant regarding the use of oxygen masks. The clear and essential instruction parents are given is: make sure your own oxygen mask is securely fastened and you are getting the oxygen you need before helping your children with their masks. For you to be helpful to your kids, you must first make sure that you have the "oxygen" — the inner strength and support you need — to be helpful.

By taking time for self-care — whether this means working out, joining a book club, going out with friends every week, or simply taking a breather from the daily grind — you're engaging in the ultimate act of caring for your family. Make self-care a habit — schedule the kind of activity you look forward to on a regular basis. Pay special attention to diet, exercise, stress management, and getting a good night's sleep. A stressed-out parent results in stressed-out kids. See self-care for what it is — a gift you can give to yourself and your family.

Establish a Support Network. The single parent frequently feels overwhelmed by the responsibility, tasks, and emotional overload associated with raising children alone. Two kinds of support are especially needed for single parents.

First, get *practical support* — ask for help when necessary from family, friends, and support systems in the community. Arrange car pools when possible, and ask other parents for help when you need it. There are times when you feel you need a break. Ask other single parents to trade babysitting, invite grandma or grandpa in for a while, or hire a reliable person to help with childcare or other assistance.

Second, you need *true friends* in your life, the kind of people you have trust in and who share in your triumphs and tribulations. You need people who will engage in a mutually supportive relationship, people who help you feel that you are important to them as well. Having true friends will help you not to over-rely upon your children for emotional support. This will allow your children to grow and develop without feeling overly concerned or responsible for your welfare. It's not uncommon for children of single parents to feel so responsible for their single parent that they find it difficult to develop their own separate lives and to prepare for leaving home. This is especially the case with single parents who have little or no life outside of their relationship with their kids. Developing and making friends is a contribution you can make to the whole family. Many communities have available support groups for single parents, often sponsored by churches, women's centers, adult education or recreation programs, mental health clinics, and other agencies. This is an excellent resource to consider; no one understands what a single parent is going through better than another single parent.

Help Your Kids Feel Needed. One true benefit of being raised in a single-parent family is the opportunity it provides for children to participate more in the day-to-day responsibilities of managing a household. Kids today are too often exempt from the work required to manage a household. This has a detrimental effect on development of our children. Kids who don't learn the importance of work, of shared responsibility, while growing up in their families will struggle later in life. Learning to handle basic household responsibilities — cooking, cleaning, pet care, simple maintenance chores — is a key part of growing up to become an independent adult. Moreover, being counted on to do one's share of the household tasks adds to the feeling of being important — of being needed. There is, after all, just one parent in this household. You need the help.

Share the Responsibility Through Family Meetings. While we recommend family meetings for all families, there's no other family situation where family meetings are more warranted. The burdensome feeling that comes from being a single parent is greatly reduced when the single parent experiences cooperation and shared responsibility in the family. The purpose of holding a weekly family meeting is to provide a regular opportunity for parents and kids to come together and work out differences, solve problems, develop plans, and encourage each other. (See chapter 9.)

Help Kids Rise to the Challenge. Kids raised in a single-parent home face many challenges. They miss out on having role models from both genders present in their lives at home. Outside of the home, circumstances can arise that are disappointing and hurtful. For example, an activity specific to dads and sons, or moms and daughters may exclude your child's participation. Some kids live with the pain of having little or no contact with a non-custodial parent, one that they may nonetheless care deeply about. Some kids live in circumstances where there are just not the financial resources to participate with their friends in all of the activities they are interested in. These challenges, while difficult to witness, will help your children to learn valuable lessons: life is challenging, filled with problems, and demands courage. Having problems in childhood is important. We have counseled many adults who have found life overwhelming in their twenties and thirties. When we began evaluating the factors involved, we discovered that these people had life just too easy as kids. They were spared hardship and strife, and their parents protected them from life's discomforts. Consequently, as adults, their expectations of life are too high, and their ability to tolerate and solve problems too low. Out of the challenges your kids will face will come their internal strength. This will be the basis of their resilience.

Elena is a single parent whose children, Miguel and Isabel, are fifteen and eleven. Their story is quite typical of the challenges facing single-parent families. One of the authors was privileged to provide counseling to Elena and her family on and off over several years. Their progression as a family was very impressive. Things didn't start out that way. The family was in considerable turmoil when counseling began, and there were several serious problems to face. The family became a single-parent family when Paulo, Elena's husband and the children's father, abruptly left the family to pursue another romantic relationship. The kids were thirteen and nine then. A divorce followed, changing everything for this family. Paulo moved out of state, started a new family, and had very little contact with Miguel and Isabel. Elena had never held a job before and the requirement that she go to work changed everything about their daily schedule. Elena was used to being at home and always there for her kids. She felt sorry for them and felt she needed to be everything for her family. Over the next year, Elena worked so hard at her job and at home that she didn't have the energy for anything else. One day following a bad case of the flu, she received a call from Miguel's school and discovered that he was failing several of his classes. This was Elena's crisis point, and she made the most of it. She made an appointment with the school counselor and discovered that Miguel also exhibited behavior problems at school. The school counselor referred the family for counseling.

Everyone soon recognized that Elena was indeed out of energy and needed some help. Isabel was able to share that she had wanted to help all along, but didn't feel her mother wanted her to. Elena was able to identify her own struggle in attempting to be both parents and make up to the kids for all that they had suffered. It was decided that the chores would now be divided up and that they could also now afford a housekeeper at least once a month to help them keep up on the household tasks. Miguel was able to discuss in counseling how sad and mad he was with the loss of his father, and how he felt that there must be something wrong with him for his father to no longer want him in his life. Everyone understood and accepted his feelings and his belief about his own lack of value was successfully challenged.

A touching moment in the counseling came when the kids together made a pitch for Mom having more a life of her own. The kids believed they were old enough and responsible enough to be alone in the evening once or twice a week. After working through her resistance to being at home even less,

Elena agreed to devote one night almost every week to get together with friends. At one point when addressing the school problems, Miguel offered to participate in an after-school tutoring club to help him get caught up with his academic work. The family also started holding regular family meetings, which opened up a place for them to regularly communicate, problem solve together, and share responsibility.

There remain lots of challenges ahead — and perhaps an occasional storm — for Elena and Isabel and Miguel. There was no magical transformation for this single-parent family, only solid progress after they had reached a point of crisis.

Yours, Mine, And Ours: Making Stepfamilies Work

Stepfamilies contain the "whole ball of wax" — kids, parents, a couple, extended families, and all of the issues of divorce. They experience grief and loss, confusing relationships, unrealistic expectations, loyalty issues, changing living conditions, and yes . . . anger.

While we won't address all of the issues involved in stepfamily living, here are some of the concerns that are common and central to how well stepfamilies are able to adjust to all of this complexity and transition.

Realize that Bringing Two Separate Families Together Is No Simple Matter. Making a stepfamily is a process that takes time and patience. Parents who believe that the family should quickly become a loving and cooperative unit are prone to frustration and anger. Parents who understand the challenging nature of this undertaking and accept that an ongoing adjustment period will be necessary, and who demonstrate patience and persistence, will fare much better in this process of creating a new family.

Take Time for Joy and Excitement, and Time for Grieving and Mourning. Stepfamilies are in two different places at the same time. There's natural excitement about everything that's new.

Parents are excited about their new relationship and a new chance for a successful marriage. Everyone is excited about everything that's new in their lives. At the same time, stepfamilies in a sense are born of loss — including a divorce (or two), separation from a parent (or two), and loss of familiar roles, people, and places. Sadness and anger are common. So it's important as a parent to celebrate the new, as well as allowing ample time to grieve what's been left behind.

Realize that Unrealistic Expectations Are a Setup for Misery. Unrealistic expectations are very common in stepfamilies, especially by the parents. Parents may expect that their new partners will be everything the divorced partners were not. There may be little room for common human imperfection. Be aware of these and reconsider these expectations more realistically.

In addition, a stepparents may expect their spouse's biological children to love and accept them as a mom or a dad. Realize that in most cases children already have two parents. A stepparent determined to take the place of a child's own mother or father is inviting resentment and rejection. While stepparents clearly have a role of leadership in the family, it's very important to realize that this new relationship between stepparent and stepchild must be built — slowly, carefully, and maybe painstakingly. Respect and love can't be demanded; it must be developed over time. We have found that a stepparent who sees himself or herself as an adult developing a friendship with the child, and working toward becoming a trusted person in the life of the child, will usually be much more successful.

Conversely, it's also unrealistic for stepparents to expect that they'll love their stepchildren in the same way they love their own children. This expectation is a setup for guilt feelings. Accept that you will have different feelings for each family member, and that your feelings toward your own children will be different from those you have toward your stepchildren. As your relationship with your stepchildren grows and develops, so also will your feelings toward them.

Beware of Loyalty and Rivalry Issues. Naturally, parents and kids who are biologically related have a closer bond, a longer history, and a greater familiarity with one another. When two families are brought together, these bonds continue. Parents tend to be loyal to their own children and vice versa. Whenever disagreements or conflicts arise, the stepfamily can split along the lines of closer, more familiar bonds. Stepfamilies that are not prepared for these loyalty and rivalry issues can become polarized. To offset this tendency, accept that loyalty and rivalry issues exist and, at the same time, the family needs to work toward achieving greater balance. Resist the tendency to see your own children as always good or right and your stepchildren as bad or wrong. Stay out of the conflicts between the children whenever possible. Let them work it out, just as they must with friends and schoolmates. As you work on your part in the relationship with your children and stepchildren, and apply the principles of mutual respect presented in this book, loyalty and rivalry issues will diminish over time.

Resolve the Discipline Dilemma. Discipline can be a tricky matter in stepfamilies. Kids resent it when a stepparent attempts to take the position of their mom or dad, and issues of loyalty and rivalry are common., For these reasons, we suggest that during the beginning stages of the formation of a stepfamily, new stepparents leave much of the disciplining to the biological parent. There are exceptions, such as when safety or property are at stake, or when the stepparent is the only parent at home, or when a child's misbehavior is directed toward the stepparent. Over time, as relationships form, as trust develops, and as the parents become more compatible with each other in their parenting styles, discipline from either parent will be more natural and accepted by all the children.

Hold Stepfamily Meetings. As there is so much to work out in stepfamilies, including relationships, rules, roles, chores, conflicts, and plans, stepfamilies can benefit tremendously by building in family meetings right from the beginning. Meetings give everyone a role in shaping the new family, increasing the sense of belongingness and significance for all family members. (See chapter 9.)

Seek Support and Guidance. Since stepfamilies frequently experience stress, conflict, and turmoil, they can benefit tremendously from the support and guidance professional counseling can provide. When seeking the services of a counselor for your stepfamily, look for someone who has training and experience not only in family counseling, but also with stepfamilies and their unique challenges.

> *The Weed family was a union of two pre-existing families. Don had joint custody of his son Aidan, nine. Lisa had sole custody of Jeremy, thirteen, and Kristina, ten. After a "honeymoon period," where everyone was more or less enthusiastic about their new life, the problems came fast and furiously.*
>
> *Don's parenting style was coercive, and he expected that all of the children would demonstrate obedience to his authority. Jeremy especially resented Don's dictatorial ways, and an intense power struggle ensued. Lisa, who had always had a close and affectionate relationship with her two children, expected to have the same with Aidan, believing he would recognize her as his new mother. Her feelings were hurt when she quickly noticed Aidan resisting her overtures of affection, and in spite of her stated preference for being called "Mom," he referred to her as "Lisa." Lisa's daughter Kristina began quickly to feel insignificant. As a youngest child she wasn't prepared for all of the attention she would be losing from her Mom, who now had an additional youngster to attend to, in addition to a new husband. Kristina began to misbehave more than ever before just to get her Mom to notice her.*
>
> *As conflicts in this new family grew, and as every routine the parents attempted to initiate was disputed by one child or another, their interactions were frequently colored by anger,*

sarcasm, and defiance. At this point loyalty issues began to emerge. During family conflicts, Don began siding with Aidan, and Lisa began siding with her two children. Soon Don and Lisa began feeling like enemies. The parents could readily see that their blended family was not blending smoothly. In fact, the family appeared headed for serious trouble.

Don and Lisa began to educate themselves about stepfamilies by attending a series of community classes on the subject. Following the series, the whole family began counseling. As the counselor worked with them on the main points we've addressed in this section, these caring stepparents began to recognize that bringing their families together and forming a new family was going to take time and effort.

Counseling helped the family members to deal with the grief and loss they experienced as a result of losing their first family. The parents were able to adjust their expectations to more realistic ones. Don decided to back off from disciplining Lisa's kids and, when he needed to respond to their challenging behavior, began to do so with the new, more respectful methods he learned in the class and in counseling. Lisa was able to talk with Aidan about honoring his relationship with his biological Mom, while allowing his relationship with Lisa to grow naturally. Lisa learned how neglected Kristina had been feeling, and how her "misbehavior" was intended to get attention from her mom. The family agreed to carve out special time each week to provide reliable opportunities to connect with each other. The family also began to have family meetings. These didn't go smoothly at first — all of the conflicts seemed to show up during the early meetings. Don and Lisa reminded themselves that forming a new family is a process that will take time. It took a major effort, but they surprised themselves with the amount of conflict they were able to tolerate. Their patience paid off as the family meetings became more and more cooperative and productive.

The challenges involved in divorce, single parenting, and stepparenting often invite anger. In this chapter, we've discussed how anger can be reduced in each of these situations through becoming aware of the issues involved in each and by applying the skills you've learned in this book.

In the next chapter, we'll discuss the most serious anger issue — abuse. Child abuse and domestic violence are more prevalent than many people think. In chapter 16 (and in Appendix B), we will show you how to get help should you or someone you know be in a family violence situation.

MAJOR POINTS

- Children benefit tremendously when their divorced parents find a way to work out their relationship respectfully and cooperatively.

- Important steps to recover from a divorce: take time; create a support network; journal; examine your belief system; keep your conflicts in check; move on; consider how you will handle your ex-spouse's anger; consider professional help.

- If you sincerely believe that your children's safety is at risk as a result of your ex-spouse's behavior, legal action must be taken.

- If you are struggling with your own mental health and cannot adequately care for your children, seek the support of family members, professionals, and the relevant agencies in the community.

- Avoid criticizing, blaming, or condemning your ex-spouse in front of your children; don't use your children as messengers between you and your former spouse; reassure your children that they are loved, that the divorce is not their fault, and that they have value; support your children's relationship with both parents; focus your attention on your own relationship with the kids, don't try to control you ex's relationship with them; resist the temptation to make it up to them; understand your children's desire to live with both parents; don't let the kids act as your caretaker; pay your child support if it's your responsibility; maintain stability and routine; get professional help if needed.

- Recognize that single parents are capable of raising healthy and happy kids.

- Don't try to be both mother and father. You are one parent, one parent is all you can be, and one parent can do a fine job raising kids.

- Take care of yourself. Take time for doing the kinds of things that are restorative. Establish a support network.

- Help your kids to feel needed. Being counted on to do one's share of the household tasks adds to the feeling of being important and needed. Plus, you can use their help!

- Use family meetings to and work out differences, solve problems, develop plans, and encourage each other.

- Stepfamilies face many challenges and feelings that invite anger: grief and loss; confusing relationships; unrealistic expectations; loyalty issues; changing living conditions.

continued

- Making a stepfamily is a process that takes time and patience. Celebrate the new, and allow ample time to grieve what's been left behind.

- Don't expect a new partner to be everything the divorced partner was not. Allow room for human imperfection.

- Parents often expect their spouse's biological children to love and accept them as a mom or a dad. A new relationship between stepparent and stepchild must be built over time.

- Accept that your feelings toward your own children will be different from those you have toward your stepchildren. As your relationship with your stepchildren grows and develops, so also will your feelings toward them.

- Resist the tendency to see your own children as always good or right and your stepchildren as bad or wrong (or vice-versa). Stay out of the conflicts between the children whenever possible. Let them work it out.

- There is much to work out in stepfamilies, including relationships, rules, roles, chores, conflicts, and plans. Build in family meetings right from the beginning.

16

When Anger Turns
to Violence

Most people believe that family violence could never happen in their own lives or in the life of someone they care for. Unfortunately, however, it does happen, all around us, and to families we know; perhaps even our own. Our purpose for including this chapter on family violence is to raise awareness of an issue that is very real, and too often minimized or denied.

As we begin our look at this difficult topic, now is a good time to reflect back on what you've already learned about calming the family storm with effective anger management:

◆ The anatomy of anger,

◆ The democratic revolution and family relationships based on mutual respect,

◆ Techniques to interrupt your anger on the spot,

◆ Five steps to less anger in your life,

◆ The power of encouragement, communication and problem-solving skills,

◆ The family meeting,

◆ The twelve principles for effective couple and marital relationships,

◆ Understanding and disengaging from children's goals of misbehavior,

◆ Effective approaches to discipline,

◆ Helping your kids manage their anger.

In our many years working with families we have found that, when parents dedicate themselves to the concepts and principles covered in this book, all family relationships improve over time, mutual respect and cooperation begin to replace anger and conflict, and the potential for violence is reduced.

Nevertheless, violence happens — unfortunately all too often.

If anger persists or turns into violence in your family, in spite of your best efforts to more effectively manage your family storm, it's time to put the book down and go for help. This chapter will give you some concepts and resources that can begin to provide that help, but a single chapter in a book on family anger cannot be a thorough treatment of violence in the family, nor can it stop violence that is already happening.

Research repeatedly shows that family violence doesn't end naturally; rather it has a definable cycle and escalates over time. The only way family violence ends is through outside support and intervention, or — tragically — through the death of a family member.

If you or someone you know is experiencing family violence, either in an intimate relationship with a spouse or partner, or between parents and children, it's vital that you take action and seek assistance — immediately. In Appendix B we have listed resources to help you do that. Please take advantage of these resources if violence touches your life.

Let us begin by clarifying how we use the terms "domestic violence" and "child abuse" in this chapter:

- *Domestic violence* refers to the violence that occurs between domestic partners — married or unmarried couples.

- *Child abuse* refers to the abuse that is perpetrated by adults and parents onto children.

DOMESTIC VIOLENCE

Marla and Victor had experienced a great deal of stress in their four-year marriage. Parents of two young children, they both had full-time jobs. They had been attracted to each other immediately when they met at a mutual friend's party, and they quickly became very close — inseparable, it seemed. Many friends considered them the ideal couple. Early in their relationship, Marla had noticed a tendency for Victor to be controlling in subtle ways, and jealous of the other relationships in her life, including her friends and family. He got angry when she spent time with other people. While Marla was concerned about this behavior, she also felt flattered by how important she was to him. She convinced herself that, once they were married, he would feel more secure and have less reason to be so protective.

After they married, however, and especially after the children came, their family stress increased. Victor became more and more critical and condemning of Marla as a mother, wife, and person. His anger occasionally erupted, and he often threatened to hit her. As time went on, Marla saw less and less of her family and friends. She began to feel trapped, and started to believe that she wasn't worthwhile enough to be treated better. Victor's anger increasingly turned violent. After he shoved or hit Marla, however, he became very affectionate and apologetic, and promised it would never happen again. But it did happen again, and again; each time followed by a period of relative calm. She feared for the children and herself, but didn't know what to do to stop Victor's attacks.

Marla became increasingly depressed and eventually confided in her best friend Sophie. They hadn't seen each other for nearly a year, and Sophie was alarmed by the changes she noticed in Marla, her depression, her low self-esteem, and her many excuses for Victor's conduct. Sophie pleaded with Marla to seek safety for herself and the children, but Marla remained confident that Victor would change.

After an incident in which Marla was hit and seriously injured — the hospital staff filed a police report — she secretly began to see a domestic violence counselor. As counseling helped her to regain some of her self-confidence and to under-stand the dynamics and pattern of domestic violence, Marla and the children moved in with her mother and father. Meanwhile, as a result of the police report, Victor had been required to enter treatment for his anger and violent behavior.

Whether they stay apart or are able to get back together, there is now hope for this couple and for their lives to be restored. Most important is the opportunity for their children to live in a healthy, violence-free environment.

As this example illustrates, and as we've discussed throughout this book, anger can turn to violence. When this occurs in families, a heavy toll is taken on both individual and family mental health, and can often impact family members for generations. Domestic violence is so serious and overwhelming to our sensibilities that a standard response is to minimize or deny its existence. It's hard to believe that it could be happening to someone we care for, or even in our own life. The following sample of statistics on domestic violence shed light on the reality of this grave matter, too often involving issues of life and death:

◆ Twenty-five percent of the women in the U.S. (twelve million) will be abused by their current or former partners at some point during their lifetime. Three to four million women are physically abused each year.[31]

◆ In the United States, *every nine seconds* a woman is physically abused by her husband.[18]

- Research suggests that wife beating results in more injuries requiring medical treatment than rape, auto accidents, and muggings combined.[52]

- Four women each day, and more than a thousand women each year, are killed by their partners.[31]

- Each year, over three million children witness one parent abusing another.[49]

- Children of battered women are fifteen times more likely to be battered than children whose mothers are not abused.[61]

- Boys who have witnessed abuse of their mothers are ten times more likely to batter their female partners as adults.[61]

COMMON MYTHS OF DOMESTIC VIOLENCE[1]

There are several myths about domestic violence. Below is a list of those myths and the corresponding truths.

Myth: Domestic violence is rare.
Truth: As the statistics above indicate, domestic violence is more common that most people realize.

Myth: Domestic violence is confined to people of color, or to those living in poverty.
Truth: Reports from police records, victim services, and academic studies show domestic violence exists equally in every socioeconomic group, regardless of race or culture.

Myth: Alcohol and drug abuse are the real causes of domestic violence.
Truth: Because many batterers also abuse alcohol and other drugs, it's easy to conclude that these substances may cause domestic violence. While alcohol or drug use may increase the intensity of the violence, research shows that batterers may or may not have substance abuse problems, and when batterers are treated for substance abuse this doesn't guarantee an end to battering behavior. There are many factors involved in battering behavior

including childhood experiences and the belief systems formed from these experiences, the level of self-centeredness (ego-esteem) versus empathy for others, and the ability to manage stress and anger.

Myth: Battered women provoke the abuse. They must like it or they would leave.

Truth: Victim provocation is no more common in domestic violence than in any other crime. Battered women often make repeated attempts to leave violent relationships, but are prevented from doing so by increased violence and control tactics on the part of the abuser. Other factors which inhibit a victim's ability to leave include economic dependence, few viable options for housing and support, unhelpful responses from the criminal justice system or other agencies, social isolation, cultural or religious constraints, a commitment to the abuser and the relationship, and fear of further violence including threats of being killed. It's been estimated that the danger to a victim increases by seventy percent when she attempts to leave (but does not go), as the abuser escalates his use of violence when he begins to lose control.

Myth: Domestic violence is usually a one-time, isolated occurrence.

Truth: Battering is a pattern of coercion and control that one person exerts over another. Battering is not just one physical attack. It includes the repeated use of a number of tactics, including various forms of intimidation such as threats, economic deprivation, isolation, and psychological and sexual abuse. Physical violence is just one of these tactics. Batterers use many forms of abuse to maintain power and control over their spouses and partners. Research repeatedly shows that domestic violence exhibits a cycle and pattern. It doesn't stop on its own. With specialized treatment, however, domestic violence can be stopped.

THE DYNAMICS OF DOMESTIC VIOLENCE

According to domestic violence expert Belinda Lafferty, M.A., LMHC,[33] "When anger turns to violence between couples and marital partners it is almost always about power and control. Anger is a tool used by the abuser to maximize the ability to dominate."

In most cases, the cycle of domestic violence is predictable. The following model of domestic violence was first developed by Colorado psychologist Lenore Walker.[58] In the late 1970s, Dr. Walker interviewed fifteen hundred battered women and discovered that each of them described a similar pattern of spousal abuse. She identified this pattern as the "Cycle of Violence." The first stage of the cycle, the "tension" stage, begins with positive or close relations that develop into tension, stimulated by anything from a bad day at work to a major life crisis. The second stage of the cycle, called the "explosion" stage, is when the battering incident occurs, which may or may not include physical contact; it may be verbal abuse. This occurs so that the abuser can gain power and control. The third and final stage of this circular cycle is the "honeymoon" stage, when the batterer tries to make up with the partner. He may feel guilt, but will often minimize the event by claiming that it was the fault of some external source — stress at work, for example, or frustration with the children, or concern about money problems. Very commonly, the partner — the victim — is blamed for the assault. "If you hadn't provoked me, I wouldn't have hit you!" Both partners deny or minimize the severity of the abuse, and the cycle continues. The couple is convinced that each abusive episode is isolated, and that the incidents are unrelated to each other. Without intervention, the violence becomes more serious, and eventually the third stage of apology and denial is abandoned.

Dr. Walker[58] also explains how three dynamics in the mind of the abuse victim — love, hope, and fear — make it hard to end violent relationships, and therefore perpetuate the abuse, keeping the cycle of violence in motion. The three elements are:

- Love for your partner, recognizing that the relationship has its good points, that it's not all bad.

- Hope that things will change, that the abuse will end. After all, the relationship didn't begin like this.

- Fear that the threats to hurt or kill you or your family will become reality.

Is It Always Men Abusing Women?

No, men can be the victims of a violent partner. This occurs in approximately five percent of domestic violence cases.[17] Usually, when this happens, it's like the pattern of men abusing women that we've described, and the cycle will continue similarly until outside help is accessed. There are important factors which are specific to male victims of abuse that keep them from seeking help. Since domestic violence is often described as a problem that places women at risk, men are more likely to see their situation as abnormal and without credibility. In our culture, men tend to believe that as the "stronger" gender, they should be able to handle the problems in their marriage or family, and are reluctant to let anyone else know about the violence. To admit that he is being abused by his wife or female partner is an embarrassing threat to a man's "masculinity," and his competence as a man. So it remains an embarrassing secret. Nonetheless, this is a severe matter, with serious implications for the whole family. Like any other situation involving family violence, getting outside help is essential.

Domestic Violence — Getting Help

We can't emphasize enough the importance of getting help the first instant you become aware of any violence in the relationship. Your own inner barometer in response to the following simple question is your best indicator of whether you need to reach out for help: "Do you feel safe in the relationship?" If the answer is "No," or "I'm not sure," it's time to look for help from people who are trained and dedicated to assisting families affected by violence. If doing this for yourself doesn't seem to be a sufficient reason to get help, do it for your children — for their safety and their future. Research shows that ninety percent of children are aware when there is violence in their home. Research also shows that children in homes where domestic violence is occurring are at greater risk for child abuse, developmental problems, anger management problems, and stress-related physical ailments, as well as having a much greater likelihood of being in violent relationships as adults.[17]

Domestic violence expert Belinda Lafferty, M. A., LMHC[33] suggests, "All children who live in homes where domestic abuse is occurring are affected by the experience. The best thing parents can do is to get the help and support that they need for themselves in addressing the violence, with the goal of working toward creating a safe, violence free environment for their children."

Appendix B lists several resources for getting help with domestic violence. If you're experiencing domestic violence, check the Appendix B now!

CHILD ABUSE

Kristina, mother of seven-year-old Kevin and five-year-old Bethany, had noticed her stress level rising for years. Life always seemed to her to be complicated and unmanageable. She had no idea that raising two children would be at least three times more difficult than raising one. In addition, she'd been working longer hours at her job since her husband, Jay, suffered an accident at work that required him to take several months off to rehabilitate. She was attempting to manage her office at work, the household, and the kids, along with supporting her husband through his difficult period. It was hard for her to ask anyone for help. Raised by a stay-at-home mom, and as a first-born daughter with significant responsibilities for her younger siblings, Kristina's belief was that she should be able to handle anything and everything.

She wasn't handling things well, however. She began noticing how frustrated she'd become with the children: barking orders at them, yelling at them to quit doing this and start doing that, and, actually shaking them and slapping them when they were misbehaving.

One afternoon, when she was especially frustrated, Kristina found herself shaking with anger while disciplining the children. She broke down in tears, and the incident became the turning point. She found the Child Abuse Hotline number (listed in Appendix B), and was very relieved to talk with someone who understood what she was going through. The hotline counselor applauded her strength in realizing there was a problem and reaching out for help. During the call, she became aware that what she was feeling was a normal reaction to what she was going through. She admitted that this was the time for her and her family to receive some extra support. She realized how close she was to abusing her kids.

Kristina followed through on the referral information provided through the hotline and arranged for herself and her family to receive help from a reputable family counseling agency in her community. This continued to be a stressful period for her family, but with the assistance of her counselor the family was able to better address its many issues and she was able to learn alternative ways of coping and responding to stressful family situations.

As with domestic violence in adult couples, anger leading to violence between parents and their children occurs all too often. Child abuse is a horror that exists far beyond our level of tolerance, perhaps even more than the violence that takes place between adults. It's for just that reason that it's important to be educated on the topic, to know of its existence, know that it can be happening right next door and, given enough stress, could possibly occur in your own home.

What Is Child Abuse? How Common Is It?

In this chapter, we're focusing attention on emotional abuse and physical abuse, two of the four categories of child abuse; the others are neglect and sexual abuse. All four are extremely serious, and most states or communities have laws that require teachers, physicians, counselors, and other professionals who work with children and families to report evidence of abuse. Throughout the nation, there are systems and resources in place to protect and aid children who are victims of any of the four types of abuse.

The American Medical Association offers these definitions for child abuse:

♦ *Emotional abuse* is "when a child is regularly threatened, yelled at, humiliated, ignored, blamed or otherwise emotionally mistreated. For example, making fun of a child, calling a child names, and always finding fault are forms of emotional abuse."[4]

♦ *Physical abuse* is "when a child is hit, slapped, beaten, burned or otherwise physically harmed."[4]

It's very important to realize that all forms of abuse, including physical abuse effect a child's emotional development. While a physical injury will most often heal, the memory of abuse remains for a lifetime.

In order to get a glimpse of the extent of the problem, the following is a sample of recent child abuse statistics:

♦ Child abuse is reported — on average — *every ten seconds*.[25]

♦ Based on approximately three million child abuse reports per year, an estimated 903,000 children were victims of abuse and neglect in 2001.[25]

♦ Nine in ten Americans polled regard child abuse as a serious problem, yet only one in three reported abuse when confronted with an actual situation. [45]

♦ The actual incidence of abuse and neglect is estimated to be three times greater than the number reported to authorities.[55]

- ◆ Nineteen percent of child abuse reports involve physical abuse of a child and seven percent exclusively emotional abuse (versus neglect or sexual abuse[10]).

- ◆ In 2001, an estimated thirteen hundred children died in the United States of abuse, an average of more than three children per day.[10]

- ◆ The long-term impact of physical abuse is severe. Common effects are poor school performance, poor peer relationships, use of anger and violence to solve problems, injuries and health problems, depression and other mental health disorders, and a greater likelihood of becoming an abusive parent in adulthood.[25]

GETTING HELP IF CHILD ABUSE TOUCHES YOUR LIFE

If child abuse is happening in your family, or in the family of anyone you know, it's vital that you take steps to make sure that the problem is addressed and support is provided. Nearly every community has laws to protect children from abuse, a child protective agency with a number to call to report abuse, a process to investigate reports of child abuse, and supportive services to help families affected by abuse. The Child Abuse Hotline number listed in Appendix B is a wonderful resource for information about child abuse laws, systems, and services. The Hotline also offers immediate telephone counseling to help you work through and make a plan to address child abuse issues in your own family, or another family you care about.

There are a number of common myths about the reporting of child abuse. Here are the myths and the facts:

Myth: Child abuse cannot be reported anonymously.
Fact: In most states, you don't need to provide your name when making a report.

Myth: The person reported for abuse is entitled to know who made the report.

Fact: They are not. Most child abuse laws protect the confidentiality of the person making the report.

Myth: Most people believe that according to law, abused children must be immediately removed from their homes.
Fact: Removing children from their homes is the least likely outcome. Most children are able to remain at home, while the family stabilizes and services are provided.

CHILD ABUSE WON'T GO AWAY BY ITSELF

Much like the issue of domestic violence described earlier in this chapter, when child abuse begins to occur in families, it becomes a repeating pattern for the parents involved, and a continual source of despair, alienation, pain, and danger for all family members.

The life of a family will be mildly to significantly disrupted when child abuse reports are made. Investigations will occur, decisions will be made for the short- and long-term safety of the child, services will be provided to treat the effects, and steps will be taken to prevent future incidences of abuse. It's critically important to admit, however, that *the problem won't go away by itself.* When the choice is between a family's life being disrupted and the ongoing and often escalating cycle of violence and abuse against a child, the best interests of the child must come first.

Realize that when children are abused, the impact is for a lifetime — and often several lifetimes — as the legacy and the impact of child abuse often affects succeeding generations. If you're in the position of deciding whether or not to face this issue head on and get outside help, we urge you to always *err on the side of safety.* Most parents never intend to seriously harm their children. However, they do when overreacting to their children with intense anger. As you now know, this happens in far too many families. For the sake of the safety and the future of your family, or another family that you care for, make the right choice.

In this chapter, we've discussed the serious and sometimes deadly problems that occur when family anger turns into domestic violence between adult partners or child abuse between parents and children. We've suggested that you "err on the side of safety" if you or anyone you know is experiencing violence in their family. The Appendix provides you with vital resources to help you get started. You just may save life and a future.

The final chapter will offer ideas about what you can do after the family storm. Since anger is a natural human emotion, and under the best of circumstances you will occasionally hurt and be hurt by anger, it's important to know what you can do to repair the damage that's been done. We also want to help you to think "beyond anger," and to help you recognize that there is a connection between the progress you can make in your own family and the future of humankind on this planet we all share together.

Major Points

◆ Anger can turn to violence. When this occurs, a heavy toll is taken on individual and family mental health, which may impact family members for generations.

◆ Family violence doesn't end naturally; it has a definable cycle that escalates over time, and ends only through outside support and intervention — or a death.

◆ Domestic violence and child abuse are so serious and overwhelming to our sensibilities that a typical response is to minimize or deny their existence.

◆ Domestic violence is more common than most people realize. It is usually not a one-time, isolated occurrence or a single physical attack, but is a pattern of coercion and control.

- About five percent of victims of domestic violence are men.

- If violence is an issue, ask yourself: "Do I feel safe in the relationship?" If the answer is "No" or "I'm not sure," it's time to look for professional help.

- As with domestic violence between adult couples, anger leading to violence between parents and their children — child abuse — occurs all too often.

- All forms of abuse, including physical abuse, affect a child's emotional development. A physical injury will most often heal, but the memory of abuse remains for a lifetime. Emotional abuse can involve frequent threats, yelling, humiliation, ignoring, and blaming.

- Nearly every community has laws to protect children from abuse, a child protective agency, an anonymous number to report abuse, a process to investigate reports of abuse, and supportive services to help families, Find the resources in your town.

- Child abuse is a lifetime issue, affecting future generations as well. If you're wondering whether to get outside help, err on the side of safety.

17

After the Family Storm — and Beyond

Anger, as we have stated many times and in many ways throughout *Calming the Family Storm*, is a natural human emotion. We all experience anger and will for the rest of our lives. You will, from time to time, hurt others with your anger, and you'll be hurt by others. Family storms are inevitable. We sincerely hope that, as a result of what you have learned from this book, you will be able to manage your own anger, respond respectfully to anger in others, and teach your children to manage their anger effectively, so that rage, aggression, and resentment are strangers to your family. May your family storms be mild and infrequent!

This final chapter offers some inspirational ideas that will help you after the storm — after anger has caused harm. Our focus here is on the power of apology and forgiveness. Both are powerful tools for mutual respect and healing. We also want to help you to be optimistic about the future of humankind, to help raise your sights, and to imagine a day when destructive anger — "storms" that cause real damage — are no longer part of life in our families or life on our planet.

AFTER THE FAMILY STORM: THE POWER OF APOLOGY

An apology sincerely given is one of the most powerful tools available to bring peace, stop arguments, and restore broken bonds in any family or any relationship. An apology can bring solace and comfort to the offended, relief to the offender, and healing to the relationship. A genuine, effective apology is an act of honesty, humility, and generosity. It's a sign of courage, and not, as many people fear, a sign of weakness.

A genuine apology is, in fact, so vital that our experience reveals that there are some situations where nothing short of an apology will repair the relationship. Why, then, is it so difficult for some — most? — people to apologize when they know they have done harm to others; when they know they have played a role in creating the family storm?

Part of the problem is a cultural one. Apologies seem to have gone out of style in recent years. Admitting mistakes is hardly ever modeled in our modern culture. In fact, what seems to be modeled more and more by political leaders, television celebrities, and the media in general is the importance of being above all wrongdoing, of never admitting fault, of always being right. This rigid, inflexible, and self-serving position is exactly what prevents us from resolving the harm we cause in our relationships.

In addition to the modeling that influences us, psychological issues get in our way as well. Pride, fear of shame, and belief that apologizing is a sign of inferiority, of weakness, also presents barriers. The irony is that by maintaining our rigid and self-righteous position, people will tend to look down on us. On the other hand, when we allow ourselves to be genuine, humane, and humble, and apologize to those we've hurt, people tend to look up to us with admiration.

Apology expert and licensed therapist Beverly Engel[26] has conducted years of research on the benefits of apology. She summarizes her research by stating the following: "Apologies sincerely given can prevent divorces, family estrangements, lawsuits, and even atrocities like school shootings. Giving and receiving apologies for mistakes, oversights or offenses — which many people avoid — are crucial to our mental and physical health and well-being. Failing to admit error and express regret adds insult to injury, and is one of the most blatant ways of showing disrespect."

She offers three "R's," or steps for effective apologies:

◆ *Regret* — sincerely recognize that you have hurt someone you care for and that what you have done matters to you;

◆ *Responsibility* — recognize that it's your job to re-connect to the person you have hurt; and

◆ *Remedy* — offer, with sincerity and sensitivity, a genuine apology to the person you have hurt and propose a way to avoid future harm and make up for the hurt that you've caused.

Apologies can never be forced. This is why it's important never to insist that your kids apologize to siblings, friends, or other people in their lives. Of course, it's relevant to share with your kids why you believe an apology is called for, and how to go about it. It is, however, up to them. An insincere apology actually adds further distrust to any relationship. Your own model, apologizing when you err with your kids, is the best way to teach them.

When offering an apology, timing is important. It's helpful to wait until the emotional intensity — the "storm" — has passed, and you are able to sit down with the other person (or persons) in relative calm.

It's vital that before you apologize, you reflect upon the lessons that you've learned and are firmly prepared to avoid hurting the other person in the same way in the future. It is important, during the apology, to share what you've learned.

Finally, an apology loses its impact if you apologize with the expectation of being forgiven. That's up to the other person. An apology is like a treasured gift, to be given without the expectation of receiving anything in return.

AFTER THE FAMILY STORM: THE POWER OF FORGIVENESS

When we are subjected to the harmful anger imposed by others, by those we care for, when we experience a family storm, we have choices about how we will live with the harm that has been done to us. Too often people hold on to their anger, take it wherever they go, weigh themselves down with it, and allow it to affect their everyday lives, including all of their relationships.

We refer to the experience of being consumed by anger as resentment. We pay a heavy toll for *resentment*. It affects the overall quality of life and health. Resentment, when directed toward a member of the family you share everyday life with, drives a permanent wedge between you and your loved one, infecting the atmosphere of the whole family.

What is the remedy? How can we lighten our burden?

One way you can overcome resentment is by discovering the power of forgiveness. We have found that most people intuitively know that forgiving a person who has harmed them is the right thing to do. Indeed, all major religious traditions and wisdoms

---

"I'M SORRY" IS NOT ALWAYS AN APOLOGY

It's important to note that by apologies, we are not talking about the manipulative, meaningless practice of apologizing used by perpetrators of domestic violence during the honeymoon period of the "cycle of violence." In that situation, there is no sincere intent to learn from the experience and to improve the relationship. As described in chapter 16, an apology doesn't help in that situation; lives are at stake. The only thing that will help is outside professional assistance.

Also, we are not talking about those people who, due to their low self-esteem, are continually apologizing. If you find yourself "over-apologizing," this is more likely a problem than it is a solution, and a signal that obtaining professional counseling help is in order.

"I'm sorry for what happened to you" is not an apology either. It's common to hear public figures express sympathy for victims of devastating events with those words. While *sympathy* may be appropriate, it's not an apology unless, as Engel points out, you accept *responsibility* for your part in the hurt.

extol the value of forgiveness. We've also seen these same people, who know forgiveness is the right thing to do, unwilling to forgive. So just what are the barriers to forgiveness?

First and foremost, when you are wronged by another person, your anger and resentment seems justified and you become attached to it. When you are hurt deeply, holding onto your resentment provides a sense of justice and revenge. Forgiveness can seem like letting the other person off the hook, making what they did to you okay, when it's not okay at all. Forgiveness can also seem dangerous. If you forgive, you might let your guard down and be hurt all over again.

Adlerian counselor and forgiveness expert Dale Babcock addresses these common barriers, with the following story and perspective:[5]

> *When I was a small boy I was riding my bicycle on a hill that was paved with crushed rock. I fell off my bike and hurt myself. I got a deep cut with rocks stuck in the skin. It was cleaned out and that hurt a whole bunch. I have a scar on that arm. When I look at that scar I remember the hurt but I don't feel the pain anymore. I think forgiveness is like that. When we forgive someone we begin to let go of our pain, we look past the hurt that was caused. We attempt to understand the person who hurt us and look for value in them. If the person continues the behavior that hurt us, it doesn't mean we have to continue to have contact with that person. With forgiveness there continues to be the need for responsible self-protection. When one forgives it helps to take away the anger and resentment. Forgiveness is not for the other person as much as it is for ourselves. The purpose is to free ourselves of the bitterness so we can go on with our lives in a more loving and meaningful way.*

So forgiveness may or may not be accompanied by reconciliation or a renewal in the relationship. If an abusive (and therefore estranged) ex-spouse is the source of your resentment, for the sake of safety as well as self-respect, you may choose to forgive without altering the relationship at all. If the source of the resentment is a child, spouse, or partner you are sharing day-to-day life with, your forgiveness will have a dramatic and positive change on the relationship.

It's important to realize that forgiveness is a process, and depending on the size and nature of the hurt, may take some time. You begin with the goal of forgiving for your own sake, and if the resentment you are holding is toward a member of your family, for the sake of the family. Dale Babcock suggests *journaling* as a way to help you through the forgiveness process — writing down your experiences, thoughts, and feelings that relate to the hurt and the goal.

Some things to consider along the path of forgiveness include:

◆ Identify and accept the painful feelings that come with what the other person has done, and accept that your resentment has been justified.

◆ Evaluate the price you are paying for holding onto your resentment. If possible, reflect upon what you know about the other person's life that may have led to the hurtful behavior, and how the hurtful behavior may have been a misguided effort to fulfill a wish or desire.

◆ Consider that the other person may also be suffering from what she did to you. If you sense in the other any possible regret, and if it's safe, let her share it with you.

◆ Focus on how moving past the resentment and coming to a place of forgiveness is in your best interest.

◆ Recognize that forgiving is not forgetting, and that remembering is a part of your ability to protect yourself.

Recent research conducted by the Stanford Forgiveness Project at Stanford University demonstrates that chronic anger and human resentment are dramatically reduced by the process of forgiveness. Research participants burdened by resentment were trained in understanding the benefits of forgiveness and the process involved. Compared to a control group who did not receive the training, the participants demonstrated a measurable reduction — seventy percent — in their chronic anger and resentment.

In his comments about the study, researcher Dr. Frederick Luskin states, "We, as a culture, suffer from the lack of forgiveness. Forgiveness as an area of scientific interest is brand new. I just believe it's such a valuable skill to learn, and such a neglected aspect of interpersonal behavior, that its absence is chilling and telling culturally, knowing the fact that so many of us everywhere hold grudges and carry resentment."[51]

After the Family Storm: Forgiving Yourself

Self-forgiveness is just as important as forgiving others. You are human, you are not designed to be perfect, and you will make mistakes. If you have contributed to the family storm and consequently hurt any member of your family, allowing yourself to feel bad and inadequate for very long is not helpful, and is, in fact, very harmful. If you have learned from your mistake, sincerely apologized to the family member you have hurt, and developed a plan to respond more respectfully in the future, you have done what you can to remedy the situation. Be kind to yourself, encourage yourself; you can learn, you can grow, you can improve, but you can't be perfect.

Adlerian psychiatrist Dr. Rudolf Dreikurs is well known for his stirring and passionate speech titled *The Courage to Be Imperfect*.[54] In it he said:

> *Perfectionism is rampant today . . . People who try so desperately to avoid mistakes are endangering themselves . . . Most people who make mistakes feel degraded; they lose respect for themselves; they lose belief in their own ability. And I have seen it time and again — the real damage was done not through the mistakes they made but through the*

discouragement which they had afterwards . . . We become overly impressed with what is wrong in us and around us. If I am critical of myself, I naturally am going to be critical of the people around me . . . To be human does not mean to be right, does not mean to be perfect. To be human means to be useful, to make contributions for oneself and for others — to take what there is and to make the best out of it.

BEYOND THE FAMILY STORM

Perhaps if there were fewer storms in families, there might be less turbulence in the world.

Imagine for a moment a world without anger, and especially a world without rage, aggression, and resentment. Is it even a possibility? Could the day ever come? What would it take? If you've been following the themes of this book, you have a glimpse into what it might take.

John Lennon put it this way:[34]

Imagine all the people, living life in peace . . .

Imagine, if you will, that parents, teachers, and all other leaders and influencers of children decided together at one time that they will treat children with absolute respect. This would need to include leadership that would encourage our children without indulging them, that would be firm with our children without dominating them. Think about the impact of this. Children would no longer have reason to feel inferior to adults. Their significance as human beings would no longer be in question, and their value as people assured. They would have no need to misbehave and meet the goals of attention, power, revenge, and inadequacy.

Imagine that couples applied the same principles to their relationship, and that a relationship of tenderness, love, and respect was then modeled to children everywhere. Imagine that there would therefore never be the need to strive for the purposes that anger serves, for any of us to need to seek power, revenge, or to protect our rights or the rights of others.

Imagine that we could see the differences in our children and between our children and all people not as something strange and frightening that we want to restrict or put an end to, but as something wonderful and interesting that adds to the variety and strength of our families, community, and world.

It's so easy to become cynical, to look around us and see nothing but growing problems, growing anger, rage, aggression, and resentment, not just in our families but everywhere.

We invite you to back up and peer through a wide-angle lens for a moment, taking a look historically at our shared existence as human beings living together on this planet.

A central theme of this book has been how the cultural development we call the "democratic revolution" has impacted human relationships. We've described how the many social movements of recent times, including the labor movement, the civil rights movement, and the women's movement, have forever changed our social landscape. We've discussed how each of us is now operating on an "equality identity," and that this applies to our children as well. We've emphasized how the traditional methods of control and punishment in this democratic world of ours once "worked," but now result in anger, conflict, alienation, power struggles, and violence. We have proposed many ways in which we can better work through life's difficulties together, and offer relationships that will work in our democratic world — work because the ideas we suggest are all based on mutual respect.

Realize for a moment just how recently, considering our long human history, all of these challenges have come our way. To place it in perspective, if we were to compress the tens of thousands of years that human beings have been on this planet into one calendar year, this period of social upheaval, the democratic revolution, and the time we've had to adapt to it, would have occurred in the last fifteen minutes!

We're new at this; we need time. There is room for justifiable hope. We can and we will get better at applying respect in all of our relationships.

A world of mutual respect and peace may seem a long way off. It won't happen by itself. The world is influenced most by the individual people in it. We all count. We each have impact — especially where our own choices and our own families are concerned. We can move our planet one step closer to harmony.

Change always begins with one person, one couple, and one family at a time.

And calming your family storm begins with you.

APPENDIX A

Finding a Counseling Professional in Your Community

Throughout this book we have encouraged you and your family to consider obtaining professional counseling assistance to help you with issues such as family conflict, couple or marital difficulties, divorce, single parenting support, stepfamilies, substance abuse, domestic violence, and child abuse. Finding just the right counselor for you and your family can be a challenge, but it is worth it. The following are some suggestions about how to get started.

There are many ways to find counseling professionals. Your school counselor or principal, leaders at your place of worship, or your family doctor often know of qualified and competent counselors that they can recommend. You also may have a friend who's faced similar problems who can make a recommendation. Local professional societies often have referral services. In addition, you will find listings in your local yellow pages for helping professionals in your area. For private counselors look under the sections titled "counselors," "psychologists," "social workers," or "marriage and family therapists."

Agencies providing counseling assistance may be more affordable than private therapists; they are usually listed in the yellow pages under "social service agencies." Many communities have public mental health centers, often part of a hospital or public health department. Some colleges and universities make free or low-cost counseling clinics available to the public. A "women's resource center" or similar group may also provide counseling services or referrals. There may be a "family services center," or "community counseling center" in your area, staffed with volunteer professionals who provide low-cost or sliding-scale counseling. A local United Way office may provide referral information.

A resource manual listing the agencies and professionals in your community, along with their areas of focus or expertise, may be published by a local organization, such as United Way, a "hotline" crisis telephone service, one of the local professional societies (e.g., psychological association, social work society), or other local agencies. Check your public library for this valuable source of information.

The following websites represent professional organizations who provide access information for counseling professionals throughout the country. Most have local affiliate groups that may be listed in your yellow pages:

American Association for Marriage and Family Therapy, www.aamft.org.

American Counseling Association, www.counseling.org.

American Mental Health Counselors Association, www.amhca.org.

American Psychological Association, www.helping.apa.org.

National Association of Social Workers, www.naswdc.org.

National Board of Certified Counselors, www.nbcc.org.

North American Society of Adlerian Psychology, www.alfredadler.org.

Psychology Today therapist listings nationwide, www.psychologytoday.com.

It's important to be particular when seeking out prospective counselors. Your concerns and your family's welfare are important. Make sure that the counselor you entrust to help your family is professionally qualified. A qualified counseling professional should have a minimum of a master's degree, and preferably should be licensed as a mental health counselor, clinical social worker, marriage and family therapist, or psychologist. In addition, be sure to ask whether the counselor has training and experience in the specific area you are dealing with, e.g., couple and marital counseling, counseling young children or teens, family counseling, help with issues of divorce, domestic violence, child abuse, single parenting, stepfamily issues. If the issue you need help with is drug or alcohol abuse, the counselor should also have specialized training in chemical dependency treatment, and should also be licensed or certified as a chemical dependency or substance abuse counselor.

It is also important that the professional you find is a good fit for you and your family, and that his or her style is one you feel comfortable with. If you see a counselor and it just doesn't "seem right," or if you don't feel respected or understood, or if the counselor seems not to be helping you or your family make reasonable progress, don't hesitate to move on and locate one that is a good match. Keep in mind however, that if real progress is to occur, the counseling process will be uncomfortable at times. The counselor's job is to help you grow, not to help you "feel good."

Resources for Family Violence

DOMESTIC VIOLENCE:
ABUSE IN ADULT MARITAL AND COUPLE RELATIONSHIPS

The National Domestic Violence Hotline provides immediate crisis intervention. Callers can receive counseling and be referred directly to help in their communities, including emergency services and shelters. Also, operators can offer information and referrals, counseling and assistance to survivors of domestic violence, family members, neighbors, and the general public. The service is available 24/7: **1-800-799-SAFE (7233).** There is a TDD number for the hearing impaired: **1-800-787-3224.** Help is also available to callers in Spanish and to other non-English speakers. The hotline also has a website: **www.ndvh.org** that includes valuable information about domestic violence as well as resource information for every state.

Canada also has a nationwide National Domestic Violence Hotline: **1-800-363-9010.** The service is bilingual: English and French. The website **www.kimberly chapman.com/abuse/ canada_abuse.html** provides information. There is also a website which lists shelters in all provinces: **www.hotpeachpages.net/ canada/index.html.**

In many areas of the United States and Canada, there are local domestic violence agencies which can provide crisis services such as shelter, counseling, and legal assistance. These numbers can be obtained from the national hotlines/websites or state, provincial or regional coalitions, the phone book, or by calling directory assistance.

The Hot Peaches Organization has links to domestic violence resources throughout the world. Website: **www.hotpeachpages. net/a/countries.html.** For example, for resources in the **United Kingdom,** visit the website:

www.hotpeachpages.net/europe/europe1.html#UK

CHILD ABUSE

The Childhelp USA National Child Abuse Hotline serves the United States, Canada, U.S. Virgin Islands, Puerto Rico, and Guam. Crisis intervention is available from professional counselors 24/7: **1-800-4-A-CHILD (1-800-422-4453).**

289

The hotline counselors also provide referrals to local agencies throughout the United States and Canada for ongoing support. There is also a website: **www.childhelpusa.org** that provides important information about child abuse and child abuse resources.

In the United Kingdom, the National Society for the Prevention of Cruelty to Children has a website with child abuse information, resources and useful links: **www.nspcc.org.uk/nspcc/helpline.** They also have a 24/7 hotline: **[44] 0808 800 5000.**

Resources for Effective Parenting

JOIN A PARENT STUDY GROUP

If you liked the ideas in this book, you may want to join with other parents in a study group. Parent groups offer the opportunity to discuss what you're learning with other parents and the group leader. Following are programs for parent study groups.

Systematic Training for Effective Parenting (STEP). *Systematic Training for Effective Parenting* is a program based on the same ideas as this book. It includes a Leader's Resource Guide, Video and parent's manual. Based on over 25 years of research, *STEP* is the world's leading parent education program and has been translated into several languages including Spanish, German, French and Japanese. *STEP* has influenced over four million parents in the United States alone. The program is designed to be taught in seven weekly two-hour sessions.

Coauthored by Dr. Gary D. McKay, one of the authors of this book, *STEP* comes in three levels: *STEP* (for parents of elementary school aged children), *Early Childhood STEP* (children under 6) and *STEP/Teen* (preteens and teens). Each program has its own parent's manual: *STEP* — **The Parent's Handbook,** *Early Childhood STEP* — **Parenting Young Children,** and *STEP/Teen* —**Parenting Teenagers.** (See book list in Appendix D for full descriptions of the books.)

STEP is offered in a variety of settings such as schools, churches and counseling agencies. If a *STEP* group is not available in your area, consider starting one yourself. *STEP* is designed to be taught by both professional and lay leaders. *The Leader's Resource Guide* has specific instructions on how to lead a group and conduct discussions and exercises. The leader doesn't have to be an expert, the *STEP* materials serve as the authority. The leader's job is basically to get the group involved with the materials and guide the discussions.

Each *STEP* program is available from the publisher American Guidance Service **800-328-2560, www.parentingeducation.com.** The parent books for each of the three *STEP* programs can be purchased from Impact Publishers **800-246-7228, www.impactpublishers.com**

Other Parenting Programs. There are two programs which have philosophies similar to *STEP* and may be available in your community:

Active Parenting by Michael Popkin, Ph.D. Contact Active Parenting Publishers: **800-825- 0060, www.activeparenting.com**

Positive Discipline by Jane Nelsen, Ed.D. Contact Empowering People, Inc. **800-456 7770, www.positivediscipline.com.**

FORM A GROUP TO STUDY *CALMING THE FAMILY STORM*

You may want to get together with other parents to discuss this book. You can discuss each chapter using the following questions:

1. What did you learn from the chapter?

2. Which ideas in the chapter were particularly helpful. Why?

3. How would you apply the ideas in the chapter in your family?

4. Any questions about the chapter?

APPENDIX D

More Resources for
Family Anger Management

BOOKS BY THE AUTHORS

McKay, Gary D., Joyce L. McKay, Daniel Eckstein and Steven A. Maybell. (2001). *Raising Respectful Kids in a Rude World: Teaching Your Children the Power of Mutual Respect and Consideration*. Roseville, CA: Prima. ISBN: 0-7615-2811-3

McKay, Gary D. and Don Dinkmeyer. (2002). *How You Feel Is Up to You*. (Revised Edition) Atascadero, CA: Impact Publishers. ISBN 1-866230-50-1

Dinkmeyer, Don, Gary D. McKay and Don Dinkmeyer, Jr. (1997). *The Parent's Handbook*. (from the Systematic Training for Effective Parenting — STEP — program.) Circle Pines, MN: American Guidance Service. ISBN: 0-7854-1188-7.

Dinkmeyer, Don, Gary D. McKay, Don Dinkmeyer, Jr., James S. Dinkmeyer. and Joyce L. McKay. (1997). *Parenting Young Children*. (from the Systematic Training for Effective Parenting of Children Under Six — Early Childhood STEP— program.) Circle Pines, MN: American Guidance Service. ISBN: 0-7854-1189-5

Dinkmeyer, Don, Gary D. McKay, Joyce L. McKay and Don Dinkmeyer, Jr. (1998). *Parenting Teenagers*. (from the from the Systematic Training for Effective Parenting of Teens — STEP/Teen — program) Circle Pines, MN: American Guidance Service. ISBN: 0-7854-1468-1

Dinkmeyer, Don, Gary D. McKay. and Joyce L. McKay. (1987). *New Beginnings: Skills for Single Parents and Stepfamily Parents*. Champaign, IL: Research Press. ISBN 0-87822-286-2

293

Other Recommended Books

Bilodeau, Lorraine. (2001). *Responding to Anger: A Workbook.* Center City, MN: Hazelden. ISBN: 1-56838-624-9

Barrish, Harriet H. and I.J. Barrish. (1989). *Managing and Understanding Parental Anger.* (Revised Edition). Leawood, KS: Barrish and Barrish. ISBN: 0-933701-41-1

Carlson, Jon and Don Dinkmeyer, Sr. (2002). *Time for A Better Marriage: Training in Marriage Enrichment.* Atascadero, CA: Impact Publishers. ISBN 1-866320-46-3

Ellis, Albert and Ted Crawford. (2000). *Making Intimate Connections: Seven Guidelines for Great Relationships and Better Communication.* Atascadero, CA: Impact Publishers. ISBN: 1-866230-33-1

Ellis, Albert and Raymond Chip Tafrate. (1997). *How to Control Your Anger Before It Controls You.* New York: Citadel Press. ISBN: 0-8065-2010-8

Fisher, Bruce and Robert E. Alberti. (2000). *Rebuilding: When Your Relationship Ends, Second Edition.* Atascadero, CA: Impact Publishers. ISBN 1-886230-17-X

McKay, Matthew, Patrick Fanning, Kim Paleg, and Dana Landis. (1996). *When Anger Hurts Your Kids: A Parent's Guide.* Oakland, CA: New Harbinger Publications. ISBN: 1-57224-045-8

McKay, Matthew and Peter Rogers. (2000). *The Anger Control Workbook.* Oakland, CA: New Harbinger Publications. ISBN: 1-57224-220-5

Nelsen, Jane. (1999). *Positive Time-Out.* Roseville, CA: Prima. ISBN: 0-7615-2175-5

Ricker, Audrey and Carolyn Crowder. (1998). *Backtalk: 4 Steps to Ending Rude Behavior in Your Kids.* New York: Fireside. ISBN: 0-684-84124-X

Note: If you can't find these books in the bookstore, try on-line books stores such as **www.amazon.com** and **www. barnesandnoble.com.** You can also search for titles available from online bookstores by visiting **www.bookfinder.com.**

How You Feel Is Up to You, The Parent's Handbook, Parenting Young Children, Parenting Teenagers, Time for A Better Marriage, Making Intimate Connections and *Rebuilding* can be ordered from Impact Publishers, Inc., P.O. Box 6016, Atascadero, CA 93423-6016. 1-800-246-7228. Website: www.impactpublishers.com.

References

1. Adapted from *Preventing Violence Against Women, Not Just a Women's Issue*, (1995). Washington, DC: National Crime Prevention Council.

2. Adler, A. (1998). *What Life Could Mean to You*. Center City, MN: Hazelden Foundation.

3. Amata. (1987). As reported in Cullen, Loanda. (1995). "Confronting the Myths of Single Parenting" www.parentsplace.com.

4. *American Medical Association, Child Abuse and Neglect*. (1999**).** Medem: Medical Library, American Medical Association website, medem.com.

5. Babcock, Dale, M.S., LCPC, Adlerian Counselor. (4/30/04). Boise, ID. Personal correspondence.

6. Ballinger, Joni Mayde, M.Ed. (9/23/03). Anger Specialist, School Counselor, Marysville School District. Bellevue, WA. Interview.

7. Barrish, H.H., & Barrish, I.J. (1989) *Managing and Understanding Parental Anger*. (Revised Edition). Leawood, KS: Barrish and Barrish.

8. Bryant, Boudleaux & Bryant, Felice. Lyrics from song: "Problems." (1958). (Performed by Don and Phil Everly). Nashville, TN: RCA Victor Studios.

9. Charlesworth, E. A. & Nathan, R.G. (1991). *Stress Management: A Comprehensive Guide To Wellness*. New York: Ballantine.

10. *Child Maltreatment 2001*. (2003). U.S. Department of Health and Human Services, Administration on Children, Youth and Families. Washington, DC: U.S. Government Printing Office.

11. *Children with Single Parents — How They Fare*. (September, 1997). U.S. Census Bureau — Census Brief. Washington, DC: U.S. Government Printing Office.

12. Cullen, Loanda. (1995). "Confronting the Myths of Single Parenting" www.parentsplace.com.

13. Dinkmeyer, D., Sr., McKay, G.D., Dinkmeyer. D., Jr., Dinkmeyer, J.S. & Carlson, J. (1985). *PREP for Effective Family Living*. Circle Pines, MN: American Guidance Service.

14. Dinkmeyer, D., Sr., McKay, G.D. & Dinkmeyer, D., Jr. (1997). *The Parent's Handbook*. Circle Pines, MN: American Guidance Service.

15. Dinkmeyer, D. Sr., McKay, Gary D., McKay, Joyce L. & Dinkmeyer, Don, Jr. (1998). "STEP/Teen Session Guide" (in the Leader's Resource Guide for *Systematic Training for Effective Parenting of Teens*). Circle Pines, MN: American Guidance Service.

16. Dylan, Bob (1964). "The Times They Are A Changin'. "

17. *Domestic Violence — A Guide for Health Care Professionals*. (1990). State of New Jersey, Department of Community Affairs.

18. *Domestic Violence Report* (1991). New York: The Commonwealth Fund.

19. Dreikurs, R. & Soltz, V. (1991). *Children: The Challenge*. New York: Plume.

20. Dreikurs, R. (1990). *The Challenge of Marriage*. Philadelphia, PA: Accelerated Development.

21. Dreikurs, R. (1967). *Psychodynamics, Psychotherapy and Counseling*. Chicago, IL: Alfred Adler Institute of Chicago (Now called Adler School of Professional Psychology).

22. Dreikurs, R. (1983). *Social Equality: The Challenge of Our Times*. Chicago, IL: Adler School of Professional Psychology.

23. Ellis, A. & Tafrate, R.C. (1997). *How to Control Your Anger Before It Controls You*. New York: Citadel Press.

24. Ellis, A. (1998). *A Guide to Rational Living*. North Hollywood, CA: Wilshire Books.

25. *Emerging Practices in the Prevention of Child Abuse and Neglect*. (2003). U.S. Department of Health and Human Services, Administration on Children, Youth and Families, Washington, DC: U.S. Government Printing Office.

26. Engel, B. (2001). *The Power of Apology*. New York: John Wiley and Sons.

27. Gordon, T. (2000). *Parent Effectiveness Training: The Proven Program for Raising Responsible Children*. Pittsburgh, PA: Three Rivers Press.

28. Hanson. (1986) as reported in Cullen, Loanda. (1995). "Confronting the Myths of Single Parenting" www.parentsplace.com.

29. Haudenschield, Lynne, M.Ed., LMFT. (10/17/03). Youth and Family Counselor, Youth Eastside Services, Bellevue, WA. Interview.

30. Horton, A. (Spring 1996). "Teaching Anger Management Skills to Primary-Age Children." *Teaching and Change 3:3. 281-96*.

31. Illinois Department of Public Health. (1996)

32. Kaperick, Peter, M.S.W., LICSW. (8/26/03). Youth and family counselor and divorce expert, Youth Eastside Services, Bellevue, WA. Interview.

33. Lafferty, Belinda, M.A., LMHC. (9/23/03). Domestic Violence Program Coordinator, Youth Eastside Services, Bellevue, WA. Interview.

34. Lennon, John. (1971). Lyrics from song "Imagine," album: "Imagine," Parlaphone

35. Lennon, John & McCartney, Paul. (1969). Lyrics from song: "The End," album: "Abbey Road," EMI Records Ltd.

36. Logan, Mac, Scottish business consultant, favorite saying.

37. McKay, G. D. & Christensen, O.C. (May, 1978). "Helping Adults Change Disjunctive Emotional Responses to Children's Misbehavior." *Journal of Individual Psychology*. 34:1. 70-84, and in Carlson, J., & Slavik, S. (1997). *Techniques in Adlerian Psychology*. Bristol, PA: Accelerated Development, 413-427.

38. McKay, G. D. (1992). *The Basics of Anger* (Booklet). Coral Springs FL: CMTI Press.

39. McKay, G.D. & Dinkmeyer, D., Sr. (2002). *How You Feel Is Up to You*. (Revised Edition) Atascadero, CA: Impact Publishers

40. McKay, G. D., McKay, J.L., Eckstein, D. & Maybell, S.A. (2001). *Raising Respectful Kids in a Rude World: Teaching Your Children the Power of Mutual Respect and Consideration*. Roseville, CA: Prima.

41. Mosak, H. H. (2000). "Adlerian Psychotherapy." In Corsini, R. & Wedding D. (eds.) *Current Psychotherapies* (6th Edition). Itasca, IL: F. E. Peacock.

42. Mosak, Harold H., Ph.D. (1999). Personal communication.

43. Nelsen, Jane. (1999). *Positive Time-Out*. Roseville, CA: Prima.

44. *Partner Abuse: Knowing the Facts and Breaking the Cycle*. (1996). Report to the General Assembly. Illinois Department of Public Health.

45. Penn, Schoen & Berland. (June 3, 1999). *How America Defines Child Abuse*. National survey. Los Angeles: Children's Institute International.

46. Powers, Robert L. (1984). Psychologist and Teacher, "Applying Psychological Skills" course, San Francisco, CA. Lecture.

47. Powers, R. L. & Griffith, J. (1987). Understanding *Lifestyle: The Psychoclarity Process*. Chicago, IL: The Americas Institute of Adlerian Studies.

48. Powers, R. L., Griffith, J. & Maybell, S.A. (September/December, 1993). "Gender Guiding Line Theory and Couples Therapy." *Individual Psychology: Journal of Adlerian Theory, Research, and Practice.* 49:3-4.

49. Schechter, S. and Ganley, A. (1995). *Domestic Violence: A National Curriculum for Family Preservation Practitioners.* San Francisco, CA: San Francisco Family Violence Prevention Fund.

50. Shaw. (1991) as reported in Cullen, Loanda. (1995). "Confronting the Myths of Single Parenting" www.parentsplace.com.

51. Stanford Forgiveness Project, Research Abstract Report. (1999). Stanford University, Frederick Luskin, Ph.D.

52. Stark, E & Flitcraft, A. (1994). "Violence Among Intimates: An Epidemiological Review," in Vincent B. Van Haslett et al (eds.). *Handbook of Family Violence.* NY: Plenum Publishing Corporation.

53. Tavris, Carol. (1989). *Anger: The Misunderstood Emotion.* New York: Touchstone.

54. Terner, J. & Pew, W.L. (1978) *The Courage To Be Imperfect: The Life and Work of Rudolf Dreikurs.* NY: Hawthorn Books, Inc.

55. *Third National Incidence Study of Child Abuse and Neglect: Final Report (NIS-3).* (September, 1996). U.S. Department of Health and Human Services, National Center on Child Abuse and Neglect. Washington, DC: U.S. Government Printing Office.

56. U.S. Census Bureau Household and Family Characteristics. (March, 1998) Washington, DC: U.S. Government Printing Office.

57. U.S. Census Bureau Supplement to the Current Population Survey. (March, 1998). Washington, DC: U.S. Government Printing Office.

58. Walker, L. E. (1979). *The Battered Woman.* New York: Harper & Row.

59. Walton, F. X. (June, 1988.) "Teenage Suicide: A Family Oriented Approach to Prevention." *Individual Psychology,* 44:2. 185.

60. Williams, R. & Williams, V. (1998). *Anger Kills: Seventeen Strategies of Controlling the Hostility that Can Harm Your Health.* NY: Harper Collins.

61. *Women and Violence.* (August/December, 1990). Washington, DC: U.S. Senate Judiciary Hearing.

62. Wong, Ken, M.S.W. (9/23/03). Director of Teen Programs, City of Redmond, WA. Interview.

References

More Books With *Impact*